REVIEW COPY

White Slave Crusades
Race, Gender, and Anti-vice Activism, 1887-1917
Brian Donovan

U.S. Cloth Price: $30
Publication Date: January 9, 2006

Contact: Michael Roux, (217) 244-4689
mroux@uillinois.edu

Please send TWO copies of your review to:

University of Illinois Press
1325 South Oak Street
Champaign, IL 61820-6903
Fax: (217) 244-8082
www.press.uillinois.edu

White Slave Crusades

White Slave Crusades

RACE, GENDER, AND
ANTI-VICE ACTIVISM,
1887–1917

BRIAN DONOVAN

UNIVERSITY OF ILLINOIS PRESS
Urbana and Chicago

Library of Congress Cataloging-in-Publication Data
Donovan, Brian, 1971–
White slave crusades : race, gender, and anti-vice activism, 1887–1917 /
Brian Donovan.
p.   cm.
Includes bibliographical references and index.
ISBN-13: 978-0-252-03025-3 (isbn 13 - cloth : alk. paper)
ISBN-10: 0-252-03025-7 (isbn 10 - cloth : alk. paper)
1. Prostitution—United States—History—19th century. 2.
Prostitution—United States—History—19th century. 3. Racism—
United States—History—19th century. 4. Racism—United States—
History—20th century. 5. Social classes—United States—History—
19th century. 6. Social classes—United States—History—20th century.
7. Women—Suffrage—United States—History—19th century. 8.
Women—Suffrage—United States—History—20th century. I. Title.
HQ144.D57   2006
363.4′4′089′00973—dc22   2005012424

For my parents,
Mary and Kerry Donovan

Contents

Acknowledgments

I owe my greatest intellectual debt to Nicola Beisel, whose own work inspired me to study anti-vice activism and social inequality. Time and again, she proved to be a model scholar and wonderful mentor. I greatly benefited from our conversations and all of the red ink she spilled on my chapter drafts. Wendy Griswold and Orville Lee III read various versions of this manuscript and gave me helpful feedback that resulted in a much better final product. My colleagues at the University of Kansas Department of Sociology created a wonderful academic environment where I could discuss and receive feedback on my work. I would like to extend special thanks to Joane Nagel for her ongoing interest in my intellectual pursuits. Friends inside and outside academic life provided crucial emotional support and gracefully endured many conversations about moral reform, anti-vice crusades, and related topics. In this regard, I'd like to thank Lisa Amoroso, Sarah Babb, Khamisah Barger, Will Berg, Michelle Boyd, Gary Castañeda, Mark Donovan, Sarah Gatson, Alan Graler, Kathy Hull, Ann Johnson, Jordan Mills, and David Stevens.

Archivists and librarians at the Bancroft Library, University of California, Berkeley; the Chicago Historical Society; the Lloyd Sealy Library at the John Jay College of Criminal Justice, New York City; the Joseph Regenstein Library at the University of Chicago; Northwestern University Library, Evanston, Illinois; Newberry Library, Chicago; the Rockefeller Archive Center, Sleepy Hollow, New York; the Social Welfare History Archives, University of Minnesota, Minneapolis; Stanford Special Collections, Stanford University, Palo Alto, California; the Watson Library, University of Kansas, Lawrence; and the Woman's

Christian Temperance Union Archives in Evanston, Illinois, offered invaluable assistance.

The Sexuality Research Fellowship Program sponsored by the Social Science Research Council with support from the Ford Foundation provided me with a generous fellowship at a crucial juncture in my research and writing. I would like to thank Diane Di Mauro and the SSRC for their help. I'm also grateful for a grant from the Rockefeller Archive Center that allowed me to access important documents vital for my study. A National Science Foundation Graduate Research Fellowship and a grant from Northwestern University supported the early stages of this project.

A version of chapter 5 was published as "The Sexual Basis of Racial Formation: Anti-vice Activism and the Creation of the Twentieth-Century 'Color Line'" in *Ethnic and Racial Studies* 26, no. 4 (2003). I would like to thank Taylor and Francis Limited (http://www.tandf.co.uk) for their permission to reproduce this material.

My editor Joan Catapano has offered great support and encouragement. The manuscript was greatly improved with the help of reviewers and editors at the University of Illinois Press.

I owe an enormous debt to my wife, Natalie Donovan, for her steadfast tenderness and devotion. Over the decades, she changed from a high school sweetheart to my lifelong companion, confidante, and love. I couldn't have done it without her.

This book is dedicated to my parents for their endless encouragement, assistance, and loving support.

White Slave Crusades

Introduction

During the early twentieth century, individuals and organizations of different political stripes launched an extraordinary effort to eradicate forced prostitution, or what was commonly known as "white slavery." The topic drew interest from lawmakers, journalists, moral reformers, and average citizens. Stories of sexual danger fascinated white Americans during the Progressive Era (1900–1920), and they consumed increasing numbers of white slavery narratives in the form of plays, films, books, pamphlets, and magazine articles.[1] At least fifteen white slavery plays and six white slavery movies were produced in the early twentieth century. In 1913, over 30,000 people viewed the white slavery film *Traffic in Souls* during its opening week in New York City, sparking controversy over its moral effect on viewers.[2] In the years leading up to World War I, over thirty cities launched vice investigations, and forty-four states passed laws to stop coercive prostitution. At the federal level, Congress passed the Mann act, or the "White Slave Traffic Act," in 1910, which criminalized the transfer of women across state lines for "immoral purposes." In its first eight years, law enforcement officials arrested over 2,000 people for Mann act violations.[3] Kevin Mumford observes that "the ideology of white slavery was in fact a staple of early-twentieth-century American culture."[4]

White slavery narratives reflected the social and historical conditions of their production. The political, economic, and cultural environment of the Progressive Era provided a fertile soil for these stories to take root in public consciousness. The white slavery genre in the United States developed during a period marked by rapid urbanization, the rise of women in the workforce, and the changing racial composition of American cities.[5] These social shifts converged in white slavery narratives. The poetics of white slavery storytelling created a powerful voice for expressing concern over the pace and direction of social transformation. As such, these stories are rich sites for understanding important dimensions of American culture. Scholars have examined white slavery narratives for the light they shed on diverse topics such as American liberalism, American legal institutions, monopoly capitalism, and important developments in journalism.[6] Many scholars have used white slavery narratives to explore the perpetuation of gender inequality at the turn of the century;[7] much less attention has been paid to their role in the historical construction of racial difference.[8] Early-twentieth-century anti-vice campaigns played a critical role in creating racial hierarchy and demarcating racial and ethnic boundaries. My foregoing analysis of anti-vice campaigns does not replace scholars' previous emphasis on gender with race, nor does it simply add race as another variable to be discussed. Rather, the approach offered here seeks to understand how dimensions of race, ethnicity, gender, and sexuality converge in anti-vice activism and the production of white slavery stories. This adds needed complexity to the existing accounts of this topic while forging new terrain in our theoretical understanding of the intersection of race and gender.

Just as scholars have plumbed white slavery stories and the white slavery phenomenon for insights into diverse historical and sociological questions, Americans living in the Progressive Era used them for a wide range of political projects. Some Progressive Era reformers lobbied for legal restrictions on red-light districts, some preached in front of brothels, and others established rescue homes for prostitutes. Reformers used white slavery stories to criticize police corruption, working-class amusements, consumerism, urbanization, the sexual double standard, male violence, women's public roles, and immigration. They deployed white slavery stories to advance often-contradictory projects: suffrage, female domesticity, mass scientific sex education, religious revival, protection for immigrants, and immigration restrictions. White slavery stories were circulated by organizations as diverse as the Immigrant Protective League, the Ku Klux Klan, and the Woman's Christian Temperance Union.[9] From the Right, social movement organizations used white slavery narratives to advocate immigration restrictions, tougher legal sanctions against vice, surveillance of saloons and hotels, and the regulation of working-class amusements. On the Left, reformers used white slavery stories for small- and large-scale reform agendas including tenement reform, immigration protection, minimum wage campaigns, and women's suffrage. The white slavery issue created strange alliances among socialists, anarchists, wealthy philanthropists, evangelists, suffragists, and anti-suffragists.

Given the enormous range of purposes to which white slavery narratives were put, and given the scholarly attention that many of these topics have drawn, this book limits its focus to the mobilization of gender and racial ideologies in anti-vice efforts. I do not pretend to provide a full account of the white slavery phenomenon, yet, given the primacy of race and gender as determinants of life chances, I made a methodological decision to cast my spotlight on those topics. This book explores the role of white slavery stories and anti-vice activism in processes of racial group-making and boundary maintenance during the late nineteenth and early twentieth centuries in the United States. I will also show how white slavery narratives offered a cultural resource that people used to make different arguments about gender and sex in the early twentieth century. The men and women who fought to abolish white slavery advanced conflicting ideas about the place of immigrants and African Americans in American society, and they also advanced divergent views on manhood and womanhood. In offering a rhetorical template for arguments about where and how to draw the color line in urban America, anti-vice activism and white slavery stories also suggested how one should think about the roles and identities of white men and women.

White slavery narratives leveraged and cultivated specific cultural sensibilities about race, gender, and sexuality. In addition to illuminating an important period in American culture, this book seeks to contribute to sociological accounts of culture, race, gender, and sexuality by analyzing the sex and gender foundations of race and the racial foundations of sex and gender. My analysis of these stories and the social movement activism they recorded and inspired shows that the creation and maintenance of racial categories depend upon characterizations of people as sexual actors. Narratives of sexual deviance comprise an important part of what Michèle Lamont refers to as "the cultural territory of race."[10] The discursive fields of sexuality and gender—where humans negotiate the meaning of sexual practices and the definitions of authentic masculinity and femininity—directly shape institutionalized forms of racial inequality. Nicola Beisel has shown how organized efforts to curb sexual immorality in the Victorian era embodied struggles over social class and the reproduction of wealth and privilege.[11] Likewise, the crusades against white slavery used dominant ideas about gender and sexuality to construct durable racial hierarchies. Michael Omi and Howard Winant argue that racial formation is a product of large and small "racial projects."[12] Accounts of white slavery crusades in the following chapters will show that racial projects are often inextricably tied to sex and gender projects.

I used a wide range of archival materials, including organizational records of anti-vice movements, speeches, books, pamphlets, and legal records. This study relied extensively on several stories about white slavery published in the early twentieth century. Borrowing from interpretive methods developed in the sociology of culture and new cultural history, I analyzed these accounts with attention to their explicit and implicit arguments about race and gender.[13] Recognizing that history is more than words and ideas, I show how ideologies translated into political, legal, and social practices that had real consequences in peoples' lives.

This study compares anti-vice efforts in three U.S. cities: Chicago, New York, and San Francisco. I compare reform efforts within each city as well as across them in order to explore the historical and regional contours of racial formation. This approach represents the "illustrative type" of comparative/historical research, juxtaposing similar historical events, processes, and actors to contribute to theoretical explanations of social life.[14] Although anti-vice reformers in Chicago, New York, and San Francisco shared overlapping goals, I focus on distinct racial projects in each locale. Specifically, I examine reactions of native-born whites to new immigrant groups in Chicago; to African Americans in New York City; and to Chinese immigrants in San Francisco.

1

White Slavery and the Intersection
of Race and Gender

The crusades against white slavery occurred during a pivotal moment during the construction of racial groups in the United States. As stories describing the sexual slavery of native-born white women proliferated in the beginning of the twentieth century, the racial category of "white" fragmented and reconsolidated in different social spheres.[1] From 1900 to 1910, the rate of immigration relative to the national population soared to the highest rate in U.S. history.[2] Moreover, rates of immigration from supposedly good and assimilable immigrants from northern Europe declined as the rates of immigration from reputedly bad and unassimilable immigrants from southern and eastern Europe drastically increased. Many native-born whites, working with a very different racial worldview than twenty-first-century Americans, regarded southern and eastern European immigrants as racially distinct and inferior. Beginning in the early twentieth century, Russian and Polish Jews, Italians, and Hungarians—and other groups that many now consider in terms of ethnicity and/or nationality—were slowly incorporated into the racial category that we now know as "white."[3] The racial status of immigrant groups and the question of whether or not they should be afforded the privileges of racial whiteness were hotly contested in discussions about municipal politics, immigration, and labor.[4]

The Progressive Era also witnessed an intensification of the "one-drop rule" with respect to African heritage that coincided with large numbers of African Americans migrating from the South to northern and midwestern cities. Americans with partial African ancestry were increasingly considered "black," although in previous decades their "mixed blood" set them cate-

gorically apart from "Negroes." New miscegenation laws, immigration restrictions, and heightened residential segregation accompanied these changes
in racial categories. White slavery narratives reflected and refracted these
transformations in racial populations and helped shape the meaning of whiteness during a time when the category of "white" was largely unsettled.

Anti-vice efforts also coincided with changing definitions of masculinity
and femininity. A wide array of gender ideologies and practices circulated in
the Progressive Era, complicating any simple portrait of its gender norms. Yet,
in many societies, the gender order arrays masculinity and femininity hier-
archically, and a single model of masculinity and femininity is deemed legitimate and embraced by individuals who may or may not embody it. Robert
Connell terms a society's prevailing definition of manhood as "hegemonic
masculinity," and one can reasonably make a case for the existence of hegemonic femininity.[5] Hegemonic gender ideals, while not describing the lives
of all or most men and women, nonetheless structure their emotional, personal, and productive lives in important ways. Thus, the fight over the cultural meaning of true manhood and womanhood has serious consequences
for the lived reality of men and women.

White masculinity underwent profound changes during the transition
from the nineteenth to the twentieth century. The nineteenth-century notion
of middle-class manliness rested on character-centered criteria. Coinciding
with an economic climate that allowed many white middle-class men autonomy and self-employment, true manhood was rooted in gentility and self-
control. In response to a host of cultural and economic shifts, the dominant
definition of manhood changed in the Progressive Era to become more body-
centered. Perhaps best personified in Theodore Roosevelt's self-created image
of rugged individualism, white middle-class American men living in the early
twentieth century embraced a new model of manliness that emphasized mus-
cularity, sexual prowess, and bodily strength. Weight lifting, boxing, and other
formerly working-class activities became ways through which men could assert their manliness.[6]

Other changes helped to transform gender and sexual norms during the
first two decades of the twentieth century. The term "New Woman" gained
popularity in the late nineteenth century to refer to women who exercised
control over their personal lives. The concept of the New Woman meant different things to different generations of men and women, and use of the term
varied regionally; some commentators emphasized the economic freedom
of New Women, while others highlighted their sexual mores. The notion of
autonomy—be it financial, personal, or sexual—remained common to most

characterizations of New Women. According to Carroll Smith-Rosenberg, the rise of the New Woman, "more than any other phenomenon of the 1910s and 1920s, signaled the birth of a new era."[7] Many New Women entered reform work, participated in political organizations, and created ways of life very different from what their mothers experienced.[8]

Working-class women, too, helped create a new gender landscape in the early twentieth century. Women's opportunities for employment skyrocketed in major urban centers, and women were employed in record numbers as clerks, typists, secretaries, and phone operators. In 1890, 19 percent of the U.S. female population worked outside the home; by 1910, nearly a quarter of U.S. women had entered the paid labor force.[9] New employment opportunities gave working-class women a growing public presence in major U.S. cities. This, coupled with mass advertising and a maturing industrial economy, fed a new consumer ethic as men and women became progressively more interested in material goods and leisure and spent more of their money on personal consumption.[10] Elaine Tyler May writes that "around the turn of the century, as the nation's concern for production began to shift toward a preoccupation with consumption, there was a parallel trend away from work toward leisure, away from sacrifice toward satisfaction, and a corresponding decline of sexual repression in favor of gratification."[11] Spurred partly by the rise of the automobile, dating became a commonly accepted practice across social classes between 1890 and 1925.[12] The development of urban amusements also helped change courtship patterns for young men and women by increasing areas of what Alan Hunt calls "heterosocial space," such as dance halls, amusement parks, ice cream parlors, and skating rinks.[13]

These renovations in courtship helped cause the Victorian idea of inherent female passionlessness and moral purity to lose currency, primarily among young working-class men and women. Many working-class women no longer considered premarital chastity as an important sign of moral worth, and some participated in the "treating system" by exchanging affection, companionship, and sexual favors for an evening's entertainment.[14] According to Barbara Meil Hobson, the overt sexuality of young women in the cities contradicted the "conventional view of women as asexual, passive, and primarily interested in the ideals of domesticity: the management of home, care of husband, and rearing of children."[15]

This chapter explores the intersection of race and gender to help explain contests over racial and gender formation embodied in white slavery activism and narration during the early twentieth century. Throughout U.S. history, boundary work around racial categories has brought into play gender and sexuality, and discussions about what it means to be a proper man or woman has invoked racial distinctions.[16] In this way, creators of social hierarchy simultaneously mobilize gender and racial ideologies to impose a logic of social difference. Definitions of kinship and family ties, as basic units of racial belonging, fuse gender, sexuality, and race. Racialized notions of lineage and family weld sexual purity and impurity to specific racial categories. Steve Martinot contends that this "purity condition" lies at the very heart of "race" as a conceptual category in American history.[17] Due to the dependence of racial categories on ideologies of sex and gender, racial formations contain crisis tendencies because different sexual practices have the potential to threaten group boundaries. This chapter will show that the maintenance of racial boundaries requires not only racial projects, but also projects centered on gender and sex.[18] Thus, a theoretical approach that considers the intersection of race and gender is needed to appreciate the social impact of white slavery narratives and moral reform efforts.

A Cultural Account of Racial Formation

I use the term "race" to refer to a set of historically specific ideas about human difference and practices based on those ideas. Race should not be thought of as representing natural or biological characteristics of people; it is an ideological system that organizes people into groups based on perceived moral, cultural, and/or bodily distinctions. Mara Loveman argues that race operates as "a principal of vision and division of the social world across time and place."[19] Insofar as most people accept racial categories as legitimate and true, perceived racial differences become a central principle of social organization. Consequently, scholars of race have searched for the origins of racial thinking in enduring institutions and patterns of human practice. A dominant thread in the scholarship on race and ethnicity considers race in structural terms, both as a structure itself and as a product of social structural change, such as shifting labor markets, immigration rates, and the unequal possession of socioeconomic power.[20]

Some scholars of race have called attention to the "structural" basis of racial taxonomies to highlight the enduring and institutionalized aspects of an otherwise arbitrary system of difference. Eduardo Bonilla-Silva uses the phrase "racialized social system" to refer to "societies in which economic, political, social, and ideological levels are partially structured by the placement of actors in racial categories or races."[21] He emphasizes the "racial structure of a society" to correct what he sees as an unsystematized and purely ideological notion of race in contemporary scholarship.[22] According to his theoretical framework, racism is an ideological product of a racialized social system.[23] Bonilla-Silva discerns a direct causal relationship between racial structures and racial ideologies, arguing that ideology emanates from institutionalized racial divisions.

Following a similar strategy, some have examined the interdependence between constructions of race and material inequality. Labor historians have analyzed race and racism as the product of shifting class interests, demonstrating how racial categories have changed based upon the nature of capitalism, labor markets, and white working-class activism.[24] For Theodore Allen, the expansion and contraction of racial categories in the nineteenth century reveals a deliberate divide-and-conquer strategy by capitalists.[25] Allen argues that American capitalists, in essence, invented the white race in the beginning of the nineteenth century to gain economic and political control over poor freemen. The ruling classes selectively conferred privileges to European immigrants that they denied African slaves, such as the right to bear arms, to plead and testify in criminal proceedings, and to marry. Capitalists warded off a potentially unified working class by unevenly allocating material resources and political rights to different groups of immigrants.

While Allen works within a structural Marxist framework, David Roediger and Noel Ignatiev use the insights of new labor history that emphasize the agency of the working class.[26] Roediger argues that the creation of racial whiteness in the Jacksonian era represented native-born white workers' fears of dependency on wage labor. Their new economic reliance on a wage blurred the line between wage labor and slavery, prompting workers to assert a white identity in order to obtain civil rights, jobs, and political influence. Similarly, Ignatiev argues that immigrant Irish Catholics effectively became white in the nineteenth century through political and labor struggles. Irish immigrants allied themselves with white workers against free African American laborers. During the 1830s and 1840s, they gained a strong political voice within the Democratic Party and frequently made vicious attacks against African American workers. White Democrats supported slavery, fearing that African American migration to the North would disrupt their hard-won economic gains. Although they were oppressed in their home country, Ignatiev argues that the Irish became part of the oppressor class in America through the process of attaining whiteness.

Despite the enormous contribution of the labor history perspective in understanding race, this approach is hindered by its tendency to reduce racial hierarchies to class formation. The transformation of racial and gender tax-

onomies and the changing face of racism depend upon large-scale transformations in economic and political systems, but the ways in which race is
understood and practiced depend on forms of cultural production and ongoing cultural practices. Michael Omi and Howard Winant argue that racial formation is the "sociohistorical process by which racial categories are
created, inhabited, transformed, and destroyed."[27] Racial formation entails
the practice of "group-making" whereby people create, defend, and close
ranks around their classifications.[28] In this sense, race refers to the ideas and
practices that create categorical distinctions, not to preexisting groups.[29] Racial and gender formations require what Mary Poovey calls "ideological
work" to create perceived differences among groups of people.[30] Therefore,
the creation and transformation of these social categories necessitate struggles over symbolic, as well as material, resources.[31]

Racial formations group people according to perceived socially significant
traits and provide a vocabulary with which to comprehend those groups. Racial categories often become codified in policies and laws that distribute resources along racial lines. These categories form a mechanism for creating social hierarchies by restricting or providing access to jobs, credentials, and legal
rights to marry and emigrate. Omi and Winant refer to this institutionalization of racial categories as representing the "racial state." Yet, despite its tremendous legal and political power, the state's ability to legitimate racial taxonomies is never total. The racial categories used by the state do not necessarily
correspond to folk or popular conceptions of race. The respondent to a census questionnaire, for instance, might have a different mental map of race than
the authors of the survey. These categories, being ultimately arbitrary, are open
to challenges from politicians, scientists, professionals, social movements, political parties, and legal actors. In the struggle to name and describe perceived
racial groups, social actors attempt to institute taken-for-granted taxonomies
and impose a vision of the social world deemed legitimate by its inhabitants.[32]

Racial taxonomies direct people's vision of the social world in a literal sense
by pointing them to physical characteristics considered markers of race.
Hence, racial formations give humans ways of seeing race, embodied in different principles of classification that change over time. Matthew Jacobson
contends that understanding racial difference "depends upon the play between social consciousness and literal vision."[33] Americans for much of the
twentieth century read racial categories through skin color. However, other
physical qualities had racial meaning at different moments in U.S. history,
such as head shape, hair, physiognomy, and eye color. Visual cues help social
actors categorize people according to race, allowing them to interpolate the

essential attributes of people based on their phenotypic characteristics. Features that give social meaning to racial categories include designations of morality, industriousness, intelligence, and other affective human properties. Supposed race-based traits of humans give social significance to the visual perception of race. In the words of Barbara Fields, "Race is a concept that we can locate at the level of appearances only. A material reality underlies it all right, as must be true of any ideology; but the underlying reality is not the one that the language of racial ideology addresses."[34] The inner properties of humans, indexed by physical markers, often become the focal point of racial difference. Racial formations link the visual cues that allow people to "see" race to human attributes, propensities, and motives. In this way, racial formations ascribe essential characteristics and dispositions onto human bodies.

Gender and the Creation of Racial Boundaries

Racial boundaries are sites of contestation about racial membership. The maintenance of racial boundaries depends upon ideologies that justify segregation, interracial sexual prohibitions, and other forms of social separation. Standard actions used to maintain racial boundaries include discrimination, segregation, ghettoization, and racial violence. These practices derive their rationale from the moral boundaries that people draw around the groups to which they consider themselves members. In turn, these boundaries and distinctions help solidify forms of inequality.[35]

Interdisciplinary scholarship has demonstrated the limits of understanding racial boundaries without considering their dependence on other forms of inequality. This body of work challenges the existence of universal forms of patriarchy and racism and suggests that inequality must be addressed as a complex set of overlapping, interlocking, and intersecting locations in social space.[36] While scholars generally recognize that social class, gender, sexuality, race, and ethnicity cannot be studied in isolation, some have attempted to specify how these interrelationships are created and maintained.[37] Historically, the ideological work required to create and preserve racial boundaries drew much of its strength from ideas about gender-specific forms of sexual expression and claims about masculinity and femininity.[38]

In the nineteenth century, racial ideologies became increasingly rooted in ideologies of blood purity.[39] Modern racial ideologies upheld the supposed naturalness of race based on ideas of lineage and descent; we belong to a particular race if only because our parents belong to that race. In this way, racial categories relied upon an image of the family as a unit of racial belonging. Struggles for "racial purity" exemplify the boundary work required of racial formations. To maintain racial boundaries, people often mobilize ideologies of gender, sexuality, and reproduction, deeming racial outsiders as sexually dangerous and racial insiders as racially restorative.[40] While the mythical bond between race and blood gave racial formations new authority and power, it also gave them a great vulnerability: sexual desire.

The maintenance of racial boundaries requires regulating sexual intimacy within and between groups. The management of women's sexuality is imperative for making racial categories because women can produce babies and biological kinship ties that others see as an expression of racial purity or impurity.[41] Tessie Liu argues that the reproduction of racial groups rests upon efforts to restrain the sexual activity of women: "Considered in these terms, race as a social category functions through controlling sexuality and sexual behavior."[42] Students of social inequality must carefully consider the intersection of race, gender, and sexuality because racial group-making depends upon specific ideas about who men and women can associate with, have sex with, and produce children with. Sexual identity and sexual practices form a "substructure" of social life that helps define and reinforce racial hierarchies and regimes.[43] The following discussion of lynching in the Jim Crow South illustrates the nexus between race, gender, and sexuality. It also foreshadows the substantive and theoretical contributions of this book by showing a process of racial boundary maintenance in the South—predicated on stories of sexual danger—that parallels the efforts to stop white slavery in northern and western cities.

Lynching and the Myth of the Black Rapist

After Reconstruction, southern whites created a white-over-black racial hierarchy through legal and extralegal means. In 1883, after the Supreme Court nullified the Civil Rights Act of 1875, southern legislatures passed several segregation laws from the late 1880s to 1910. This system of legal segregation, known as Jim Crow, prohibited interracial marriage and mandated separate schools, restrooms, and drinking fountains as well as separate seating in trains, buses, theaters, libraries, and stores.[44] Concerns about sexual and racial purity shaped racial domination in the post-Reconstruction South. According to John D'Emilio and Estelle Freedman, "The institutionalization of segregation in the late-nineteenth-century South rested upon a deep-seated fear that social mixing would lead to sexual mixing."[45] The existence of mixed-race persons who confounded the white/black racial binary and the sexual relationships between African American men and white women were points of crisis for the Jim Crow caste system.

Mixed-race persons in the South often fell into an ambiguous space between racial categories, challenging the sureness of the color line. This compelled the architects of Jim Crow to arrive at exact definitions of racial groups. James Davis argues that southerners strengthened the one-drop rule during the Progressive Era by legally defining people as "black" or "Negro" if they had any trace of African ancestry. The one-drop rule erased fine-grained distinctions that nineteenth-century Americans made among categories such as "mulatto," "colored," "Negro," "quadroon," and "octoroon."[46] State legislatures strengthened the one-drop rule in their anti-miscegenation laws. For example, Virginia abandoned its one-fourth rule in 1910 and imposed a standard that defined a person as "Negro" if they had one-sixteenth African ancestry.[47]

In addition to creating a sharper distinction between racial categories, southern whites sexualized the content of these categories by attributing certain sexual proclivities and desires to blacks and whites. The image of sexually passive southern white women was supported by an opposing image of lusty and lascivious black women. The image of the civilized and chivalrous white southerner found its opposite in the image of the black rapist. These racial and sexual ideologies converged in the practice of lynching, the South's most vicious method of maintaining black/white racial boundaries. Throughout the nineteenth century, native-born whites used lynching as a means of racial control, but until the 1880s, most lynching victims were Italian, Chinese, and Mexican immigrants. By the 1880s, the practice of lynching moved from the western frontier to the South, and African Americans became the primary targets of white lynch mobs.[48] Incidence of lynching peaked in 1892 when 161 African Americans were lynched, and until World War I, the average number of lynchings never fell below two or three per week.[49] D'Emilio and Freedman conclude that "from its start, the system of Jim Crow relied on lynching as its ultimate weapon of enforcement."[50]

During the late nineteenth and early twentieth centuries, some lynchings were attended by hundreds, sometimes thousands, of white spectators. These "spectacle lynchings" became a form of entertainment and ritual for the New South, and they were frequently accompanied by the torture, castration, and mutilation of the victims.[51] After 1893, railroad companies arranged special trains to transport spectators to lynching sites. Despite their barbarity, or perhaps because of it, lynch mobs acted with community approval and regularly

included whites of all social strata, including some of the community's leading citizens.[52] In the course of ritualistically marking the color line, spectacle
lynchings also gave rise to new forms of cultural production and consumption.[53] With the expansion of communication systems and the development
of photography, images of lynching circulated throughout the country. Whites
eagerly sought and collected souvenirs from lynchings, including postcards,
photographs, and body parts of the victim. Eyewitness reports spread widely
after spectacle lynchings in the form of "lynching narratives." Lynching narratives circulated as an enduring reminder of the penalties for crossing the
color line.[54]

Lynching narratives and justifications for lynchings often summoned the
image of the "black beast rapist." Stories of animalistic African Americans
raping white women provided a powerful rationale for racial violence in the
New South. Although the idea that African American men were unable to
control their sexual desires was a staple of white racial thinking throughout
the nineteenth century, the myth of the black rapist gained wide acceptance
only in the late 1880s.[55] Gail Bederman notes, "As the myth of the Negro rapist
spread throughout the South, the incidence of Southern lynching soared."[56]
Jacquelyn Dowd Hall argues that stories and rumors about African American
men raping white women became "the folk pornography" of the South, and
"as stories spread the rapist became not just a black man but a ravenous brute,
the victim a beautiful young virgin. The experience of the woman was described in minute and progressively embellished detail."[57] The practice of
lynching received both tacit and open support from outside the South as
well.[58] Although the majority of African American lynching victims had not
been accused of rape, it remained the South's primary justification for the
practice.[59]

The popular image of African Americans as a sexual threat required ideological work. Influential spokespersons from both the North and South described African American men as susceptible to bouts of uncontrollable lust,
and many women's rights activists used stories of black rapists to their political advantage. Rebecca Felton, a leader in the Georgia chapter of the
Woman's Christian Temperance Union, repeatedly stressed the importance
of lynching as a way to deter sexual violence against white women. In 1897,
she gained support by declaring, "If it takes lynching to protect women's
dearest possession from drunken, ravening beasts, then I say lynch a thousand a week if it becomes necessary."[60] Her remarks, delivered at the annual
meeting of the State Agricultural Society of Georgia, received national pub-

licity. After concluding a lecture tour to warn women about black rapists, Felton in 1922 became the first woman elected to the U.S. Senate.[61]

* * *

While southern whites enforced Jim Crow, native-born whites in the northern and western cities faced their own racial boundaries crises stemming from the uncertain racial status of new immigrant groups. Since the dawn of slavery, "white" and "colored" racial categories were consistently defined in opposition to one another, but membership within those categories shifted in the years leading up to World War I.[62] Throughout U.S. history, African Americans were relegated to the bottom of the racial ladder, but European immigrants in the nineteenth century complicated the binary black/white caste system. Anglo-Saxons considered Jews, Italians, and Irish as nonwhite races, occupying an intermediate status between black and white. During the nineteenth century, "white" did not stand as a monolithic group but was arranged into a hierarchy of different white races: Anglo-Saxons, Celts, Slavs, Hebrews, Iberics, Nordics, Teutons, Mediterraneans, and others. Anglo-Saxons regarded the Italians as savages, and in 1891 an Anglo-Saxon mob lynched eleven Italians in New Orleans.[63] Native-born whites considered the Irish racially inferior through much of the nineteenth century.[64] Jews, as well, clung to what Jacobson has called "probationary whiteness," and like other non-Anglo-Saxon immigrants, Jews "gradually became Caucasians" during the twentieth century.[65] Although now, in the twenty-first century, Americans would regard them as white or Caucasian, members of these groups saw themselves, and were seen as, racially different from other groups of "whites."

The color line between African Americans and whites permeated twentieth-century America, but as Jacobson observes, "Between the 1840s and the 1920s it was not altogether clear just where that line ultimately *would* be drawn."[66] In the North, the rapid influx of new immigrant groups and the northern migration of African Americans created new challenges for the continuing hegemony of native-born whites. In the West, native-born whites considered the Chinese as both a source of cheap labor and a threat to white racial purity. Like the development of Jim Crow, the creation of northern and western racial boundaries depended upon racialized images of sexual depravity and sexual innocence. Native-born whites in the North and West did not borrow the southern narrative of the black rapist, but they created their own story of sexual danger that drew upon the memory of abolitionism; they claimed to have discovered a new form of slavery.

Stories about immigrants abducting native-born white women and forcing them into prostitution proliferated during these crucial decades in U.S. history. White slavery narratives, like spectacle lynchings and stories of black rapists in the South, provided a resource for racial boundary maintenance in the North and West. The white slavery genre provided a touchstone for a new set of racial and gender projects, making the crusades against white slavery part and parcel of the ideological work of gender and racial formation in the early twentieth century. The next chapter analyzes the qualities of white slavery stories that made them a powerful discursive resource for maintaining and transforming racial boundaries. Subsequent chapters examine how reformers used white slavery narratives to shape the meaning of race and gender in early urban America.

2

The New Abolitionism:
The Cultural Power
of the White Slavery Genre

White slavery narratives—stories about women forced into prostitution—circulated in many formats. From 1905 to 1910, newspapers and
popular magazines frequently published accounts of white slavery.[1] At the
height of the agitation against white slavery from 1909 to 1910, at least eight
books were published on the subject. Some recounted a single story about
the plight of a white slave, while others contained several stories detailing the
fate of different women abducted into prostitution.[2] Many books about
white slavery included essays from physicians, religious leaders, missionaries, and moral crusaders emphasizing different aspects of the problem. Some
were explicitly fictional, but most books about white slavery claimed to have
a factual basis.

White slavery narratives represented an elaboration of two genres of American literature: captivity narratives and seduction narratives. A long-standing
tradition of American captivity narratives found new expression in stories
about white slaves.[3] Early American settlers penned stories about Indians on
the frontier abducting white women. The writers, sometimes using first-
person accounts, tried to convey the alleged barbarity wrought by ruthless
natives. Indian captivity narratives mobilized two mutually reinforcing stereotypes: the savage Indian and the helpless white woman.[4] These stories provided justification for violence against Indians and the acquisition of their
native land. They also enabled white men to retain control over women by
imploring them to remain close to home.

White slavery narratives also continued the tradition of the nineteenth-
century seduction narrative. In these stories, wealthy men preyed upon the

economic insecurity of working-class women, had sex with them, and betrayed them. Journals from the growing purity movement, such as the *Advocate of Moral Reform* and the *Friend of Virtue,* regularly explored these themes. The plots of many nineteenth-century novels focused on seduction and betrayal, while seduction narratives of a more lurid variety were a popular feature of newspapers called "penny presses."[5] These stories offered moral reformers a cultural template with which to make political claims.[6] Reformers created and disseminated seduction narratives as part of a broad effort to raise public awareness of prostitution, the age of consent, and the dangers of unrestrained male sexuality.[7] By the early twentieth century, the rudimentary elements of this genre provided a foundation for white slavery stories. Timothy Gilfoyle writes, "By the turn of the century, this image of the fallen woman has been replaced by that of the 'white slave.'"[8]

Borrowing the basic elements of captivity and seduction stories, white slavery narratives describe the plight of a "white slave," typically a native-born white girl from the countryside who travels to the city in search of employment. Once in the city, she falls prey to a white slave procurer—often an immigrant from southern or eastern Europe—who offers to secure employment for her. In some stories, the victim is lured to the city on false promises of marriage. In others, she leaves the countryside to pursue employment in the city and falls into the trap of the white slave procurer, or "white slaver," soon after her arrival. The procurer forces the girl into a life of prostitution by physical coercion or trickery, and once inside the brothel doors she finds it impossible to escape.

Published accounts of white slavery emphasized the dangers of city life, the threat of new immigrants, and the equivalence between chattel slavery and white slavery. Despite the commonalities among white slavery stories, they express a range of possible subject positions. The core elements of the white slavery genre allow for criticism of a number of people and institutions, including industrial capitalism, new amusements, immigrants, lackadaisical parents, and the white slaves themselves. The characters and themes of white slavery narratives reveal why these stories were so useful for Progressive Era reform projects.

White Slaves

During the 1830s and 1840s, Democratic politicians and labor leaders frequently made comparisons between chattel slavery and wage labor. They used the term "white slavery" to describe the plight of working-class men. Democratic politicians favored the term because it was broad enough to unite different class factions. Yet, while the term "white" provided a consolidating platform, the word "slavery" created a linguistic association with blacks and degradation. To avoid a sustained comparison with blacks, white working-class laborers eschewed the term by mid-century.[9]

The association between prostitution and the phrase "white slavery" emerged as early as 1839 in England, but "white slavery" remained a slogan of protest against class exploitation for much of the nineteenth century.[10] During the 1880s, British reformers began to use the phrase "white slavery" to refer to both class and sexual exploitation. British social purity organizations focused on the problem of forced prostitution in an effort to raise the age of consent, and their successes inspired the American moral reform community. With the efforts of the Woman's Christian Temperance Union (WCTU), the white slavery issue entered American public and political discourse by the end of the nineteenth century.

White slavery narratives made different estimates of the scale of forced prostitution in the United States. F. G. Tyrrell's 1908 *Shame of the Human Race* declared, "At the present time it is next to impossible to compute the number of white slaves in this country. It is safe to say there are thousands."[11] Norine Law wrote that "some 65,000 daughters of American homes and 15,000 alien girls are prey each year of the procurers in this traffic."[12] Former police chief of New York City Theodore Bingham estimated that 2,000 women were brought into the United States and were subsequently enslaved in brothels.[13] A representative from the Florence Crittenden Mission contended that 20,000 women entered the white slave trade every year.[14] Leona Prall Groetzinger in *The City's Perils* quoted FBI director Stanley Finch, who "estimated that not less than 25,000 young women and girls are annually procured for this traffic."[15] Charlton Edholm cautioned that "your little girl is not any more safe than any of the 46,000 that are every year trapped in houses of shame."[16] H. M. Lytle in *Tragedies of the White Slaves* wrote that in Chicago, "5,000 young innocents" are "led forth to the slaughter, annually."[17] Likewise, John Dillon in *From Dance Hall to White Slavery* stated that every year in Chicago 5,000 girls are "offered up as sacrificial victims to the Social Evil."[18]

Scholars who view the crusades against white slavery as a "moral panic" or exaggeration point to the claims of reformers as a gross overstatement of the extent of forced prostitution.[19] Rather than offer evidence of social hysteria, different estimates of the extent of white slavery simply represent different definitions of the term. Theodore Bingham in *The Girl That Disappears* pointed to the lack of consensus about white slavery: "In the minds of one part of the public every woman of the under-world is a 'white slave.' Another half of the population scouts the idea that any woman is a white slave, and there we are."[20] For some authors, white slavery referred to the drugging and abduction of chaste women. Others used the term to refer to a number of exploitive situations: pimps abusing their prostitutes, child prostitution, seduction and betrayal, economic compulsion to enter prostitution, or confinement in a brothel. The slippery definition of white slavery offered by reformers reflects real changes that occurred in the prostitution trade. Coercion and violence became an all too common fact of life for prostitutes as increasing numbers of middlemen profited from the vice trade, including informal consortiums of brothel proprietors, ward politicians, saloon owners, and real estate agents. Along with the commercialization of prostitution, pimps attained a greater role in the lives of prostitutes.[21]

Reformers' quantification of the extent of white slavery depended largely on their definition of the archetypal "white slave." White slavery narratives offered different images of the white slave that pivot on the question of women's sexual agency: the extent of control women have over their sexual practices. The white slave's lack of sexual agency distinguished her from willful prostitutes, yet white slavery narratives revealed a range of opinions on how much responsibility a woman should assume for entering the vice trade. For some authors, white slavery described a system whereby virgin girls were forced into prostitution by physical coercion. Others suggested that some women entered prostitution willingly and became white slaves only after they found that they could not escape the brothel. Although these accounts point to forces beyond the woman's control, some authors attributed blame directly to the immorality or foolishness of the enslaved girl. These varying constructions of the white slave implicated different strategies for fighting prostitution. White slavery narratives had no single political valence but were an elastic cultural resource for a range of political agendas.

White slavery narratives often depicted previously chaste girls forced into prostitution. According to Edward O. Janney, the author of *The White Slave Traffic in America*, "The white slave traffic is the widely accepted term for the procuring, selling or buying of women with the intention of holding or forcing them into a life of prostitution. The term is not fairly descriptive, since the traffic reaches to every race and color, originating in Europe, where its victims are white, but it is generally used to designate the system by which vice markets are kept supplied."[22] This definition established force as a criteria in determining who was and who was not a white slave. Janney also asserted that white slaves were not necessarily white or European but were drawn from a wide range of racial groups. U.S. District Attorney Edwin Sims, quoted in Chicago evangelist Ernest Bell's *Fighting the Traffic in Young Girls,* offered a definition of white slaves as women forced into prostitution who would not otherwise be prostitutes:

> The term "white slave" includes only those women and girls who are actually slaves—those women who are owned and held as property and chattels—whose lives are lives of involuntary servitude. The white slave trade may be said to be the business of securing white women and of selling them or exploiting them for immoral purposes. It includes those women and girls who, if given a fair chance, would, in all probability, have been good wives and mothers and useful citizens.[23]

Another reformer, Norine Law, argued that most brothel workers qualified as "white slaves" because of their unwilling entry into prostitution and because they could not escape the brothels where overseers compelled them to live and work. She wrote, "It is true beyond any question that the majority of women who become inmates of brothels have been deceived, lured or trapped."[24] Law emphasized that most women who entered prostitution were victims of trickery and added, "Another fact which the public finds hard to believe—especially the public of mothers—is that girls who are lured into the life of shame find it impossible to make their escape, and that they are prisoners and slaves in every sense of the word."[25] For Law, white slavery referred to the coercion used before and after women entered the brothel.

Another image of the white slave suggested that they lacked morality or common sense before the brothel experience warped their virtue. These accounts expressed a measure of sympathy for the white slaves yet claimed that they were ultimately responsible for their initial downfall. In *White Slave Hell,* Rev. F. M. Lehman and Rev. N. K. Clarkson wrote, "We know that many young females fall victims to their own improper conduct. An excessive love of finery beyond their means, bold and forward behavior in the presence of men, light and frivolous conversation, Sunday walks with merry companions, attending theaters and singing-saloons, keeping late hours and neglecting home duties—all these are judged to be indications of easy virtue; and, as a rule, the judgment is correct."[26] Under this definition, girls who became white slaves were bad to begin with, and their enslavement was ultimately their own doing.

Along these same lines, Ernest Bell wrote in *Fighting the Traffic in Young Girls* that the sexual slavery of Asian women involved coercion that far surpassed that experienced by white slaves. He argued: "The system of Chinese brothel slavery differs from the white slave trade, in that Chinese brothel slaves are not weak or wicked women who have fallen into the clutches of traffickers, as so many of our European and American white slaves unquestionably are, but are good girls who have been sold by their actual owners into a life of shame for money, sometimes sold by their own parents."[27] Here, Bell asserts that the depravity of American and European prostitutes make them susceptible to the machinations of the white slave traffic. In a section of his book entitled "Good Women Are Not Protected by Bad," Bell responds to a popular argument that segregated prostitution offers protection for respectable women by allowing men to satisfy their sexual appetite apart from their wives or marriage-minded girlfriends. He argues that venereal diseases fester in districts of segregated prostitution and that men will bring pestilence home to their families. In short, "harlots and their patrons are the worst enemies in every way that good women can have."[28] Bell uses arguments from the social hygienist Prince Morrow to claim that men who visit prostitutes give diseases to their wives that eventually affect their offspring: "'The cruelest link in the chain of consequences,' says Dr. Prince Morrow, 'is the mother's innocent agency. She is made a passive unconscious medium of instilling into the eyes of her newborn babe a virulent poison which extinguishes its sight.'"[29] In contrasting the mother's passivity and "innocent agency" with diseased prostitutes, his writing demonstrates that the authors of white slavery narratives were not always entirely sympathetic to the plight of the white slave.

The Dangers of the City

From 1860 to 1910, large American cities increased in population nearly sevenfold. By 1910, almost half of all Americans were city dwellers.[30] The disorders of America's major cities—evidenced by slums, crime, hunger, sweatshops, and disease—elicited concern from Progressive Era muckrakers and activists. White slavery narratives flourished in this spirit of reform, bolstering the image of the city as a cruel, dangerous, and unforgiving place. Many of these stories commenced with a description of an unsuspecting country girl leaving the safety of her rural town and ended with a description of her abduction in a large city.[31]

White slavery narratives reflected these changes by expressing concern about job-seeking white women in large cities. According to reformers, white slave procurers typically offered false promises of city employment to lure fresh victims from the countryside. The rise of wage-earning women coupled with newly developed forms of recreation worried many members of the white middle class. Public spaces such as city streets, train stations, dance halls, department stores, amusement parks, and even ice cream parlors were considered dangerous places for young independent women because of the constant presence of white slave procurers.

FALSE EMPLOYMENT AND MARRIAGE

With different images of the "white slave" in mind, white slavery narratives detailed diverse scenarios of abduction and downfall. They outlined the varying methods that white slave procurers used to trick women into prostitution. Many described the evil machinations of "confidence men" who gained the trust of women and girls, then led them to ruin.[32] In Reginald Wright Kauffman's white slavery novel *The House of Bondage*, a teenage girl named Mary meets a German Jew named Max Crossman who offers to take her to New York in order to marry her.[33] She agrees, not because of her attraction to him, but because she marvels at his exciting description of life in a big city: "As he spoke, though she did not know it, the far-off orchestras were calling her, as if the sound of the city deafened her to all other sounds, as if the lights of New York blinded her to the lights of home."[34] Upon arriving in New York, his promise of marriage sours, and Mary soon finds herself an inmate of a brothel after drinking too much wine. In *White Slave Hell*, Lehman and Clarkson describe a girl leaving her family for employment in Chicago: "The beautiful green of the far rolling meadow, the music of the brawling brook and the quaint old farm stead have suddenly lost their charms. The city with its smoking chimneys, roaring traffic and blinding pleasure accelerates the fever-tides of desire, as she plans for this easy, money-making position."[35] Both of these accounts recognize the appeal of city life for young women and contrast its dangers with the pastoral security of the countryside. Like a siren's call, the lights of the city lured these women to their destruction. For Mary, "the lights of New York blinded her to the lights of home." For the other, the "blinding pleasure" of Chicago and a promise of quick employment led her to her doom.

In *White Slave Hell*, Lehman and Clarkson accompanied their story about the abducted farm girl with illustrations that detail her downfall. In the first, titled "The Last Farewell," the girl waves good-bye to her father with an outstretched hand. The second illustration, "The Cab Route," shows the same young woman in a busy city being led into a taxi. A well-dressed man with a moustache holds her right arm and gestures to the cab, while tall buildings dwarf the people milling on the street. The caption at the bottom indicates that the man is leading the naive woman to a brothel: "A pander from the Madam's low retreat / Makes ruin of our Innocence complete." The final illustration de-

"The Last Farewell. With breaking heart he bids his child farewell / Enroute to languish in a living hell." In F. M. Lehman and N. K. Clarkson, *The White Slave Hell, or With Christ at Midnight in the Slums of Chicago* (Chicago: The Christian Witness Company, 1910).

picts an elderly couple praying for the return of their daughter. The mother has her hands clasped above her head and looks longingly to heaven. While her parents pray for her return, the white slave languishes in the brothel. *White Slave Hell* describes images of bucolic innocence that move through the mind of the victim as she plies her trade: "The lewd loveless lout leering at her side drags her still deeper into the depths and—then a picture of old dog Tray, the parting at the farmstead and the drooping figure on the depot platform flashes before her tear-dimmed vision. As she lies on her couch of shame after the night-orgies are over the music of the babbling brook steals softly down the halls of memory and she longs for 'Home, Sweet Home.'"[36]

False promises of employment ensured a consistent source of white slaves. In *The Tragedies of the White Slaves*, Lytle wrote, "Probably the greatest agency through which girls are lured is the fake 'theatrical agency.' In Chicago there

"The Cab Route. A pander from the Madam's low retreat / Makes ruin of our innocence complete." In F. M. Lehman and N. K. Clarkson, *The White Slave Hell, or With Christ at Midnight in the Slums of Chicago* (Chicago: The Christian Witness Company, 1910).

exists many of these clearinghouses for the vice trust."[37] Drawing upon a distinction between the innocence of the countryside and the depravity of the city, Lytle described an employment contract as a death warrant for a young woman: "The kiss she places fondly on her mother's brow is that of a person going to her grave. The laughing farewells she has with her young friends are the last. The homecoming within a few months' time is never to be realized. The signing of her name to the contract is the signing of her death warrant and—yes, even worse than that. In the stroke of the pen she signs away her body to the slavers."[38]

CHEAP AMUSEMENTS

Several new institutions that accompanied urbanization also put women at risk. In the early twentieth century, dance halls, five-cent theaters, and amusement parks—what historian Kathy Peiss has described as "cheap amusements"—became immensely popular among the urban working class.[39] The authors of white slavery narratives described these places as notorious hunting grounds for white slave traders. *White Slave Hell* lists several sources of white slavery: "From the dance hall; from the beer garden; from the saloon; from the ball room; from the nickel theater; from the respectable (?) theater; from the ice cream parlor; from the hotel; from the church; from the depot; from the excursion boat; from the park; from the street; from the village and from the quiet farmstead home in the hills the Octopus on the Lake draws our nation's fairest daughters into its unsatisfied maw of lust."[40] According to Lehman and Clarkson, white slave procurers patrolled seemingly safe places, such as ice cream parlors. Procurers' outward appearance of respectability belied a fiendish appetite for young women, "and as for the girl, shielded and kept ignorant at

"The First Step. Ice cream parlors of the city and fruit stores combined, largely run by foreigners, are the places where scores of girls have taken their first step downward. Does her mother know the character of the place and the man she is with?" In Ernest Bell, *Fighting the Traffic in Young Girls* (Chicago: G. S. Ball, 1910).

"The Octopus on the Lake. The monster's slimy tentacles drag in / The fairest forms to grace the dens of sin." In F. M. Lehman and N. K. Clarkson, *The White Slave Hell, or With Christ at Midnight in the Slums of Chicago* (Chicago: The Christian Witness Company, 1910).

home, any day they may meet the polished and winning 'procurer,' in the street, the railway station, the hotel, the waiting-room of a department store, the ice-cream parlor, at an entertainment, or even on the very school-grounds."[41]

White slavery narratives depicted dance halls as particularly dangerous places for young women. Norine Law in *Shame of a Great Nation* concluded, "There are very few girls who visit the public dance hall, that do not in the end come to grief."[42] Bell wrote that "the route to the abyss is commonly by way of dance halls and amusement resorts of all kinds having drinking attachments. . . . The girl who dances is in very great peril, and she puts young men with whom she dances under greater temptation than herself."[43] Florence Dedrick, a rescue missionary for the Moody Church in Chicago, concluded, "One of the most fascinating allurements of city life to many a young girl is the dance-hall, which is truly the ante-room to hell itself. Here indeed, is the beginning of the white slave traffic in many instances."[44]

Anti-vice crusaders argued that the amusements and employment opportunities found in major urban centers had a powerful effect on the moral condition of women by transforming "country girls" into "city girls." Chicago anti-vice crusader Clifford Roe declared that "these pandering cases, and

"Dangerous Amusements—The Brilliant Entrance to Hell Itself. Young girls who have danced at home a little are attracted by the blazing lights, gaiety and apparent happiness of the 'dance halls,' which in many instances leads to their downfall." In Ernest Bell, *Fighting the Traffic in Young Girls* (Chicago: G. S. Ball, 1910). A sign to the right of the entrance reads "Hotel Rooms by Day or Week."

many more, bring out clearly that the cities are indeed great melting pots where foreign girls are cast in the crucible to be made Americans, and where the country girls are being transformed into city girls."[45] For Roe, cities had a transformative effect on foreigners and country girls, giving them an urban sensibility. Although both were vulnerable to the white slaver, Roe claimed that all girls were at risk from the white slave trader: "The panders make no distinction between girls who are innocent, quiet and modest and those who are more wayward, flirtatious and frivolous. The procuring of the former adds zest and sport to the hunt, while the latter are easy prey for them."[46] Many reformers argued that the innocence of country girls made them vulnerable to the schemes of white slavers. *White Slave Hell* quoted Florence Dedrick: "The country girl is more open to the enticements of city life, being more truthful, perfectly innocent, and unsuspecting of those whose business it is to seek their prey from girls of this class. The city girl has had it drilled into her from the time she could walk that she must regard people with distrust, not speaking to strangers anywhere, accepting nothing from any one, and making confidants only of her own people."[47]

Edwin Sims described at length the dangers facing country girls. His remarks were reprinted in several white slavery books: "In view of what I have learned in the course of the recent investigation and prosecution of the 'white slave' traffic, I can say in all sincerity, that if I lived in the country and had a young daughter, I would go to any length of hardship and privation myself rather than allow her to go into the city to work or to study."[48] Sims urged parents to keep their daughters in the country, citing "imminent peril to every girl in the country who has a desire to get into the city and taste its excitements and its pleasures."[49] He continued: "[Y]ou feel like saying to every mother in the country: Do not trust any man who pretends to take an interest in your girl if that interest involves her leaving your own roof. Keep her with you. She is far safer in the country than in the big city."[50]

THE WHITE SLAVE PROCURER

White slavery narratives depicted the dangers facing young independent women in the city. Its new forms of recreation and opportunities for employment drew young women into precarious situations. Also, the shifting racial population of American cities vexed reformers. White slavery authors worried openly about the migration of African Americans to northern cities and the rapid influx of immigrants from southern and eastern Europe. Embedded in the contrast between the country and the city was a contrast between American and foreign.

A central feature of white slavery narratives is the depiction of foreigners as a sexual threat. Sims declared, "Many of these white slave traders are recruited from the scum of the criminal classes of Europe."[51] Descriptions of the white slave trade often expressed nativist hostility against new immigrants. Norine Law pinned the blame on new immigrants in *The Shame of a Great Nation:*

> [T]he stock of the immigrants entering the United States, and especially its cities, is growing constantly worse. Drawn first from the higher and more intelligent types of northwestern Europe, our immigration has degenerated constantly to the poorest breeds of the eastern and southern sections of the continent. We have made the United States an asylum for the oppressed and incompetent of all nations, and have put the government into the hands of the inmates of the asylum.[52]

Law iterated a common distinction made by native-born whites about older immigrants from northern Europe and newer immigrants from southern and eastern Europe. Immigrants from southern and eastern Europe were considered less desirable than older waves of immigrants because they were perceived as lacking the positive elements of the Anglo-Saxon race.[53] In *White Slave Hell*, Lehman and Clarkson contended, "A great deal of this evil is done by foreigners, and I do believe that the root of the trouble is laziness. They come from countries where the highest good is just to lie in the sun and sleep. They do not, they cannot, understand the love of work, the dignity of labor, the joy of accomplishment."[54]

White slavery narratives often singled out eastern European Jews for creating white slave markets in American cities.[55] In *Chicago and Its Cess-Pools of Infamy*, Samuel Paynter Wilson described his excursion into Chicago's red-light district where he witnessed American girls toiling in brothels managed by Russian Jews:

> My heart kept going faster and faster until I could bear it no longer. American "fillies" and body and soul under a brutal Russian Jewish whoremonger! I slipped quietly out into the street; night was coming on as I walked down Madison street and south on Peoria. Yes, there were the shanties—poor, wretched hovels, every one of them. Out shone the flickering red lights, out came the discordant, rasping sound of the rented piano, out belched the shrieks of drunken harlots, mingled with the groans and curses of task-masters in a foreign tongue, attracting the attention of the hundreds of laborers, negroes and boys, as they walked home on Peoria street from their day's work.[56]

For Wilson, Chicago's immigrant population threatened to erode spatial boundaries between natives and the foreign-born. Vice districts created spaces for social and sexual intercourse among people of different races and nationalities—what historian Kevin Mumford has termed "interzones."[57] Brothels were a site of scandalous intermingling, bringing together working-class men from all races and classes. Wilson continued, "I discovered in the wine and back rooms of the wretched place a crowd of perhaps fifty drunken, dirty men and women, young white girls, huddled in with the worst mob of negroes, whites and Chinese I have seen in Chicago's slums, all cursing, drinking, singing and blaspheming in plain view and hearing on the street."[58] In contrasting "young white girls" with depraved "negroes, whites and Chinese," Wilson makes a comparison that binds gender and race by aligning whiteness with femininity. Gender and race are fused together in these passages to create a characteristically lurid description of white slavery.

The French, too, were often described as notorious white slave procurers. Ernest Bell wrote, "Paris, the capital of such kings and the scene of such debauchery, became the source and headquarters of the world-wide white slave trade of the present time."[59] He maintained that the French—although joined by other races and nationalities in perpetuating white slavery—were primarily responsible for establishing the vice traffic in the United States. He continued, "By no means all the traffickers are French. Many are Jews, many Italians and Sicilians, some are Austrians, Germans, English, Americans, Greeks. But it is Paris that has made vice a fine art, and has made the white slave trade a wide-spread systematized commercial enterprise."[60] Bell described the growth of the vice trade in racial terms, claiming that "the outrageous French system of giving legal standing to vice" is "utterly repugnant to the Anglo-Saxon conscience."[61] Anti-vice reformers frequently blamed eastern Europeans, Jews, and the French for developing white slavery syndicates in American cities. White slavery narratives were amenable to different racial projects based on different visions of citizenship and racial hierarchy.

White Slavery versus Chattel Slavery

Stories about white slavery took the primary elements of captivity and seduction narratives into new directions by evoking the specter of antebellum slavery. In this way, the white slavery narrative drew strength from another nonfiction genre from the nineteenth century: the abolitionist tract. Consistent with the northern history of abolitionism, urban reformers claimed to have discovered a new form of slavery that demanded an attack as vigorous as the one waged against chattel slavery. The comparison of white slavery and chattel slavery had several rhetorical elements that frequently appeared in white slavery books and stories. White slavery authors stressed the equivalence of white slavery and chattel slavery and often argued that white slavery represented a more egregious system of inhumanity compared to chattel slavery. They also brought into play the touchstones of the abolitionist movement. Urban reformers made these comparisons in their book-length narratives as well as in their public statements about prostitution.

"THE BLACK TRAFFIC IN WHITE GIRLS"

Authors of white slavery stories attempted to place white slavery on a par with chattel slavery. Many reformers tried to accomplish this with the linguistic juxtaposition of "black" and "white," referring to white slavery as a "black slavery." For instance, Madeline Southard in *The White Slave Traffic versus the American Home* referred to the "black tragedy of white slavery."[62] Chicago missionary Jean Turner Zimmermann authored a book entitled *Chicago's*

Black Traffic in White Girls.[63] Ernest Bell manned a float in the 1909 temperance and law enforcement parade that read "End Black Traffic in White Girls."[64] He also used this phrase in an article he wrote for the WCTU's journal, the *Union Signal.*[65] Likewise, the cover of his book *Fighting the Traffic in Young Girls* promised "thirty-two pages of striking pictures showing the workings of the blackest slavery that has ever stained the human race." Elizabeth Andrew and Katharine Bushnell in *Heathen Slaves and Christian Rulers* referred to white slavery as "one of the blackest chapters in the history of human slavery."[66] Reformers used the metaphorical relationship between black and white to punctuate the evils of the forced prostitution of native-born whites. Referring to forced prostitution as a "black slavery" marked it as bad and immoral, but it also implicitly compared forced prostitution to the enslavement of African Americans.

Reformers often went one step further and argued that the system of white slavery was worse than chattel slavery. Clifford Roe stated:

> A great many persons were skeptical of the existence of a well defined and organized traffic in girls. They seemed to think that those advocating the abolition of this nefarious trade were either fanatics or notoriety seekers. . . . The first task therefore was to enlighten about ninety-five per cent of the people; to bring home to them the realization that a vast system of slavery, far more debasing than that of the blacks, was flourishing under their very eyes.[67]

Norine Law argued "that there is an actual, systematic and widespread traffic in girls as definite, as established, as mercenary and as fiendish as was the African slave trade in its blackest days."[68] Tyrrell stated that "a white slave is a vassal as much as was ever the blackest African that came over from the dark continent in the reeking hold of a slave ship."[69] Sims claimed that "things are being done every day in New York, Philadelphia, Chicago and other large cities in this country in the white slave traffic which would, by contrast, make the Congo slave traders of the old days appear like Good Samaritans."[70] In *White Slavery in Los Angeles,* Charles Locke stated, "Stealthily like poisonous serpents these devils ply their ingenious schemes, and the result is the most horrible slavery which has been known in civilization."[71] Likewise, Roe argued, "The words describe what they stand for. The white slave of Chicago is a slave as much as the negro was before the Civil War, as the African is in the Belgian districts of the Congo."[72]

Some white slavery authors de-emphasized the brutality of chattel slavery in order to punctuate the horrors of white slavery. For example, Roe described the living conditions in brothels as more degrading than what slaves experienced before their emancipation:

> This country could not bear the spectacle of black folk enslaved in the south, and the most terrible civil war in all history was the result. And yet here in Chicago the good citizen, his wife, and his sons and daughters ride down town on the street cars with never a thought of the fact that ere he reaches down town his way will take him within pistol shot of dens where women, white of skin and civilized of mind, are kept in slavery under conditions worse than that of the slave quarters before the war.[73]

Roe suggested that the vice and depravity that existed in their community should outrage the "good citizen" and his family. If men were willing to go to war because of slavery in the South, then northerners should be motivated to address slavery in their own cities. Roe compared the victims of forced prostitution with enslaved African Africans, suggesting that women "white of skin and civilized of mind" were more worthy of a war fought on their behalf. Likewise, in *Chicago and Its Cess-Pools of Infamy*, Wilson contends that "in the dives and dens of our city's underworld I have heard shrieks and heart cries and groans of agony and remorse that have never been surpassed at any public slave auction America has ever witnessed."[74]

In a similar vein, B. S. Steadwell, president of the American Purity Federation, maintained that the traffic in young women was far more pernicious than chattel slavery: "We thought that we had gotten rid of chattel slavery years and years ago. But now we learn of a state of affairs which is worse than the chattel slavery of olden times. For the slave of former times had at least a long lease on life and frequently enjoyed health and some measure of freedom, but the white slave of today is crushed body and soul, beaten and humiliated—then left to perish."[75] For Steadwell, the conditions surrounding the white slave ensured her early death, whereas African slaves had health, freedom, and longevity. In a section entitled "Worse Than African Slavery," Lehman and Clarkson summoned the stereotype of the "happy slave" to argue that the hideousness of white slavery surpassed the horrors of chattel slavery:

> It is as if the old times before the war had come back and white girls were enslaved even more than the black ones. How long would slavery have lasted, if every white man knew that his own daughter was in danger of being bought and sold? It is far worse than African slavery, for many of the black slaves were happy and many of them were good, even deeply religious; while no woman,

though she be deceived and made an innocent victim, can be happy after she
has been ruined, can live happily in sin, or when surrounded by vice.[76]

According to Lehman and Clarkson, white slaves were irreparably ruined
by their imprisonment while chattel slaves were able to retain their religion
and morals.

Some authors suggested that the efforts to stop white slavery could help rec-
oncile regional divisions between the North and South. Lehman and Clarkson
argued that the practice of white slavery surpassed the cruelty of chattel slavery and presented a new problem to be fought by the now-united American
public: "The kindly earth drank up the crimson life-tides of the Blue and Gray,
and the passing years have healed the wound and we are brothers again. Under
the shadow of the dear old flag has sprung into existence a slavery that to-day
outrivals in cunning and cruelty that of the Black Slave Master; viz., the White
Slave trade."[77] A WCTU worker reiterated this sentiment when she noted, "This
state of affairs is only possible because the subject has never been put before
the masses of the people. An arousement is needed! There can be but one opinion—there will be no North, no South, no 'wet,' no 'dry.'"[78]

THE NEW ABOLITIONISM

In addition to arguing the equivalence between white slaves and chattel slaves,
authors of white slavery narratives compared themselves to abolitionists.
Katharine Bushnell, an important moral entrepreneur of the white slavery
problem, delivered a speech in Chicago entitled "Slavery Up North." Following her speech, the audience drafted two resolutions, one of which declared, "[I]t is the sentiment of this meeting that another occasion has arisen
in this country which calls for action as determined and heroic as was the great
anti-slavery movement of thirty years ago."[79] Writing about white slavery for
the WCTU, a worker for the organization asked, "We have freed the black people—shall white women remain in bondage?"[80] Likewise, the opening chapter of Jane Addams's book on white slavery, titled "An Analogy," compared
white slavery with chattel slavery and compared the abolitionist movement
with Progressive Era anti-vice organizations. Addams wanted to illuminate
the horrors of coercive prostitution as a form of slavery "as old and outrageous as slavery itself and even more persistent."[81]

Reformers tried to garner support for their new abolitionist cause by using
the symbols and hallmarks of the nineteenth-century abolitionist crusade. The
image of Abraham Lincoln as the emancipator of slaves appeared repeatedly
in the cultural products of anti-vice activists. For instance, Ernest Bell hung a

picture of Lincoln in his office. He also passed out leaflets to several Chicago brothels that stated, "'It is a penitentiary offense to detain any woman in a house of prostitution against her will . . .' No 'white slave' need remain in slavery in this State of Abraham Lincoln who made the black slaves free."[82] The 1907 inauguration of the National Vigilance Committee occurred at the Lincoln Center on Lincoln's birthday to symbolize its connection to abolitionism.[83] Joseph Flint from the American Purity Federation—an organizational precursor to the National Vigilance Committee—claimed, "The prophet soul of Abraham Lincoln foresaw the doom of slavery. Gifted with equal insight, choice souls are today foreseeing the dethronement of carnality and the bringing in of the peaceful reign of purity."[84] Ellen Henrotin invoked the memory of Lincoln during a 1909 public speech in Chicago. She proclaimed, "We are celebrating here in Chicago this week the birthday of the liberator of slaves. Perhaps a hundred years from today America will be celebrating the birth of some woman wise enough and brave enough and noble enough to be the liberator of women from a slavery far worse than that from which Lincoln freed the negro."[85] According to the transcript of her speech, her audience offered applause when she concluded: "When our citizens fully realize its importance and truth, they will rise to the occasion as they did in Lincoln's time, and stamp out white slavery forever."[86]

Like the memory of Lincoln, Harriet Beecher Stowe's *Uncle Tom's Cabin* provided a touchstone with which to compare anti-prostitution efforts with abolitionism. For instance, in the late nineteenth century, British reformer William T. Stead declared that he was ready to become the "new Mrs. Stowe" by popularizing the prostitution issue.[87] Jane Addams commented on the "growing literature" about white slavery that was "not only biological and didactic, but of a popular type more closely approaching 'Uncle Tom's Cabin.'"[88] Frances Willard, daughter of an abolitionist and leader of the WCTU, recalled a seduction narrative from her youth: "The first time the thought ever came to me that a man could be untrue to a woman was when on entering my teens I read a story in the [*Advocate of Moral Reform,*] entitled, 'The Betrayer and the Betrayed.' It haunted me more than any story in all my youth, except [*Uncle Tom's Cabin*]."[89] Suffragist Helen Hamilton Gardener wrote two popular seduction narratives in the late nineteenth century. The WCTU distributed her novels to legislators and the public to generate support for its age of consent campaign. Gardener said that she hoped that the depiction of "fallen women" in *Pray You, Sir, Whose Daughter?* would generate the same outrage accomplished by the depiction of African Americans in *Uncle Tom's Cabin*.[90]

Reginal Wright Kauffman's novel *The House of Bondage* is perhaps the closet imitator of *Uncle Tom's Cabin*. The bestseller chronicles the victimization of a teenage girl from rural Pennsylvania at the hands of an immigrant Jewish white slave procurer, a French brothel madame, Chinese opium addicts, and corrupt Irish policemen. The villain in *Uncle Tom's Cabin* is a slave master named Simon Legree; Kauffman's chief villain is "Rose Legere," the brothel madame who enslaves the innocent teen. A reviewer in the *New York Times* compared the book to *Uncle Tom's Cabin,* and so did John D. Rockefeller Jr. in a letter he sent to over 200 prominent citizens, accompanied by a copy of the novel. Rockefeller's mailing of *The House of Bondage* brought the novel to the attention of prominent Americans. Businessman and philanthropist Cleveland Dodge mentioned to Rockefeller that he "had a long letter from Mr. Roosevelt, after reading the book. He is immensely stirred about the whole matter, and wants at once to meet the author."[91] Tycoon J. P. Morgan told Rockefeller, "It has haunted me ever since I read it."[92]

* * *

Some literary scholars and sociologists of literature have argued that readers actively create the meanings of texts. To understand the power of a cultural object, be it a play, magazine article, painting, or news broadcast, it is insufficient to focus on the intrinsic or immanent qualities of the work. The analyst must consider how the audience interprets the object in question and must recognize the legitimacy of these interpretations, however far they veer from the author's intent. The "reader response" approach analyzes the interaction between cultural objects and their audience, emphasizing the expectations and background that cultural consumers bring to the objects that they are reading, listening to, or viewing.[93] Yet, some cultural objects, like white slavery narratives, avail themselves to multiple interpretations more so than others.[94]

Reformers used stories about forced prostitution to address popular political and social issues of the time. The range of political and social agendas that found expression in white slavery narratives testifies to the usefulness of the genre. The following chapters analyze how reformers used white slavery narratives for different projects centered on race, gender, and sexuality. Tracing the crusades against white slavery in Chicago, New York City, and San Francisco will show that anti-vice efforts were an important part of the volatile history of race and gender in the early twentieth century.

3

Suffrage and Slavery:
The Racial Politics of the Woman's Christian
Temperance Union Purity Campaign

Historians have persuasively demonstrated that the dominant ideology of femininity during the Victorian era provided a powerful moral validation for the early women's rights movement.[1] This set of ideas—what Barbara Welter termed the "cult of true womanhood"—extolled the innate virtue of women that stemmed from their sexual modesty and passivity.[2] Women's supposed lack of sexual passion ensured domestic harmony, which Victorians considered a foundation of national strength. Although outwardly restrictive, this ideology of femininity allowed middle- and upper-class women to make a strong claim for political power in the name of "social housekeeping"[3] and "home protection."[4]

Scholars have also shown that ideas about racial difference embedded in the cult of true womanhood directed the strategies of the early women's rights movement.[5] The Woman's Christian Temperance Union, the largest women's organization of the nineteenth century, produced and disseminated stories about forced prostitution and helped set the agenda for the national fight against white slavery. This chapter analyzes the racial politics of the WCTU's social purity campaign. Like other organizations that comprised the early women's rights movement, the WCTU justified its acquisition of political and social rights by its race-based sexual piety and morality and members' maternal responsibility to protect the Anglo-Saxon family. Their investigations of forced prostitution in lumber camps in Wisconsin and Michigan formed a starting point for the American crusades against white slavery.

Frances Willard and Katharine Bushnell, leaders in the WCTU, were largely responsible for introducing the white slavery issue to the American reform community in the late nineteenth century. As prominent public spokespersons, Willard and Bushnell not only reflected the cultural climate of their era but also offered new ways of understanding the connection between race on one hand and manhood and womanhood on the other. These reformers articulated images of the Anglo-Saxon family, the white slave, and the white slave procurer that others used decades later, often for different political agendas. Their investigations and revelations of forced prostitution provided arguments in support of women's suffrage, couched in notions of proper Anglo-Saxon femininity and masculinity. This chapter explores the possibilities and limitations of the WCTU's political strategy and its dependence upon an ideology of Anglo-Saxon superiority.

The Maiden Tribute of Modern Babylon

A proper account of the WCTU's fight against white slavery begins in late-Victorian London. In July 1885, English journalist William T. Stead published an article in the *Pall Mall Gazette* entitled "The Maiden Tribute of Modern Babylon." He explained in detail how poor girls were systematically drugged, imprisoned, and raped.[6] Stead's article had an explicit critique of class inequality. He described depraved aristocrats who preyed on helpless working-class girls from the East End of London. One and a half million reprints were made of the article, ensuring its widespread exposure.[7]

As editor of the *Pall Mall Gazette,* Stead practiced "New Journalism," an emerging approach that used sensational topics, interviews, and concrete evidence of wrongdoing to influence political parties and social policy. Stead's "Maiden Tribute of Modern Babylon" created an uproar that temporarily effaced political and religious differences among its readers; all could agree that the crimes that he described had to be stopped. Approximately 25,000 people participated in a demonstration in Hyde Park following Stead's revelations. Delegates from temperance organizations, purity groups, and working men's clubs carried white roses symbolizing sexual purity and raised banners calling for social purity and a war on vice.[8] Parliament soon thereafter passed the "Criminal Law Amendment Act," which raised the age of consent from thirteen to sixteen. The new law mandated that men who had sexual intercourse with girls under the age of sixteen, whether or not they consented, could be prosecuted for rape.[9]

"The Maiden Tribute of Modern Babylon" had an immediate impact on the American moral reform community. Frances Willard, then president of the WCTU, claimed that Stead's revelations allowed for candid discussions of sexual violence. She wrote, "The moral cyclone that attended the *Pall Mall Gazette* disclosures" effectively "cleared the air and broke the spell, so that silence now seems criminal and we only wonder that we did not speak before."[10] A few months after Stead's article appeared, Willard urged her organization to follow the lead of English reformers.

The issue of coerced prostitution, increasingly referred to as "white slavery," offered an unambiguous example of male cruelty and the need for the moral influence of women. Toward the goal of protecting women, Willard created a special subdivision of her organization to fight sexual violence and the sexual double standard. Prompted by Stead's article, Willard formed the Department of Social Purity of the WCTU.[11] The department focused on rescuing prostitutes and abolishing the sexual double standard.[12] Like their English forebears, purity reformers also launched a nationwide campaign to raise the age of consent. WCTU researchers discovered that the age of consent was ten in most states, twelve in others, and in the state of Delaware it was only seven.[13] Willard appointed Katharine Bushnell as an evangelist for the new department, a young woman whom Willard had learned to trust while dean of women at Northwestern University.

"Another Maiden Tribute": Katharine Bushnell and the Lumbermen's Camps

Katharine Bushnell played a critical role in bringing the problem of forced prostitution to the attention of the WCTU. Bushnell received her MD from the Woman's Medical College in Chicago in 1879. She served as a medical missionary in China for the Methodist Episcopal Foreign Missionary Society for over two years. Upon her return, she moved to Denver to practice medicine but spent much of her time working for the Colorado WCTU. In 1885, Frances Willard encouraged her to return to Evanston, Illinois, to work for the WCTU's Department of Social Purity. Bushnell began her lifelong career in social purity reform with an investigation of forced prostitution in lumber camps.[14]

Bushnell launched her investigation during the heyday of the midwestern lumber industry. During the 1870s and 1880s, lumber towns in Michigan and Wisconsin rapidly grew. Canadian lumbermen were consistently the largest group of foreign-born workers in these towns, and their numbers swelled in the 1880s. The lumber trade also attracted workers from Ireland, Poland, Germany, and England.[15] Between 1880 and 1890, foreign-born lumbermen comprised over 40 percent of the men in the three largest lumber towns in

Michigan, more than the percentage of immigrants in Milwaukee and Detroit. By 1890, French Canadians, Germans, and Poles made up 71 percent of the foreign-born population in these towns.[16]

The large percentage of young foreign men that lived in lumber towns made them an obvious target of reform. The high concentration of young male immigrants prompted one WCTU worker to worry about the lack of "Christianizing and refining influences" and the danger of lumbermen reverting "toward barbarism."[17] Moreover, lumber camps were notorious centers of prostitution. Despite the seasonal nature of logging, prostitutes were a permanent presence in the lumber towns. Historical research affirms Bushnell's observation that there were hundreds of prostitutes working in the camps.[18] Most of them were Canadian immigrants, but some prostitutes came from England, France, Ireland, and Germany.[19] Prostitutes in these settlements faced unusually harsh circumstances. They accounted for approximately one-quarter of all suicides in the camps. Also, with common laborers and sailors, prostitutes made up the most frequently arrested group in the lumber towns.[20]

Bushnell studied the lumbermen's camps from May to August 1888. In her autobiographical pamphlet, she recounted reading about "a horrible White Slave trade" in the daily newspapers, and "when we could not find anyone to investigate the conditions and get reliable facts, I determined to investigate them myself."[21] During the four months she probed the lumber towns, she visited about sixty "dens" of prostitution and recorded "the histories of some 577 cases of degraded women."[22] These reports embarrassed Wisconsin politicians who had assured the public that prostitution did not occur in the camps. State investigator James Fielding, whose own inquiry Bushnell criticized, attacked Bushnell and accused her of "unchastity." Bushnell brought slander charges against him that were eventually thrown out of court.[23] Despite these assaults on her character, Bushnell's testimony before the Wisconsin legislature led to the passage of a law that criminalized the procuring of prostitutes, nicknamed the "Kate Bushnell Bill."

In 1887, the WCTU published an article in its national newspaper called "Another Maiden Tribute," based on disturbing reports of prostitution in northern Michigan and Wisconsin. "Another Maiden Tribute" described how women were offered lucrative employment in the camps but were forced to serve as prostitutes for the lumbermen after they arrived: "Advertisements cunningly devised are used in coaxing working girls from their homes."[24] Although immigrants comprised a large number of prostitutes in the camps, the WCTU focused its attention on native-born girls. The article detailed the tragedy of a Chicago girl "of undoubtable respectability" who "was decoyed from an honorable life by an advertisement offering large wages in a boarding house. When she had nearly reached her destination, she for the first time learned the horrible life she was going to, and sought to turn back, but was compelled by force to go on."[25] The slave keepers imposed an elaborate system of fines "by which the poor wretches are kept constantly in debt to the overseers."[26] In some cases, men reportedly used force to keep women from escaping. The article noted, "Dogs are kept to guard against the girls running away. In one case, which has been fully investigated, a girl escaped, after being shot in the leg, and took refuge in the swamp. Dogs were let loose on her trail, and a gang of overseers started after her. She slept in the swamp one night, but was finally hunted down and taken back to the den."[27] WCTU workers encouraged the Department of Social Purity to research these charges and to educate women and girls about the dangers of false promises of employment:

> Meanwhile, we must devise some way of warning young girls, especially those of the working classes, against the snares of the decoyer; offers of high wages for services at distant points should be regarded with suspicion and subjected to thorough investigation. Possibly no more immediate duty devolves upon the social purity department of the W.C.T.U. than the issuing and distributing among working girls a "note of warning," cautioning against the dead falls of the procurer. Let it be published on manilla paper, and so cheap that the poorest—all are poor—can afford to do their duty.[28]

Like Stead's article in the *Pall Mall Gazette*, "Another Maiden Tribute" emphasized the particular dangers facing working-class women. The statement that "all are poor" asserts a collective identity for women as humble Christians and the need for women of all social strata to protect one another. The WCTU viewed the moral and Christian influence of middle- and upper-class women as the solution to the prostitution problem. They also sought help from the White Cross movement, an Episcopal sexual purity organization that published pamphlets and circulars about the need for sexual purity. Typical of the early WCTU's emphasis on moral education, the Department of Social Purity sponsored "mother's meetings" to teach parents how to discuss sex with their children.[29]

The WCTU also created the Lumbermen Department to inculcate lumbermen with Christian morals. The Lumbermen Department worked to create "free reading rooms, or club rooms, where the daily papers, magazines, traveling libraries, innocent games are provided in place of cards and other doubtful entertainment" in order that lumbermen "be given the idea of a true citizenship."[30] Although they did not mention the immigrant presence in lumber camps, the WCTU's appeal to give lumbermen an "idea of true citizenship" suggested that the immorality found in the camps gave immigrant lumbermen a distorted perspective of what it meant to be an American, preventing them from truly assimilating. The WCTU suggested that moralizing influences would eventually lessen the number of crimes committed by the lumbermen. When discussing the ongoing problem of prostitution in the lumber camps, WCTU worker Emma Shores claimed: "An army of men of all nationalities come to our shores from every land under the sun. These men are to make our laws, and become our citizens. Their children are to fill an important place in the body politic of our nation. A large majority of the juvenile criminality comes from the ranks of the people from other lands, and it is our duty to do our part in saving these young foreigners."[31] In her report of the missionary work among lumbermen, WCTU worker Emma Obenauer stated that improving the morals of lumbermen and the moral climate of their camps protected women from sexual violence. She said that "by helping *them* spiritually we protect *our own sex* and the scattered settlements where no preaching on temperance work is carried out."[32]

The investigation of forced prostitution in the lumber camps led the WCTU into a new moral battleground, and it substantially boosted the career of Katharine Bushnell. Enlivened by her notoriety, Bushnell began a two-year public speaking tour, delivering more than 140 lectures in fourteen different states.[33] In Philadelphia, Bushnell delivered a speech entitled "The Slavery of Women in Northern Wisconsin";[34] in Chicago, she addressed 300 women with a talk entitled "Slavery Up North." After her Chicago speech, the audience drafted and unanimously passed two resolutions calling "for action as determined and heroic as was the great anti-slavery movement of thirty years ago" in order to give "relief of their sisters who are buried in living graves, as are those now being held in the dens of Northern Wisconsin."[35]

Bushnell's speeches drew large audiences, but she sensed that they had a prurient interest in her stories about the lumber camps. She complained that "the audience wanted nothing else from me but sensational stories about Northern Wisconsin, and listened impatiently to plain moral instruction in the principles of purity."[36] Frustrated with the direction of her reform work in the United States, Bushnell left for England in 1890 to work with English reformer Josephine Butler.[37] Referring to her fight with the Wisconsin state investigator, Bushnell later recalled that "Miss Willard herself had felt that it would be better for me to pursue my purity activities where it could be done with less sensation because of the Wisconsin episode."[38] While Bush-

Frances E. Willard (1839–98). Willard acted as president of the National Woman's Christian Temperance Union from 1879 until her death in 1898. From Anna Gordon, *The Beautiful Life of Frances Willard* (Chicago: Woman's Temperance Publishing Association, 1898).

nell studied prostitution abroad, Frances Willard became the guiding force of the WCTU's social purity efforts.

Frances Willard and the Racial Foundation of Victorian Feminism

Although historical studies of Frances Willard have described her as a defender of the working class and an early feminist, she held an understanding of Anglo-Saxon racial distinctiveness that tempered the progressive aims of her organization.[39] Willard's racial ideology depended upon a particular understanding of Anglo-Saxon womanhood. As this section will show, the ways in which Willard and the WCTU framed the issues of sexual violence and white slavery expressed—and depended upon—a depiction of new immigrants and African Americans as sexual predators. In the course of this, Willard and the WCTU attributed sexual meaning to different racial categories.

The WCTU's popularization of the white slavery issue bolstered its larger efforts to expand women's political power. In fact, women's suffrage was arguably a more important goal to the leaders in the WCTU than temperance, despite the name and public face of their organization.[40] Willard shared many of the goals of the early women's rights organizations, including women's right to political participation in voting and holding office, the right of wives to retain their maiden names, the right for mothers to have custody of their children following divorce, the right for women to have control over family size, and an elimination of divorce laws that favored men. The leadership of Frances Willard also nurtured the WCTU's concern with class inequality. Unlike the antagonism toward immigrants and the working class it displayed in the early twentieth century, the WCTU championed the victims of industrial capitalism during the early growth of its organization. Beginning with Willard's presidency in 1879, the WCTU pursued a broad reform agenda that Willard called the "Do-Everything" policy. She tried to forge alliances with the major progressive organizations of the time, including the Populist and the Labor movements. Willard also supported a living wage and an eight-hour workday and maintained a close friendship with Terence Powderly, the president of the Knights of Labor.[41]

Yet, Willard's explicit support of women and the poor did not always extend to racial minorities. Like most racial ideologies, hers was multifaceted and contradictory. As the daughter of an abolitionist, Willard expressed the desire for racial equality between African Americans and whites. Under her leadership, the WCTU was a model of interracial cooperation.[42] On the other hand, Willard harbored many prejudices typical of the Anglo-Saxon Victorian upper class, and her racial worldview shaped her approach to the prostitution issue.

Willard articulated a connection between sexual immorality and foreignness in her earliest writings and public speeches. At the age of twenty-nine, a full decade before she led the WCTU, Willard toured Europe and the Middle East for two years. During her travels, Willard contemplated the problem of gender inequality by evaluating different sexual and matrimonial practices in foreign lands. In Egypt, Willard decried the practice of arranged marriage. In her private journal, she discussed the hardships faced by Egyptian women and recounted, "We looked from the lofty masses of architecture to the slim-legged Arabs crouched on fragments of rock below, and felt more than ever that they belonged to a degenerate race."[43] In Paris, Willard visited the Jardin Mabille where she observed young women, whom she assumed were prostitutes, dancing and consorting with older men. In her journal, Willard expressed outrage at the "crowds of gaily-toiletted, painted, flashing-eyed, bold-faced women who are *lost* in the direst of all sense who promenade the wide paths of the garden."[44] She wrote, "I query whether the insight into Parisian peculiarities is worth the losing from my sensibility, even for an hour, that innocent ignorance, that painful shudder at sights impure."[45] These public displays of indecency and affection made her reflect on the distinction between Anglo-Saxons and the French. In her journal, she wrote, "It is a full life—an artistic—a manifold that the Parisiens lead—but it is too public— too charged with impressions and empty of reflections for an Anglo Saxon nature to long enjoy."[46]

Her travels abroad were a crucial influence in Willard's thinking about the economic foundations of gender inequality.[47] They also gave her examples of the sexual immorality of non-Anglo-Saxons that she used later in her career. In her first paid public speech, Willard recalled her travels and the lack of economic independence of Italian women, the iniquitous dowry system of the Germans, and the licentiousness and rampant infidelity of the French.[48] Almost two decades later, at the helm of the WCTU, Willard openly worried about immigrants carrying the pervasive immorality of their native lands to American shores. In her address at the 1889 WCTU convention, Willard exclaimed, "America has become the dumping ground of European cities. The emigration has steadily deteriorated in proportion as its quantity has grown."[49] Here, Willard issued a common complaint made by native-born whites about the inferiority of southern and eastern European immigrants.

Willard used the twin problems of immigration and sexual violence as a starting point for her political claims. She made her most impassioned defense of social purity work in a pamphlet called *A White Life for Two,* in which Willard deployed her typical rhetorical strategy of appealing to Victorian notions of womanhood and Christianity at the beginning of her essay and presenting more radical feminist ideas at the close.[50] Toward the end of the pamphlet, Willard argued for "one undivided half of the world for wife and husband equally; co-education to mate them on the plane of mind; equal property rights to make her God's own free woman, not coerced into marriage for the sake of support, nor a bond-slave after she is married."[51]

Willard often concluded her speeches about prostitution and social purity with calls for women's participation in political life. In her address to the 1886 annual meeting of the National WCTU, Willard listed a series of concrete reforms that would end sexual violence and empower women. Willard also questioned the manliness of men who opposed women's legal and economic power:

> Put a money value upon a wife's industry in helping to build up and maintain a home; let this be hers out of the common income and collectable by law. Give a wife half and not one-third of the estate and let her last will and testament cover that amount. Give women the ballot, that such representatives of the people may be put into power as shall make these equitable laws and punish by a penalty as availing as death would be, the betrayer and crim-

inal whose strong arm is employed for her outrage rather than for her protection. Every true man will bid us Godspeed in all of these endeavors, for such aims "antagonize" not men, but brutes.[52]

Willard's speech at the International Council of Women in 1888 praised Anglo-Saxon men who had the moral courage to protect their wives and daughters: "Out of the long savagery and darkness and crime, I see humanity coming up into the brightness and beauty of a new civilization. I see the noblest men of the world's foremost race, the Anglo-Saxons, who made this audience possible, the men who have worked side by side with us, to bring about these great conditions, placing upon woman's brow above the wreath of Venus the helmet of Minerva and leading forward the fair divinities who reside over their homes to help them make a new and nobler government."[53]

As Gail Bederman has shown, the term "civilization" in the late nineteenth and early twentieth centuries meant more than an advanced state of human development; it referred to the evolutionary progress and superiority of the Anglo-Saxon race.[54] As Darwinian ideas increased in popularity, the WCTU and its contemporaries viewed racial and sexual traits in evolutionary terms. Willard invoked the racially loaded image of social evolution to underscore the need for male sexual purity. She also noted that Anglo-Saxon men "made this audience possible" in order to emphasize the racial aspects of their sexuality and their necessary role in reproducing their race. Using a popular discourse of civilization and evolutionary advancement, Willard suggested that the supremacy of "the world's foremost race" required Anglo-Saxon men to practice morality, godliness, and self-control.

The Racial Face of Sexual Danger

Willard saw the political power of Anglo-Saxon women and the sexual morality of Anglo-Saxon men as performing important racial functions, and she outlined the gendered responsibilities of Anglo-Saxons to preserve the integrity of their race. According to Willard's racial ideology, the maintenance of racial boundaries necessitated both the internal policing of Anglo-Saxon sexuality and the protection of Anglo-Saxons from the sexual threats of other races.

Willard's idea of sexual purity invoked a racialized villain. The terminology and metaphors Willard and the WCTU used to articulate both the threat of sexual violence and its solution offer a window into the core components of their racial ideology. When discussing the protectors of womanhood,

Willard praised Anglo-Saxon men and women. When discussing the perpetrators of sexual violence, Willard and the WCTU pointed to white men, the French, and African Americans.[55]

In some contexts, Willard referred to "white men" as a potential threat to women. In *A White Life for Two,* she used examples of male sexual violence, including sexual slavery in the lumber camps and the Jack the Ripper murders in London, to argue for an end to the sexual double standard: "The awful deeds done by white men in the great woods of Alaska, the brutal relations of our soldiery to the Indian women of the plains; the unspeakable atrocities of the lumber camps in Wisconsin and in Michigan; the daily calendar of crimes against women as set forth by the press, and the blood-curdling horrors of Whitechapel, London, have aroused the civilized world."[56] Willard highlighted a shared identity of women as victims of male lust and cruelty. Willard used a more racially inclusive category to discuss the villains of sex crimes (white men) and a more restrictive category to refer to the potential rescuers of women (Anglo-Saxon men).

The WCTU also argued that the French posed a threat to American morals. While French immigrants were often seen as more assimilable than southern and eastern European immigrants, Willard and others insisted that they were not true Anglo-Saxons. Reporting on a 1901 anti-prostitution conference in Lyons, France, one WCTU worker remarked, "It was the first of its kind in France, gay France, whose name is synonymous in our thoughts with all that is extreme in evils of self-indulgence."[57] An investigative report sponsored by the WCTU declared that "there is every reason to believe that a regular business of importation of French girls for immoral purposes between Canada and Chicago is carried on."[58]

At the 1886 WCTU convention in Chicago, Frances Willard commented on the wagons that French health inspectors used when inspecting prostitutes. She said that "law-makers tried to import the black wagon of Paris to England and America, and Anglo-Saxon women rose in swift rebellion."[59] Willard used the term "Anglo-Saxon" to refer to the protectors of womanhood, drawing a sharp contrast between French immorality and Anglo-Saxon womanhood. Anglo-Saxon women, Willard argued, had the moral power to stem the tide of sexual immorality. Willard used a racial metaphor to decry regulated prostitution, distinguishing between the blackness of regulated prostitution from the whiteness of Anglo-Saxon womanhood. She also rhetorically created an Anglo-Saxon identity that excluded the French.

The WCTU also considered African American men a sexual threat to native-born whites. In George Wharton James's *Chicago's Dark Places,* published by Craig Press and the Woman's Temperance Publishing Association in 1891, it is asserted that African Americans posed a sexual menace to white girls. The phrase "dark places" metaphorically refers to the sin and iniquity found in Chicago's poorest neighborhoods. Insofar as these neighborhoods housed a large percentage of the city's immigrants and African Americans,[60] "dark places" becomes more than a metaphor for sin; it carries a double meaning that links sexual practices and race. The WCTU's use of moral metaphors of "dark" and "light" and "black" and "white" easily slides into descriptions of race. For example, when discussing prostitutes in the west side vice district, the book declares: "Some of the girls are white and some are black, but all alike alas! have the same black purpose of heart."[61] The WCTU argued that the vice trade eroded racial boundaries by drawing people together in sin and suggested that the sexual sins of white girls gave them a common "black purpose of heart" with black prostitutes, blurring the moral distinction between white and black girls.

Although prostitution ultimately corrupted the moral and racial purity of white girls, the WCTU did not hold them responsible for their entry into the vice trade. Typical of what would become a core element of the white slavery genre, *Chicago's Dark Places* emphasized the trickery that men used to lure women into brothels: "Many are decoyed into such houses; more go there after being betrayed. They have lost caste, they are disgraced, and they think there is no other door open to them."[62] George James recounted one case where "a white girl was found in a negro house of prostitution" where she was "consorting with the vilest kind of Negroes."[63] She was arrested while soliciting on the street and held as a witness against the "keepers of the dive into whose hellish place she had been entrapped by evil machinations."[64] While awaiting trial, the girl prayed "for death to relieve her of a life that had become too painful to be borne."[65]

In another case, James reported that a "white girl had escaped from a house of prostitution" in Chicago. The girl's downfall ensued after "a negro met her on the street and asked where she was going. Her reply was, she wished to go home. He said he would take her home, and at once walked with her to a place on — avenue. The girl was pretty, and as simple as a child, and said she had no idea whatever as to the nature of the place to which she was being taken. The house was kept by a colored woman, who, seeing the childishness of the girl, determined to keep her."[66] James described how the girl was kept under strict surveillance. Her clothes were taken from her to prevent her escape. The brothel madam forced her with threats of physical violence to have sex with a racially mixed clientele. James wrote, "During the whole of her captivity she was required to pay $20 a week for her room and board, and this had to be made from negroes and Chinamen."[67]

The image of African American men as a sexual threat explains Frances Willard's reluctance to condemn lynching. As the number of lynchings of African American men climbed in the 1880s and 1890s, Willard continued to promulgate one of the most powerful justifications for lynching: the reputed sexual danger that African American men posed to white women. In an interview published in 1890, Willard said: "The grogshop is the Negro's center of power. Better whisky and more of it is the rallying cry of great, dark-faced mobs. The colored race multiplies like the locust of Egypt. The grogshop is its center of power. The safety of women, of childhood, the home, is menaced in a thousand localities at this moment, so that men dare not go beyond the sight of their own roof-tree."[68] Willard argued that intemperance fueled sexual violence by African American men. The image of the black rapist was central to her campaign against sexual violence and was also annexed to her arguments about alcohol and temperance.

Willard's comments outraged Ida B. Wells, who argued that cases of consensual interracial sex were misrepresented as rape and used as a pretext for lynching.[69] In 1893, Wells launched a two-year anti-lynching tour in Britain. Wells pointed to Willard's remark as an example of the deep-seated prejudices shared by prominent whites. While Willard hailed Anglo-Saxons as the protectors of womanhood, Wells rarely used the term "Anglo-Saxon," and then only in sarcastic, derogatory ways.[70]

In 1884, Willard responded to Wells in her address to the WCTU convention in Cleveland: "It is my firm belief that in the statements made by Miss Wells concerning white women having taken the initiative in nameless acts between the races she has put an imputation upon half the white race in this country that is unjust, and save in the rarest exceptional instances, wholly without foundation."[71] Willard found it inconceivable that white women would take the initiative in an interracial sexual relationship because, for Willard, it was impossible for an interracial couple to live "a white life for two." If white women instigated interracial sex only "in the rarest exceptional instances," then the vast majority of such unions were instances of rape.

Willard's statements probably resonated with many women in the southern chapters of the WCTU, some of whom openly supported lynching. Willard's reluctance to condemn lynching may have also stemmed from her desire to win support in the South. Willard argued that it was wrong that immigrants and African American men had voting rights and political power not shared by Anglo-Saxon women. In so doing, she described non-Anglo-Saxons as a political as well as a sexual threat. Willard wrote:

> I think we have wronged the South, though we did not mean to do so. The reason was, in part, that we had irreparably wronged ourselves by putting no safeguards on the ballot box at the North that would sift out alien illiterates. They rule our cities today; the saloon is their palace, and the toddy stick their scepter. It is not fair that they should vote, nor is it fair that a planta-tion Negro, who can neither read nor write, whose ideas are bounded by the fence of his own field and the price of his own mule, should be entrusted with that ballot from the first. The Anglo-Saxon race will never submit to be dom-inated by the Negro so long as his altitude reaches no higher than the per-sonal liberty of the saloon, and the power of appreciating the amount of liquor a dollar will buy.[72]

In an effort to win southern support for women's suffrage and temperance, Willard described the vulnerability of the Anglo-Saxon race to the political power of "alien illiterates" and the "plantation Negro." To illustrate the in-justice of African American voting rights, the WCTU helped organize mock temperance elections exclusively for whites to show that prohibition would pass if African Americans could not vote.[73]

In 1894, the WCTU succumbed to pressure from Wells and others and adopted an anti-lynching resolution at its national convention. Despite its criticism of "all lawless acts," the resolution did not refer to lynching by name, and its wording explicitly invoked the stereotypical image of the an-imalistic black rapist:

> Resolved, that the National W.C.T.U., which has for years counted among its departments that of peace and arbitration, is utterly opposed to all lawless acts in any and all parts of our common lands and it urges these principles upon the public, praying that the time may speedily come when no human being shall be condemned without due process of law; and when the un-speakable outrages which have so often provoked such lawlessness shall be banished from the world, and childhood, maidenhood, and womanhood shall no more be the victims of atrocities worse than death.[74]

By writing of the "unspeakable outrages which have so often provoked such lawlessness," the resolution implicitly blamed African American men for the horrific rates of lynching.

At the early stages of the organization, the WCTU had a strong record of interracial cooperation. Yet, as women's suffrage and prohibition became realistic goals, the WCTU barred African American women from the organization and intensified its racist representation of African American men and immigrants.[75] African American women were reluctant to join the WCTU's social purity efforts, probably because they were put off by the racial overtones of the crusade.[76] After the death of Frances Willard in 1898, the WCTU pursued a policy of white exclusivity.[77]

White Slavery and the WCTU after Willard

The WCTU inaugurated America's war on white slavery with its vice investigations in the late nineteenth century. It also helped organize in 1895 the first National Purity Congress, a convention of the American Purity Alliance, where purity workers delivered approximately thirty speeches divided among seven panels.[78] The American Purity Alliance became the National Vigilance Association in 1910, an organization devoted to fighting prostitution and associated evils. Meanwhile, the WCTU intensified its anti-vice efforts as white slavery became a nationwide concern in the early twentieth century. The organization became more conservative during these years, reflected in its increasingly strident tone when discussing the victims and villains of the white slave traffic.

The WCTU recognized that Anglo-Saxon women were not the sole victims of male violence. The WCTU explicitly stated that white slavery affected women of all races and nationalities, and it attempted to change the terminology of forced prostitution from "white slavery" to "traffic in women" or "women's slave traffic." Decades after Willard made the problem of sexual coercion central to the agenda of the organization, the WCTU urged reformers to adopt the term "traffic in women" to describe forced prostitution. At the 1910 World WCTU convention, the organization made a declaration to "alter the name 'White Slave Traffic' to 'Women's Slave Traffic,' and thus include colored races, whose women furnish a very large proportion of the victims of vice."[79] At the thirty-sixth annual WCTU convention, members approved a motion that the organization "use the designation, 'traffic in women,' instead of the commonly accepted appellation, 'white slave traffic,' in referring to the iniquitous system of ensnaring and selling women into a life of shame, since no woman, of whatever race or color, is exempt from the danger of its machinations."[80] During her presidential address at the 1910 WCTU convention, Lillian Stevens said that "although the traffic originated in Europe where its victims are white, it is claimed, and with reason, that the term 'white slave' does not fitly describe the heinous system inasmuch as it involves every race and every color."[81] Stevens simultaneously blamed Europeans for inventing white slavery and recognized the plight of African Americans and immigrant women. Also, the comment that, in Europe, "its victims are white" reflects a changing understanding of racial categories, as the tight category of nineteenth-century whiteness loosened, and immigrant groups that were previously perceived as racially distinct and inferior entered its fold.

Despite its attempt to change the terminology of coercive prostitution to encompass non-native-born whites, the WCTU suggested that white slavery posed the greatest threat to homes of native-born white Americans. In her 1907 article in the *Union Signal*, the WCTU superintendent of rescue work described the danger white slavery posed to native-born girls: "Our own girls are being hunted. Nearly every issue of the daily paper in our larger cities has its story of 'A Lost Girl.' What becomes of them? Drugged in a licensed café, lifted into a cab under the very eyes of the police and 'taken through the portals of hell.'"[82] The WCTU's Department of Rescue Work reported in 1909 that the vast majority of white slaves were from American homes: "According to authoritative estimates, some 65,000 daughters of American homes, and 15,000 alien girls, are the prey each year of 'procurers' in this traffic in women. Even marriage is used as one of the methods of capturing girlhood and 'breaking them into a life of shame.' They are hunted, trapped, in a thousand ways—sold for less than swine, and held in a slavery worse than death."[83]

The California branch of the WCTU invoked the threat of white slavery to native-born white Americans in that state's 1911 suffrage campaign. On the cover of the California WCTU's magazine, the *White Ribbon Ensign,* the WCTU featured an illustration of a white woman defending her children against several threats to her home. Standing in front of her frightened children, she clutches a large club labeled "The Ballot" to ward off several wolves that run toward them, including a wolf, ready to pounce, labeled "white slavery." This image suggests that white women's political power was the only thing that stood between animalistic immorality and the homes of native-born whites.

When discussing the villains of white slavery, the WCTU continued to blame foreigners for the white slave traffic. It accused foreign-born men of profiting from white slavery as well as of introducing Americans to immoral sexual practices. With immigrants securing a foothold in municipal politics, the WCTU worried that their involvement in the vice trade weakened the morals of the entire country. A year after Willard's death, the WCTU published an article entitled "A Study of Social Vice" by William Ferguson. He wrote:

The Woman's Christian Temperance Union used a "home-protection" discourse to make claims for women's political power. "Hand Her the Club" is from the October 1911 cover of the *White Ribbon Ensign,* the journal of the WCTU.

In the coming decades the Italian and Pole, and their like, are certain to play substantially the same social and political role that the Irishman and the German have played during the two decades past. With that thought in mind and a moment's reflection impresses one with the fact that the universities in which we are training our future mayors, aldermen, police and school commissioners, legislators, and congressmen, are on our Clark streets, our Allen streets and our little Divisions. Little Pablo Frizzecoli playing in the gutter in front of an Allen Street or Clark Street brothel may, twenty years from now be that man upon whose standards of morality the moral life of the city or state may depend.[84]

Ferguson's hypothetical example of "Pablo Frizzecoli" suggested how the vice problem threatened to corrupt immigrant children, who would later wield political power. Instilling Christian ethics in immigrant children not only ensured their moral protection but was also important for the well-being of the entire city. This quotation also pointed to the distinctions native-born whites drew between old and new immigrants. By the turn of the century, Germans and Irish experienced a slow symbolic whitening, while many native-born whites considered the reputed inferiority of Italians and Poles as a threat to American culture. Ella Thacher, a WCTU worker, commented in 1907 that "we are face to face with the most difficult race problem ever confronting a nation—that of assimilating at least sixty nationalities or races." Expressing a typical nativist sentiment, she claimed that immigrants threatened to swamp American cities and change the mental and moral characteristics of the United States.[85]

The WCTU's attention to white slavery waned late in the second decade of the twentieth century as it channeled its energies and resources into temperance work. The WCTU consequently reframed the problem of white slavery in terms of the "alcohol question." In 1909, a WCTU worker declared, "The real white slave is the life of the poor drunkard."[86] In 1910, Rose Woodallen Chapman, the superintendent of the WTCU's Purity Department, departed from the typical depiction of organized white slave traffic. She claimed that the traffic in women stemmed, not from male cruelty per se, but from the traffic in liquor:

> Moreover, we of the Woman's Christian Temperance Union know that if there is no organized "white slave traffic" as is claimed, there is an organized liquor traffic, which is the very source and root of this terrible evil. Where is it the procurers meet? In the saloon. Where is it the poor victim generally meets her terrible fate? In the back room of a saloon or in a wine-room. What is it that is responsible for nine-tenths of the immorality among men? Alcoholic liquor, say the physicians who have made the closest study of immorality and the resultant diseases.[87]

* * *

The WCTU imported the white slavery narrative from abroad and placed sexual violence on the public agenda, forcing male politicians to defend or change rape and age of consent laws. The WCTU articulated new ways of thinking about the importance of native-born white women in civil society, but racial stereotypes guided its gender and sexual politics. Ideologies of Anglo-Saxon and white superiority shaped the WCTU's feminist political projects. It drew racial distinctions between native-born citizens and immigrant groups based upon racial attributions of sexual passivity and sexual aggression. The point of this chapter is not simply to prove that the WCTU was racist in its fight against sexual violence and white slavery but also to show that its representation of white slavery fused notions of Anglo-Saxon superiority with Victorian ideas about female sexuality.

The WCTU's social purity campaign reveals the racial politics embedded in the cult of true womanhood and the racial distinctions drawn between "Anglo-Saxons" and "whites." Willard and the WCTU referred to the moral courage of Anglo-Saxon men and the political power of Anglo-Saxon women as the solutions to the problem of sexual violence. They cast white men, immigrants, and African Americans as the villains of white slavery. Their discourse about moral purity and their activities aimed at eliminating sex crimes reveal the connection that they drew between criminality and race, a connection that became more explicit in the course of their campaign.

White slavery narratives were a particularly powerful cultural resource for the WCTU. The stories about white or Anglo-Saxon girls abducted and forced into prostitution allowed the WCTU to make a strong claim for political power. Yet, the general scenario that it borrowed from William T. Stead's "Maiden Tribute of Modern Babylon" had room for reinterpretation. Once the WCTU introduced the white slavery issue to the Chicago reform community, it was used by reformers and organizations that did not share the goals or beliefs of the woman-centered movement. In the early twentieth century, the response to white slavery in Chicago developed along two main lines: a environmental approach, represented by the settlement house movement, which viewed poverty and lack of support for immigrants as the source of white slavery, and a coercive approach, represented most clearly by Chicago attorney Clifford Roe, which viewed foreigners as the root of the white slavery problem.[88]

Willard inspired a generation of college-educated women to engage in reform work. Her "Do-Everything" agenda allowed women to imagine themselves working toward a number of political goals. The settlement house movement was a notable outcome of the WCTU's trailblazing efforts. Suzanne Marilley argues, "Willard's influence on women leaders extends into the twentieth century. The most obvious ideological influence she had was on Jane Addams."[89] The white slavery problem was one of the central issues that Addams inherited from Willard. In the spirit of the early WCTU, Addams addressed the prostitution problem with efforts aimed at working-class uplift. Whereas Addams rejected the nativist cries of Anglo-Saxon superiority, her colleague Clifford Roe amplified it. He considered white slavery to be a product of pernicious foreign influences. Their arguments about the sexual and racial dimensions of white slavery will be explored in the next chapter.

4

"The Black Traffic in White Girls": Chicago's War on Vice

This chapter examines how Chicago reformers used white slavery narratives to address the changing racial composition of Chicago and the sharp increase in independent wage-earning women. Reformers' storytelling about white slavery reveals different racial ideologies that made complex connections among whiteness, sexual morality, class, and citizenship. Their ideas about race prefigured the style of their reform efforts and shaped the strategies and outcomes of their crusades. Primarily, I will compare the anti-vice activism of settlement house pioneer Jane Addams and Chicago attorney Clifford Roe. Although both were deeply concerned about the white slave trade, they disagreed about the source of coercive prostitution and the proper methods of eliminating it.

Addams's production and use of white slavery narratives shared some similarities with the themes of the WCTU and the social purity movement, but her discourse also marked a strong departure from the cult of true womanhood and the ideology of Anglo-Saxon superiority. Addams regarded new immigrant groups as a welcomed addition to urban America. Her racial ideology, broadly described as "pluralist,"[1] fit with a reform strategy that targeted socioeconomic conditions. Addams thought that coercive prostitution resulted from the poverty and lack of social support facing newly arrived immigrant groups, not from their supposed moral impoverishment. She viewed sexual morality as contingent upon economic circumstances such as employment opportunities and working conditions.

Chicago attorney Clifford Roe, on the other hand, argued that immigrants were fundamentally distinct from native-born whites. He located the source of white slavery in the moral failing of immigrants and drew a connection between foreignness and criminality. Roe's white slavery narratives suggested how proper sexual practices could restore morality, and therefore racial integrity, to white working-class men and women. His nativist racial ideology presupposed a coercive law enforcement strategy directed at white slave procurers. Addams's and Roe's analyses of the racial dimensions of prostitution drew fuel from different images of the "white slave" and different evaluations of women's sexual agency.

Independent Women and the Color Line in Chicago

Jane Addams and Clifford Roe developed their ideas about white slavery in a historical context that was vastly different from material and ideological conditions that shaped the WCTU's initial investigations in the 1880s. The racial composition of Chicago changed drastically in the first two decades of the twentieth century. Also, as the city grew, increasing numbers of young women sought employment in its department stores and business offices. Taken together, these changes concerned reformers because reformers viewed women as increasingly vulnerable at the same moment that they worried about the threat that non-natives posed to public morals.

In the early twentieth century, the rapid growth of corporations and retail markets created new sales and clerical positions for women.[2] New employment opportunities gave working-class women a growing public presence in the city, and boarding homes in the "furnished room district" of Chicago swelled to meet the demands of independent wage-earning women.[3] Chicago had three distinct furnished room districts. On the south side, the furnished room district overlapped with both a large portion of the African American community and the segregated vice district. Native-born and immigrant women populated the furnished room districts on the north and west sides.[4] Joanne Meyerowitz notes that "the prevalence of prostitution in these districts fostered a climate where open expressions of sexuality were common."[5]

The growth of Chicago's vice districts coincided with the city's shifting racial composition. After 1880, immigrants from the supposedly undesirable parts of Europe came to American cities in record numbers. Between 1870 and 1890, approximately a quarter of a million immigrants settled in Chicago. By 1890, 40 percent of Chicago's residents were foreign-born, and 38 percent were second-generation Americans. By 1900, the foreign-born and their children comprised almost four-fifths of Chicago's population, and immigrants accounted for over one-third of the population increase between

1860 and 1900.[6] Germans, Irish, and Scandinavians were the largest immigrant groups in Chicago, but after 1880 there were increasing numbers of Poles, Lithuanians, Czechs, Italians, and eastern European Jews. They comprised a small percentage of the city's 2.4 million population, but it was not the sheer number of new immigrants that troubled native-born whites as much as their perceived inferiority to older waves of immigrants.[7]

From 1870 to 1900, the percentage of northern Europeans immigrating to Chicago declined from 89.4 percent of the total number of immigrants to 66.7 percent.[8] The large percentage of immigrants from southern and eastern Europe worried native-born whites because these groups were seen as less likely to assimilate to Anglo-Saxon norms.[9] Native-born whites developed a distinction between old immigrants from northwestern Europe and new immigrants from the remaining parts of Europe. Older immigrants who arrived before 1880 had several material advantages when compared to later waves of immigrants, yet many native-born whites attributed the difference between the two to the "superior stock" of older immigrants.[10]

In Chicago, newly arrived immigrant families settled west of the central business district, crowding into a semicircular belt about two miles across from east to west and nearly ten miles from north to south.[11] The tenement settlements in Chicago stretched from the north at Fullerton Avenue near Halsted Street, then moved south and west, encompassing most of the west side of the city. The majority of immigrants lived in thirty small blocks from Halsted Street to the Chicago River. According to the Department of Labor and the Hull House settlement, twenty-six nationalities were represented in the "slum" tenement district by 1894.[12]

The development of the west side immigrant enclaves paralleled the expansion of the south side "black belt." Between 1870 and 1890, Chicago's African American community tripled in size, from less than 4,000 to nearly 15,000. This growth of the African American population kept pace with the overall increase in the city's population, yet between 1900 and 1910, the number of African Americans living in Chicago grew by nearly 50 percent, from approximately 30,000 to 44,000, exceeding the growth rate of the city as a whole.[13] African Americans did not settle throughout the city as they had done in the nineteenth century but were becoming confined to clearly delineated areas south of the central business district. They did not do this out of choice but were forced into what became known as the "black belt" by mob violence, restricted covenants, blockbusting, and "neighborhood improvement associations" that bought the land of African American families.[14] The south side black belt slowly extended farther south and began to widen as African Americans moved to neighborhoods east of State Street, toward Cottage Grove.[15]

Immigrant enclaves and African American neighborhoods were more likely than wealthier and whiter neighborhoods to be located near vice districts.[16] Progressive Era reformers were alarmed by the seemingly natural alliance among African Americans, the least desirable immigrants, and the flourishing vice trade.[17] Jane Addams expressed sympathy for "the children of the poorest colored families who are often forced to live in disreputable neighborhoods because they literally cannot rent houses anywhere else."[18] Yet not all observers were sympathetic to the immigrants and African Americans forced to live near Chicago's vice district.

Chicago's Moral Entrepreneurs

In the early twentieth century, Chicago witnessed a tremendous outpouring of concern over the white slavery issue, and many white slavery narratives focused on the Chicago vice trade.[19] Three authors in particular—two journalists and an evangelist—were responsible for drawing attention to Chicago's prostitution problem: William T. Stead, George Kibbe Turner, and Ernest Bell. These authors expressed a nativist racial ideology that connected the expansion of the vice trade to the changing racial composition of the city. Although William Stead's views of race were different from those of leaders in the settlement house movement, he drew strong support from Jane Addams because of his benevolence toward Chicago's poor. George Kibbe Turner and Ernest Bell were more closely aligned with Clifford Roe. All three set the tenor for the city's anti-vice crusade.

WILLIAM T. STEAD

After publishing the scandalous "Maiden Tribute of Modern Babylon" story about child prostitution in England, Stead played a seminal role in Chicago's war on prostitution. About seven years after his campaign to raise public awareness about white slavery in England, Stead toured Chicago's vice district. In 1894, he published a 400–page report of his investigations entitled *If Christ Came to Chicago*. His book sold 100,000 copies in its first printing, and the second edition sold 200,000 copies.[20] Stead spent much of the book condemning the aldermen who controlled the notorious First Ward: Michael "Hinky Dink" Kenna and John "Bathhouse" Coughlin. Kenna and Coughlin were known to buy votes, extort money from brothel owners, and hold outrageous public balls. They also controlled the Levee District that housed most of Chicago's brothels.[21]

Stead criticized the foreign population of the First Ward, the aldermen that depended on their support, and the influx of new immigrants into Chicago.

In *If Christ Came to Chicago,* he explained the connection between Chicago's immigrant population and the political power of corrupt Democrats: "During the last year a great change has come over the population. The negroes have diminished and the Italians have increased. The large number of lodgers are registered and they vote. Where they come from no one knows; they are a floating migratory population, but they are voted as any other resident of the ward."[22] Stead described the squalor of the First Ward and its lack of American culture. He decried one of the schools he visited in the First Ward as overrun by foreigners: "The principal of the school told me that forty per cent of the scholars are Russian or Polish Jews; a very large number of the remainder are negroes. The genuine American was in an extremely small minority."[23]

Stead's book received a mix reaction among Chicago's prominent citizens. Some regarded his work as little more than a guidebook to Chicago's underworld. Others chastised him for his bombastic tone. Wherever he went, Stead seemed to draw controversy with his observations about the city's prostitution problem. For instance, Stead offended Chicago clubwomen after he gave an inflammatory speech at a meeting of the Chicago Women's Clubs in 1893. Historian Joseph Baylen wrote that Stead lost much of the community's backing when he gave an "impromptu outburst before the leading matrons of Chicago on December 27 which completely alienated the press and seriously limited his effectiveness in the city."[24] Stead chastised Chicago clubwomen for being "self-indulgent" and "more disreputable than the worst harlot."[25] Apparently, the wealthy and well-dressed audience infuriated Stead, who continued his harangue despite the obvious hostility of the audience. He asked, "Who are the most disreputable women in Chicago? They are those dowered by society."[26] As Stead hurried out of the room, the remaining speakers set aside their prepared statements and proceeded to denounce his remarks. Jane Addams, one of the few women who defended Stead, claimed that the women misunderstood him.

GEORGE KIBBE TURNER

Journalist George Kibbe Turner sparked popular concern over white slavery in Chicago with his article "The City of Chicago: A Study of the Great Immoralities," published in *McClure's* in April 1907. Clifford Barnes, former president of the Committee of Fifteen, an anti-vice organization, recalled the effect of Turner's article on the Chicago reform community: "It was during the summer of 1907 that Chicago was startled out of her usual attitude of indifference toward commercialized vice by a series of shocking revelations, which indicated that our city was the center of a well organized traffic in women, a very real white slave market."[27] Turner first took aim at the liquor trade and its immigrant supporters: "If a new colony of foreigners appears, some compatriot is set at once to selling them liquor. Italians, Greeks, Lithuanians, Poles,—all the rough and hairy tribes which have been drawn to Chicago,—have their trade exploited to the utmost."[28] Turner blamed the city's crime problem on the large numbers of European immigrants and the African Americans who moved to Chicago in the early twentieth century:

> The European peasant, suddenly freed from the restraints of poverty and of rigid police authority, and the vicious negro from the countryside of the South,—especially the latter,—furnish an alarming volume of savage crime, first confined to their own race, and later,—as they appreciate the lack of adequate protection,—extended to society at large. None of these folks, perhaps, have progressed far along the way of civilization; but under the exploitation in Chicago they slip back into a form of city savagery compared to which their previous history shows a peaceful and well-ordered existence.[29]

Turner expressed fear about African Americans who migrated to Chicago from the South and Europeans who immigrated to the city from abroad. In the above quotation, he used the racially loaded dichotomy of "savagery" and "civilization" to depict Chicago's crime problem. Like other native-born whites in the Progressive Era, Turner used the rhetoric of "civilization" to characterize evolutionary racial progress or its opposite. As Turner looked forward into Chicago's dark future of crime and depravity, he also glanced back into the relatively "peaceful and well-ordered existence" of European peasants and African Americans in the Jim Crow South.

For Stead, the presence of immigrants and African Americans posed a threat to civilization and the racial future of America. Turner made a rhetorical appeal to Anglo-Saxon civilization and argued that it depended upon female sexual purity. He declared: "The chastity of women is at the foundation of Anglo-Saxon society. Our laws are based upon it, and the finest most binding of our social relations. Nothing could be more menacing to a civilization than the sale of this as a commodity."[30] Fusing racial concerns with reproductive ones, Turner claimed that sexual purity of Anglo-Saxon women was essential for the preservation of the Anglo-Saxon race.

ERNEST BELL

A writer for the *Northwestern Christian Advocate* stated that "when the final history of the modern campaign against the segregation of vice and the white slave traffic in America is written, the prophet of the whole movement will be

Ernest A. Bell, superintendent
of the Midnight Mission.
From Olive Bell Daniels,
*From the Epic of Chicago:
A Biography, Ernest A. Bell,
1865–1928* (Menasha, Wis.:
George Banta Publishing
Company, 1932).

the subject of our sketch, the Rev. Ernest A. Bell."[31] A Canadian-born Methodist, Bell traveled to India with his wife, Mary, shortly after the birth of their first child. He became ill and angered the Methodist Missionary Board by not fulfilling his tenure abroad. Bell preached in a small church in St. Joseph, Missouri, and moved to Chicago after learning that the missionary board refused to fund his future travel. In Chicago, Bell felt a deep conviction that ministers must rescue the souls of sexual sinners, and he soon made Chicago's Levee his second home.[32]

Bell emerged as one of the city's leading anti-vice crusaders through his work with a group of ministers and evangelists dedicated to stopping prostitution. Reverend Melbourne Boyton transformed a Clark Street brothel into a rescue home and held weekly meetings with other religious leaders to discuss the vice trade. Bell joined his coterie and coordinated their hymnal processions in the red-light district. He preached against vice late into the night, often returning to his home at three or four in the morning. Bell's biography documented numerous incidents when drunken revelers hurled stones, noxious chemicals, and death threats at him; both police and criminals harassed Bell's midnight services. Undaunted, he supplemented his nightly street-corner sermons with vigorous anti-vice organizing during the day.

Bell quickly enlisted the help of other religious leaders. He offered his assistance to Reverend Boyton and on June 6, 1905, wrote him a letter: "The summer is begun and will soon be ended. Are we likely to do some work for the darkest Chicago?"[33] About three months later, Bell asked Victor Lawson of the *Chicago Tribune* for financial help for his midnight evangelism: "If you cannot help me light darkest India, will you help me light darkest Chicago?" Lawson sent him fifty dollars.[34] On November 11, 1906, Bell mailed a letter to Arthur Burrage Farwell of the Chicago Law and Order League asking him to dine at the local YMCA with several religious leaders from Chicago. The luncheon marked the beginning of the "Midnight Mission," and those in attendance elected Bell superintendent. They stated their purpose clearly: "The Mission would now attack the organized traffic of 'White Slavery.' The iron bars of the windows in the red-light district must come down."[35] According to his biographer, as Bell walked along Chicago's streets in 1904, he experienced "smells of every race of mankind. Chicago had more Jews than Jerusalem, more Scandinavians than Christiania—more prostitutes than Babylon. God—he had dreamed about India. Something had to be done about Chicago."[36]

Bell directly blamed immigrants for the white slave trade and conceived of himself as a domestic missionary aiming to stop the invasion of non-natives.[37] He outlined his ideas about white slavery in his tome *Fighting the Traffic in Young Girls*. His book sold over 70,000 copies within the first seven months of publication and eventually sold more than 400,000 copies.[38] Bell declared:

> Unless we make energetic and successful war upon the red light districts and all that pertains to them, we shall have Oriental brothel slavery thrust upon us from China and Japan, and Parisian white slavery, with all its unnatural and abominable practices, established among us by the French traders. Jew traders, too, will people our "levees" with Polish Jewesses and any others who will make money for them. Shall we defend our American civilization, or lower our flag to the most despicable foreigners—French, Irish, Italian, Jews and Mongolians?[39]

In addition to marking the French, Irish, Italians, and Jews as foreign threats, Bell also exonerated several European countries: "I know of no resorts controlled by English, Scotch, German or Scandinavian men."[40]

For Stead, Turner, and Bell, the vice trade in Chicago threatened to shred the moral fabric of the city. They blamed white slavery on foreign influences and the growing presence of African Americans in Chicago. The settlement house movement represented another perspective on the connection between new immigrants and vice. Jane Addams saw the plurality of races and nationalities in Chicago as a potentially positive force that was undermined by poverty and squalid living conditions. The next section describes Addams's approach to white slavery, showing the comfortable fit between her ideology of racial pluralism and her environmental strategy to combat white slavery.

Jane Addams and the Economics of White Slavery

THE HULL HOUSE AND RACIAL PLURALISM

By the end of the nineteenth century, settlement houses offered a new generation of college-educated women a career in reform work. Settlement house workers acted within a set of opportunities and constraints that differed from those facing the labor movement and other class-based, male-dominated groups. The settlement movement suggested a new form of political action that helped to fill a void created by relatively weak working-class organizations.[41] Through settlement work, educated middle-class women committed themselves to improving the lives of newly arrived immigrants and the poor by living in working-class neighborhoods and engaging in hands-on social reform. The most important settlement house was Jane Addams's Hull House.[42] She founded the Hull House in 1889 to help immigrant women and children. Addams explained the purpose of her settlement as "an experimental effort to aid in the solution of the social and industrial problems which are engendered by the modern conditions of life in a great city."[43]

In contrast to nativist ideas of Anglo-Saxon superiority, Addams's racial ideology could broadly be defined as pluralist. Addams emphasized the unique gifts immigrants brought to America, advocated equal participation of immigrants in the social and political life of the city, and strove to eliminate the barriers between immigrants and native-born Americans.[44] Addams pressed for the preservation and cultivation of immigrant cultures, encouraging immigrants to observe their national holidays, customs, dress, and folklore. For example, in 1912 she lobbied for a change in the Naturalization Act that would eliminate a clause that demanded immigrants renounce their allegiance to their native land before they became American citizens.[45]

Addams highlighted nationality instead of race as the defining identity of immigrant groups. She never spoke of immigrant groups as racially distinct and spoke about Anglo-Saxonism with scorn. Although she did not view immigrant groups from Europe as representing different races, Addams's conception of pluralism was complex.[46] She wanted immigrants to assimilate into American culture and believed assimilation to be an inevitable result of their interactions with American institutions. Holding onto their heritage was the ironic motor of their assimilation. According to Rivka Lis-

sak, Addams believed that if "the immigrants were not forced to choose between two loyalties in becoming Americans, they would not lose their self-
respect. This would make it easier for them to start feeling American."[47] Addams felt that immigrants would enter the fabric of American culture only
when they felt comfortable living in America, surrounded by members of
their homeland.[48]

JANE ADDAMS AND THE NEW ABOLITIONISM

Two of the most pressing issues facing the Hull House was the apparent growth
of prostitution in Chicago and the geographic overlap between vice districts
and impoverished neighborhoods of immigrants and African Americans. The
racial ideologies of Jane Addams and the Hull House influenced how they approached the white slavery problem. Addams's ideas about the role of immigrants in American culture distinguished her from nativists like Stead, Bell,
and Turner. Instead of blaming immigrants for the prostitution problem, Addams viewed immigrant girls as the primary victims of white slavery.

In *A New Conscience and an Ancient Evil*, Addams explored the economic
and political conditions that engendered the white slave trade in Chicago.
Critical analyses of her book have consistently focused on her seemingly exaggerated stories of prostitution. Both Allen Davis and Walter Lippmann described it as "an hysterical book."[49] Most recently, English professors Janet
Beer and Katherine Joslin accused Addams of "projecting [her] own maladies
and discomforts onto the social and political world."[50] Like many scholarly
treatments of Progressive Era anti-vice campaigns, these critiques overlook
Addams's political aims. Her biographer offered a more generous interpretation, referring to *A New Conscience and an Ancient Evil* as "the most sustained and striking argument for women's suffrage she ever made."[51] Like
the WCTU, Addams used the white slavery issue as a template for making
feminist claims. She expected that the white slavery issue would eventually
draw people to the suffrage cause:

> As the first organized Women's Rights movement was inaugurated by the
> women who were refused seats in the world's Anti-Slavery convention held
> in London in 1840, although they have been the very pioneers in the organ-
> ization of the American Abolitionist, so it is quite possible that an equally en-
> ergetic attempt to abolish white slavery will bring many women into the Equal
> Suffrage movement, simply because they too will discover that without the
> use of the ballot they are unable to work effectively for the eradication of a
> social wrong.[52]

Making a comparison between abolitionism and anti-vice activism, Addams hoped that white slavery narratives would galvanize women's support for suffrage. In turn, the vote would give women the political power they needed to protect themselves from the ugly aspects of the vice trade. Women's suffrage, she argued, would be a critical step in ensuring the protection of vulnerable women from both white slave traders and police harassment.[53]

Addams's conception of white slavery was different from the WCTU's. In Addams's white slavery narratives, women were not the victims of abduction and physical coercion. Although she was concerned with male violence, none of her examples of white slavery involved drugging, abduction, or physical force. The abduction scenario did not tower as the defining feature of white slavery, nor was male cruelty the central problem needing eradication. Instead, Addams analyzed the economic roots of the vice trade. Her materialist framework deflected blame from the immigrant victims and purported perpetrators of white slavery and instead focused on the social conditions that kept non-natives from enjoying the fruits of American citizenship.

URBAN EMPLOYMENT AND THE CREATION OF WHITE SLAVES

Jane Addams used accounts of white slavery to critique industrial capitalism and to insist on state intervention on behalf of the wage-earning women in Chicago. She also advocated widespread sex education, improved working conditions for young women, and women's suffrage. Her discussion of the causes of white slavery emphasized low wages and working conditions, but it also revealed a layered understanding of female subjectivity. Poverty made certain sexual practices acceptable to working-class women that were unthinkable to those with more resources. Illness and unemployment placed women in difficult situations, making them face the "hideous choice between starvation and vice which is perhaps the crowning disgrace of our civilization."[54] In contrast to the WCTU's depiction of prostitution as a fate worse than death, Addams recognized prostitution as a choice that some women pursued, yet a choice often made under harsh circumstances. By not writing a scenario of abduction and trickery, Addams blamed employment conditions instead of individual men. For the WCTU, the false promises of employment lured women to the lumber camps; the white slaves discussed by Addams were already employed, suggesting that they belonged in the city despite its problems.

Unemployment often drove women to prostitution, but different forms of modern employment also functioned to create white slaves. Secure employment did not ensure the moral protection of young women, because the exigencies of modern industrial capitalism destroyed their spirit. When discussing the factory system, Addams implicated the literal machinery of capitalism in the creation of white slaves: "[T]he speeding up constantly required of the operators, may at any moment so register their results upon the nervous system of a factory girl as to overcome her powers of resistance. Many a working girl at the end of the day is so hysterical and overwrought that her mental balance is plainly disturbed."[55]

Addams asserted a conception of sexual morality that considered the effect of economic forces on human subjectivity. When she spoke of the injurious effects of industrial working conditions on the "nervous system" of the factory girl, Addams made morality part of the body and not simply a question of individual will, preference, or resolve. She said, "Doubtless as more is known of the nervous and mental effect of over-fatigue, many moral breakdowns will be traced to this source."[56] Addams suggested that the strain put upon the minds and bodies of working-class women put virtue out of reach. In her 1912 speech delivered before the Christian Conservation Congress, Addams called upon the church to advocate labor reforms on behalf of vulnerable young women. She declared, "If it is known that excessive fatigue and underfeeding are causes that increase the victims of social evil, it is the business of the Church to obtain laws limiting the conditions for working-women."[57]

Although Addams advocated industrial reforms, factory work did not present the easiest road to prostitution. According to Addams, "It is perhaps the department store more than anywhere else that every possible weakness in a girl is detected and traded upon. . . . No other place of employment is so easy of access as the department store."[58] Addams argued that the low wages women earned in department stores made them vulnerable to vice. Citing a report of "Women and Child Wage Earners in the United States," Addams noted that a large percentage of prostitutes held previous employment in department stores. She wrote: "The report states that the average employee in a department store earns about seven dollars a week, and that the average income of the one hundred immoral women covered by the personal histories, ranged from fifty dollars a week to one hundred dollars a week in exceptional cases. It is of these exceptional cases that the department store girl hears, and the knowledge becomes part of the unreality and glittering life that is all about her."[59]

Evidence on industrial conditions collected during this time supported her contention that a weekly wage of seven dollars made women vulnerable. A number of federal surveys of labor conditions in Chicago concluded that independent wage-earning women in Chicago required eight to twelve dollars a week to cover living expenses.[60] A survey of store and factory workers by the federal government in 1908 found that these workers earned an average of $8.17 a week. Immigrant women earned considerably less. One budget study estimated the cost of living in Chicago to be $9.70 per week, excluding expenses such as soap and medicine.[61] The discrepancy between the amount of money that women needed to live and the amount that they earned engendered the fear that women would enter prostitution because of economic necessity.

In addition to the low wages earned in these jobs, department stores encouraged women to imagine the things that they could buy if they had more money. While factories shielded girls from the opulence of the modern city, department stores dangled it in front of them. Low wages and a strenuous working environment converged on the department store girl: "Of course a girl in such a strait does not go out deliberately to find illicit methods of earning money, she simply yields in a moment of utter weariness and discouragement to the temptations she has been able to withstand up to that moment. The long hours, the lack of comforts, the low pay, the absence of recreation, the sense of 'good times' all about her which she cannot share, the conviction that she is rapidly losing health and charm, rouse the molten forces within her."[62] According to Addams, working conditions shaped the potentially excitable subjectivity of women—their "molten forces." Unequal power relationships between men and women and among members of different social classes produced a vice-prone disposition.

Considering white slavery in economic terms gave Addams a more nuanced view of women's sexuality. Unlike the abduction scenario of the WCTU, the proximate causes of prostitution were sometimes the fault of the women themselves. Addams explained: "Although economic pressure as a reason for entering an illicit life has thus been brought out in court by the evidence in a surprising number of cases, there is no doubt that it is often exaggerated; a girl always prefers to think that economic pressure is the reason for her downfall, even when the immediate causes have been her love of pleasure, her desire for finery, or the influence of evil companions."[63] Here, Addams did not retreat from her materialist interpretation of vice; she simply distinguished between proximate causes that were more or less within a woman's power and deeper reasons that women entered the vice trade.[64]

Whereas the abduction scenario illustrated a simple view of the path to prostitution, Addams considered a variety of push and pull factors that were sometimes within and other times outside of a woman's control. In telling a story about "Marie," a French immigrant girl forcibly taken as a white slave by a procurer, Addams drew a comparison between physical abduction and the psychological dynamics that often compelled prostitutes to remain in difficult situations. After Marie's rescue and the prosecution of her abductor, she tried to lead a normal life in Chicago. Yet her past experiences "warped and weakened her will" such that she continued to work as a prostitute on her own, sending her earnings to her parents in France. Addams concluded, "She is as powerless now to save herself from her subjective temptations as she was helpless five years ago to save herself from her captors."[65] Addams recognized that coercion was not always based on fear or physical abuse and that psychological pressure often kept women from leaving dismal sex work.

For Addams, white slaves were not always innocent white girls from the countryside; immigrant victims also played a prominent role in her accounts. In the twelve stories of white slavery she recounts in *A New Conscience and an Ancient Evil*, Addams identifies nine victims as immigrant women.[66] Addams also reversed the causal sequence typically found in other white slavery narratives. Instead of native-born girls becoming victimized when they moved to the city, she described their victimization as a result of having to leave the city. Familial ties did not ensure the moral protection of women but were often a catalyst for their downfall. Addams recounted the story of "an honest, straightforward girl from a small lake town in Northern Michigan" who worked in a Chicago café. Every week she mailed "more than half of her wages of seven dollars to her mother and little sister, ill with tuberculosis, at home."[67] Then she received a letter from her mother imploring her to return home because her sister was dying. While working that day, she secured a trip home with one of the café's customers:

> [S]he was suddenly startled by hearing the name of her native town, and realized that one of her regular patrons was saying to her that he meant to take a night boat to M. at 8 o'clock and get out of this "infernal heat." Almost involuntarily she asked him if he would take her with him. Although the very next moment she became conscious what his consent implied, she did not reveal her fright, but merely stipulated that if she went with him he must agree to buy her a return ticket. She reached home twelve hours before her sister died, but when she returned to Chicago a week later burdened with the debt of an undertaker's bill, she realized that she had discovered a means of payment.[68]

Addams suggested that the modern city complicated traditional family obligations. In this story, the man did not misrepresent himself or his motives. He bargained with the girl, and she later discovered the utility of casual prostitution. Her choice was set in motion by a range of unfortunate circumstances: low wages, a dying sister, distance from her mother, and an unex-

Table 4.1. Origins of the Victims and Villains in Clifford Roe's *Panders and Their White Slaves* and Jane Addams's *A New Conscience and an Ancient Evil*

	Roe's *Panders*	Addams's *New Conscience*
Victim positively identified as an immigrant	21% (7)	75% (9)
Race or national origin of victim unknown	79% (26)	25% (3)
Total	100% (33 stories)	100% (12 stories)
Villain positively identified as an immigrant	36% (12)	8% (1)
Race or national origin of villain unknown	64% (21)	92% (11)
Total	100% (33 stories)	100% (12 stories)

pected debt. Addams portrayed her as a victim but one who made conscious, albeit constrained, choices.

Given the economic causes of white slavery, families provided little protection for independent women. In fact, as the above story illustrates, certain family situations threw women into jeopardy. Another story from Addams's *A New Conscience and an Ancient Evil* described how a family illness led to a daughter's moral downfall:

> One young Polish girl had worked for two years in a downtown hotel, and had steadfastly resisted all improper advances even sometimes by the aid of her own powerful fist. She yielded at last to the suggestions of the life about her when she received a telegram from Ellis Island stating that her mother had arrived in New York, but was too ill to be sent on to Chicago. All of her money had gone for the steamer ticket and as the thought of her old country mother, ill and alone among strangers, was too much for her long fortitude, she made the best bargain possible with the head waiter whose importunities she had hitherto resisted, accepted the little purse the other Polish girls in the hotel collected for her and arrived in New York only to find that her mother had died the night before.[69]

Whereas an earlier generation of reformers focused on the family as a wellspring of virtue and moral inoculation, Addams saw families as sources of potential conflict and pressure. The solution to white slavery could not be found in the family nor in a return to rural innocence. Addams declared that "it is apparently better to overcome the dangers in this new and freer life, which modern industry has opened to women, than it is to attempt to retreat into the domestic industry of the past."[70]

Addams argued that commercialized prostitution was a symptom of dramatic reordering of economic and social structures. Her claims that economic circumstances shaped sexual practices fit with her racial pluralism. The racial status of immigrant women did not depend upon their morality. Like the WCTU under Frances Willard's leadership, Addams pursued a broad program of reform in order to heal the wounds caused by urbanization and industrialization, yet she did not speak on behalf of Anglo-Saxon womanhood. With her work for the Hull House, the Immigrant Protective League, and the Juvenile Protective Association, Addams tried to cure the ills of the modern city and to offer a homelike refuge for immigrants and their families.

Clifford Roe and the Sexual Logic of White Citizenship

Chicago attorney Clifford Roe was the nation's most prolific writer on the subject of white slavery, and he emerged as the foremost crusader against forced prostitution in the United States. A few months after the publication of George Kibbe Turner's article in *McClure's*, Roe launched a series of prosecutions against white slave traders and handled over 348 cases in 1909.[71] Canadian moral reformer John Shearer stated, "He might well be known to History as the William Lloyd Garrison of the movement."[72] Roe was a prominent member of several anti-vice organizations and acted as executive secretary of the American Vigilance Association. The legal gains in the war on white slavery owed much of their success to Roe's lobbying. Roe assisted in securing national legislation against white slavery with the Mann White Slave Traffic Act, authored by Illinois senator James Mann. Some of the document record for the Mann act came from Roe's reports; he delivered over 100 speeches in support of the act.[73]

Roe successfully prosecuted hundreds of white slavery cases in Chicago. Acting as assistant state's attorney for Cook County, he commenced the first of several criminal trials against white slave procurers in January 1907. According to Roe, the trial of Pansy Williams "marked the discovery of a trade of women in Chicago."[74] In his 1910 book, *Panders and Their White Slaves,* Roe described how a young man named John drugged a twenty-two-year-old woman named Agnes at a dance hall. She lost consciousness and awoke to a "dark negress" who assured her, "You are all right . . . and you will like it here." Agnes demanded to see the owner of the house after the maid informed her that her clothes were locked away. "The negress disappeared and

Chicago anti-vice crusader Clifford G. Roe. From Ernest Bell, *Fighting the Traffic in Young Girls* (Chicago: G. S. Ball, 1910).

came back with a stout, blond woman, wearing a kimono and a great many diamonds and other jewels."[75] Pansy Williams, the brothel madam, explained to the victim that she owed a debt to the house and handed her a red satin dress. Several days later, the police rescued Agnes after she managed to mail a letter to her father. Prosecuting attorney Clifford Roe charged Pansy Williams with holding Agnes in bondage in a brothel, noting that without an opportunity to leave, Agnes was "held practically as a slave."[76]

Agnes's story corroborated two cases that had crossed Roe's desk a year earlier while he was practicing law for a private firm. The similarities among these accounts convinced Roe that an expansive traffic in women operated in the United States and had Chicago as its headquarters. Referring to himself in the third person as "the Prosecutor," Roe recalled how the Agnes case sparked his crusade: "Agnes made the sensational charge in court that she had been drugged and held as a prisoner. It was the startling testimony in this case that caused the young State's Attorney, whom we shall hereafter for convenience designate as the Prosecutor, to delve more vigorously into the white slave business and to institute a thorough investigation."[77]

Roe claimed that white slavery thrived because of dance halls and false employment agencies. Dance halls were a favorite target of reformers in the Pro-

Table 4.2. Methods of Procuring and Scenarios of Abduction in Clifford Roe's *Panders and Their White Slaves* and Jane Addams's *A New Conscience and an Ancient Evil.*

	Roe's *Panders*	Addams's *New Conscience*
Outright coercion	6% (2)	0% (0)
Amusements, dance halls	42% (14)	0% (0)
False promises of employment	36% (12)	8% (1)
False promises of marriage	12% (4)	25% (3)
Casual prostitution that becomes coercive	0% (0)	33% (4)
Unknown, other	3% (1)	33% (4)
Total	100% (33 stories)	100% (12 stories)

gressive Era, and Roe viewed them as a chief source of white slavery.[78] A 1910 investigation by the Juvenile Protective Association found that Chicago had 190 dance halls with saloons adjoining them and that liquor was sold in 240 of Chicago's 328 halls.[79] In one instance, Roe prosecuted the organizers of a "Chicken Dance" at a club called "Little America" on 31st Street. Roe stated that if police had not stopped the dance from occurring, "I am confident at least a dozen girls who would have attended this dance by morning would have found themselves in a disorderly resort." He added that "dance halls are the greatest evil we have to contend with, for it is at these places young girls are enticed into drinking by strangers whom they meet, and the next thing they know they are ruined."[80] Roe blamed new urban amusements such as dance halls and nickel theaters in about 42 percent of the white slavery cases he discussed in *Panders and Their White Slaves*.[81]

Roe also prosecuted white slave procurers who offered false promises of employment to their victims. According to Roe, white slave panders often besieged stagestruck girls who had left their small towns to become Chicago actresses. For instance, Roe prosecuted Jesse Thomas, an Austrian army officer, for running a false theatrical booking agency. Thomas supposedly offered fourteen-year-old Ruth Hardy employment as an actress after she ran away from home. The *Chicago Tribune* reported, "Her mother received a letter from her on Monday saying that she would leave shortly to go on the stage. She said her stage name would be Clotilda Carrolton and that all the girls called her Hilda."[82] Although Thomas denied knowing the girl, Roe found a contract signed by "Hilda Carrolton" in his office and strongly suspected that he was going to sell her to a brothel. Roe said that he intended

to "hold this man for causing the delinquency of a child and on a more serious charge," probably statutory rape. Roe cited false promises of employment as the scheme used to trap women in about 36 percent of the instances
of white slavery discussed in *Panders and Their White Slaves.*[83]

AMERICAN WOMEN AND WHITE SLAVES

Roe's white slavery narratives consistently expressed sympathy for victims,
like Agnes and Ruth Hardy, who were tricked into prostitution. According
to Roe, the primary victims of panders, or white slave procurers, were native-
born girls from rural towns and communities.[84] In *Panders and Their White
Slaves,* only 21 percent of the thirty-three victims he discussed were foreign-
born. This is in sharp contrast to the immigrant victims who comprised 75
percent of Jane Addams's stories in *A New Conscience and an Ancient Evil.*[85]
Roe argued that immigrant white slave procurers abducted native-born
women for foreign vice markets: "The awakening of the people has brought
to light too that not only has the immigrant girl in America been exploited
in this foreign traffic, but American girls have been procured for the foreign market. Girls from many North American cities have been sent to South
America, to Shanghai and to Australia."[86]

Like Addams, Roe thought that different forms of employment put women
at risk. Unlike Addams's accounts of white slavery that emphasized long hours
and low pay, Roe claimed that wicked men set up sham businesses in order
to lure girls into the vice trade. When discussing a white slave case where two
seventeen-year-old girls were duped by a false theatrical agency, he said: "These
two girls are young, pretty, and have always borne good reputations. They had
a narrow escape from ending their lives as 'white slaves.' In time I hope this
class of employment agents will be driven from Chicago. Then young girls,
without fear, can apply for work and feel certain they will not be taken into
some notorious dive."[87] Here, Roe suggested that women have a right to seek
employment in the city, but he said nothing about the problems that working-
class women commonly confronted in legal employment situations. By focusing his ire on false employment agents, he deflected attention away from
the economic climate that Addams deemed central to the problems of prostitution and sexual exploitation. For Roe, the white slave trade blossomed because of the naïveté of women and the trickery of men. Low wages and dire
working conditions were only a small element of the white slave trade.

Roe conceded that a small percentage of women entered prostitution because of economic pressure, but he claimed that "most girls are inherently
good and respectable and that it takes something more than low wages alone

to drive them to the depths of despair."[88] A view of purity as something women simply possessed or lacked fit with his stark quantification of white slavery. According to Roe, "How many voluntarily go into this life? It is estimated that about twenty per cent! This shows us that eighty per cent are led into it by some scheme or entrapped and sold, and at least two-thirds of this number are from our own country, being inveigled from farms, towns and cities."[89] In 1911, he stated that "fifty per cent of the total number leading lives of vice, or in other words about one half are recruited through the white slave markets."[90] By 1914, Roe cautiously moved away from portraying women as either hopelessly depraved or helpless victims. In discussing the number of brothel "inmates" who fell to white slave procurers, Roe said, "All inmates are not white slaves, neither have all these inmates been procured, but it is safe to say that in the beginning a large percentage of them were entrapped or inveigled into the life. Very few girls would enter this commercial life voluntarily. They might even become clandestine or occasional women of their own free will, but very seldom would they become commercial women willingly."[91] Roe drew a sharp distinction between occasional prostitutes and white slaves, thereby effectively ignoring the economic circumstances surrounding "occasional women" and attributing their sexual practices to "free will."

In both his early and later writing, Roe saw female sexual agency as an internal moral quality. Women were either naturally pure and incapable of entering the vice trade without extreme coercion, or their weak will made them vulnerable to new consumerist temptations. In both instances, their choices stemmed from an essential moral disposition. Roe declared, "Vice is a moral fault, a defect of the natural character, or a defect as the result of training and habits."[92] Roe's examples of white slavery suggested that the internal morality that kept women from willful prostitution was a racial trait overwhelmingly shared by native-born whites. The case of Maurice Van Bever, recalled by Roe in *Horrors of the White Slave Trade,* reveals the difficulties Roe faced when convincing a jury of the sexual innocence of non-native white slaves.

In the heart of Chicago's red-light district, a Frenchman named Maurice Van Bever purchased two brothels called "Paris" and "White City." Roe successfully prosecuted Van Bever based on the testimony of William Simes, a bartender who worked at both places, and a Jewish girl named Sarah, whom Van Bever had "lured to the life of a white slave." The jury found him guilty of pandering but only after Roe skillfully refuted the defense attorney's closing statements, which "had made a deep impression" on several of the jurors.[93]

According to Roe's account of the trial, Van Bever's defense attorney tried to appeal to the racial prejudices of the jury. The defense attorney insisted that Sarah's Jewish greed led her to willingly work for Van Bever as a prostitute. According to Roe, Van Bever's attorney said, "You have a girl—not an innocent Jewish girl, not an innocent American girl, but a girl who is capable of coolly and calmly planning as to how she shall get the dollar." The defense attorney explained, "Sarah always has her head about her. What does that mean? It means she is always cool and calm with all the characteristics of her race; cool and calm; always her head about her. When is she cool and calm? When does she always have her head about her? When? When she is about to put money in her purse? When was a woman of her race other than cool and calm when money was the paramount issue?" The defense attorney tried to portray Sarah as a cunning Jew, striving to line her pockets with money by any means necessary. His comments invoked a stereotype of Jews as calculating and full of avarice, and he also referred to her Jewishness in racial terms. Toward the end of his remarks, he sarcastically added, "God help us and God help the Jews. If they were all innocent as little Sarah we would soon be able to pay off our mortgages."[94]

Roe knew that he "must battle hard to overcome the influence of this speech upon the jury" and argued that Sarah's race should not factor into the jury's decision-making. Roe said, "The counsel would have you think that because this girl happened to be a Jewish girl—German Jewish girl she is—he said born in St. Louis. There is no evidence here where she was born. She was board abroad, if that is to be brought into this case."[95] In many of Roe's prostitution trials, the whiteness of the victim probably assured the jury of her sexual innocence, but Sarah's Jewish origins compounded Roe's difficulty in proving his case.

Roe regarded white slave abductions as the defining feature of modern prostitution, and he usually represented prostitutes as chaste victims. This understanding of white slave victims shifted the blame from the prostitutes themselves to the white slave traders and the parents who failed to protect their children. In a 1909 public speech, Roe blamed parents' ignorance for the downfall of their children and claimed that many girls found in vice resorts were Methodists. Roe intended to point out that all young women were vulnerable to white slavery despite their religious upbringing, but his comment irritated a local Methodist pastor.[96] George H. Trevor, a pastor of a Chicago Methodist church, said, "I don't believe that girls trained in Methodist homes go into such places. The girls may be fifty-second cousins to Methodists, but in my opinion they don't come out of the church."[97] Roe did not suggest that Methodist girls were especially prone to prostitution; rather, he wanted to emphasize the threat white slavery posed to all Christian families. When accounting for the vice trade in Chicago, Roe saw only lured white slave victims while Trevor saw only immoral volunteers. Their disagreement stemmed from a fundamental difference in how they viewed prostitution. In the rare instances where women willingly became prostitutes, Roe continued to regard them as helpless victims. In his suffrage tract *What Women Might Do with the Ballot,* Roe stated, "In our efforts to abolish the traffic in girls, it does not seem fair to fight the unfortunate women who either gravitate or are tricked into lives of shame. The persons to fight are those who encourage, maintain and protect the social evil."[98] Roe's image of the white slave as a chaste white native-born girl from the countryside found its opposite in his image of the white slave procurer as an immoral foreigner.

NATIVISM AND THE WHITE SLAVE PROCURER

Although Roe had much to say about the causes of white slavery and the character of white slave victims and villains, he focused most of his energy on using anti-prostitution legislation to punish alleged white slave dealers. In 1907, the Illinois Vigilance Association presented a bill to the Illinois state legislature to criminalize pandering. The bill imposed a fine of up to $300 and a year in jail for any scheme to "induce, persuade or encourage" a woman to become an inmate of a brothel. Repeat offenders would be imprisoned for ten years. The state legislature enacted this law in July 1908, making Illinois the first state in the nation to make pandering a crime.

Roe's prosecutions garnered public attention, and soon he had the support of wealthy philanthropists. Five Chicagoans pledged their financial support for his crusade, allowing Roe to investigate white slavery on a full-time basis. Soon thereafter, Roe was forced out of his job, and he carried on his work without the formal backing of the Chicago district attorney's office.[99] During the next few years, momentum grew behind Roe's efforts. After a public conference on white slavery in 1909, Emil G. Hirsch stated, "Mr. Roe expects to have behind him a solid representation of the best that exists in organizations making for civic progress. A fund of $50,000 has been pledged for the work."[100] Armed by wealthy backers and popular support, Roe launched a sustained attack on the white slave traffic. His writings articulated a powerful connection between foreignness and criminality, and he often aimed his law enforcement efforts at the new immigrants of Chicago. In *Horrors of the White Slave Trade,* Roe listed seventy-seven cases where he obtained a successful conviction under Illinois's new pandering statute.[101] Fifty of the seventy-five defendants had last names that suggested Jewish, Italian, or French origins.[102]

In *Panders and Their White Slaves,* 36 percent of the white slave procurers he identified were foreign-born.[103]

Roe argued that white slavery in the United States originated from eastern Europe, claiming that eastern Europeans exported the systematic white slave trade to the United States. The development of the prostitution trade mirrored the growing complexity of urban commerce, with increasingly hierarchical organizations and expanding potential for profits. Roe blamed the rapid growth of prostitution on eastern European Jews: "There was a great influx of Austrian, Russian and Hungarian Jews about twenty-five years ago in New York City. Among these immigrants were disreputable men and boys who had learned the art of the kaftan of Eastern Europe, and they soon began to develop this traffic in America." He decried "the dreadful work of the Jewish cadet and pander, who had settled on the West side of Chicago."[104] Roe argued that Frenchmen developed the white slave traffic in America during this same time. He explained that the French Revolution disrupted the prostitution market, forcing French procurers and pimps to relocate in London and New York. From there, French prostitutes and their panders settled in Chicago and San Francisco.[105] Roe blamed Jews and the French for white slavery, and he also observed that "in recent years the Italians and Greeks have come into prominence in the pandering business."[106] Roe expressed the nativist fear of a foreign incursion; immigrants from all corners of the globe threatened America with their criminal culture.

As immigrants made Chicago neighborhoods their home, Roe described his unease in walking the streets and being assaulted by the smells of foreign food. In *Panders and Their White Slaves,* Roe depicted the Chicago courthouse as a swirl of alien culture and pollution. The place was

> teeming with more odours than could possibly be concocted by the ingenuity of man. Each day it is filled with the garlic and tube-rose of the Italians; the mysterious opium scent of the Chinaman; the highly perfumed sport is there, and the lodging-house bum, reeking with tobacco and whiskey; all this is mixed with the gases from the open sewerage in the underground cells, which are worse than any of those of the dark ages. . . . To top it all off comes the steam from the corned beef and cabbage and the frying of the odoriferous onion, which the cook in the cellar below is going to dish up to the prisoners for their noonday meal.[107]

He described the courthouse as invaded by the culture of non-native races. The Italian's garlic offended his sensibilities and mixed with the smell of sewage. His description of corned beef and cabbage linked a dietary staple of the Irish with prisons and criminality. Roe asserted a concrete connection between foreign-born men and the practice of white slavery, but native-born whites risked eroding the moral boundaries between themselves and other races with their participation in the vice trade. Participating in the "sporting culture" of brothels and gambling houses, or indulging in whiskey or tobacco, associated an otherwise white person with foreignness and criminality.

SEXUALITY AND RACE IN *THE GIRL WHO DISAPPEARED*

In *The Girl Who Disappeared,* Roe's 1914 book based upon "a composite historical exposition of actual cases" that he prosecuted, Roe explained how women's and men's sexual choices build white America.[108] It also offered a sustained argument against the notion that low wages cause prostitution. Roe characterized sexual agency as a quality within a person's will or sense of morality, independent from economic conditions. Roe's construction of the white slave victim suggested that working-class women have sexual desires, choices, and a measure of free will. This conception of womanhood allowed him to blame women for their downfall and praise them for their moral renewal. Roe prosecuted foreigners for their participation in the vice trade, but he thought that the solution to white slavery ultimately rested in the moral power of native-born white men and women. Roe's descriptions of the victims and villains of white slavery posited a cultural and moral basis of racial membership. For Roe, moral failing, not economic pressure, created the supply and demand for white slaves.

The Girl Who Disappeared tells the story of Jane Carr and Steve. Jane is eighteen years old and living in a small midwestern town when a man named John Randolph promises her employment as an actress in Chicago. He sells her to a brothel once they arrive in the city. Jane eventually escapes with the help of Steve, a white barber who frequents the brothel where Jane was held. Soon thereafter, Jane finds employment in a large department store. After several years, her employer places her in charge of a social service bureau that looks after the moral dangers confronting women who work at the store. Jane soon becomes an exemplar of American womanhood through her devotion to reform work. Meanwhile, Steve returns to a life of gambling, drinking, and vice. He is arrested after stealing from his employer, but he pledges himself to a pure life. Eighteen months after his arrest, Clifford Roe hires him as a detective because of his vast knowledge of the Chicago underworld. By the end of Roe's narrative, Steve redeems himself by tracking down the man that originally procured Jane.

Roe initially used eye color to mark the race of the victims and villains of his story. John Randolph claims to represent a theatrical agency and places an ad in a newspaper edited by Jane's father. When Randolph walks into her father's office, "she noticed something about his piercing black eyes that at first repelled her." Her apprehension eases as the man describes the high salaries she could expect to earn as an actress in Chicago. As she tells him of her desire to go on the stage, "her large blue eyes shone with enthusiasm."[109]

John Randolph offers to accompany Jane to Chicago. Soon after their arrival, he sells her to a brothel. According to Roe, Jane typified the girls white slavers pursue:

> They [panders] generally look for girls who are rather ignorant and have not passed the grades of grammar schools; more than half of them are country girls and from small towns. They also seek girls who are out of work, and suf-

According to Clifford Roe, white slave procurers often pursued stagestruck girls. "As Jane Carr told him of her great desire to go upon the stage her large blue eyes shone with enthusiasm." From Clifford Roe, *The Girl Who Disappeared* (Naperville: World's Purity Federation, 1914).

fering privations, girls who are dissatisfied with their home surroundings, girls who are romantically inclined and dream of an elopement or marriage at first sight, girls who have a great longing for the glare of the footlights, or silly girls who are foolish about cheap feathers and finery.[110]

The white slaves that Katharine Bushnell investigated for the WCTU had simple economic motives for seeking employment in the lumber camps: these camps offered working-class girls a substantial paycheck. In Roe's narrative, the victims of white slavery had needs, desires, and romantic inclinations that placed them in danger. He suggested that choices about sex and morality ultimately stem from inner strength or weakness, not from economic or social circumstances.

After Jane's arrival, a black maid escorts her into the lavish sitting room where she meets the brothel keeper. The maid explains the situation to Jane: "As long as she was in debt she was told that it would be necessary for her to remain at this house. This fact was confided to her by the colored maid, who seemed to sympathize with the girl, and yet was loyal to her mistress."[111] The figure of the black maid appeared in Roe's other stories about white slavery, like the case of Pansy Williams and Agnes.[112] The black maid often explained the situation to the abducted victim shortly after her arrival in the brothel. The maid stood as a referent to chattel slavery, but the brothel maids were not allied with the white slave. Roe's use of this rhetorical device contrasted the freedom of the black maid with the bondage of the white slave; in helping maintain the house of prostitution, the African American maid became part of the machinery of white slavery.

Jane escapes with the help of Steve, a white barber and frequent visitor to her brothel. Afterward, she takes a job at a confectionery store, but her boss fires her after a man who frequented her former brothel tells him of Jane's unfortunate past. Jane finds new employment at a large department store, but another former brothel customer soon recognizes her. Jane's fellow workers shun her because of this, but her employer supports her. After Jane tells him about her tragic abduction, the superintendent holds a meeting and chastises the workers for not giving her a chance. Over the next six years, public knowledge of the white slavery problem grows, and Jane sheds the stigma of her past. Prompted by the news coverage about white slavery, Jane's employer creates a social service bureau for the store and places her in charge. Jane tries to improve the climate of the workplace by giving advice to harassed girls, removing pestering men from the store, and providing escorts for girls who work long nights.

In her capacity in the social service bureau, Jane also monitors the morality of working women. Jane's treatment of a complaint by several shop girls unearths Roe's ideas about the importance of white women's sexual agency for maintaining racial boundaries. Jane hears complaints that a French-woman named Fallet is "living with a man working in the store, but was not married to him. She was a menace to all the young girls in the department, as she was very forward in her actions and used vile language." Fallet is a bad influence because "the girls would crowd about her and listen eagerly as she vulgarly discussed delicate matters."[113] Jane calls Fallet into her office and demands Fallet defend her behavior. Fallet explains her economic constraints:

> "How do you expect a woman to get along on seven dollars a week and live decently? It is the store's fault that we women have to do this. If they paid their clerks a living wage, then they could live in a respectable way." "I don't know about that," replied Jane. "If a girl or woman has the right stuff in her she'll starve before she will submit to wrongdoing. Women like you are too anxious to put the blame for your misdeeds upon somebody else. Of course I know it is hard to get along and live very well on seven dollars a week, but if one looks around, there are plenty of places where one can live decently even with that salary."[114]

Roe used the character of Jane Carr to make an argument about the racial dimensions of sexual morality. Jane's arguments about sexual morality mark boundaries between French and native-born women. Roe contrasted Fallet's sexual sins with Jane's purity, using French and American women to mark sexual immorality and morality respectively. Morality was ultimately inherent in women with "the right stuff," making them accountable for their sins despite low wages or dreary working conditions. While the Frenchwoman made excuses for her behavior and complained about her wages, Jane urged her to adhere to a higher code of morality. When Jane referred to a woman with "the right stuff in her," she spoke of an internal moral disposition that women could draw upon to protect themselves from threats to their chastity. For Roe, the "right stuff" allowed native-born white working-class women to distinguish themselves from nationalities and races that Roe deemed prone to immorality, like the French, Irish, Italians, Chinese, and Jews.

Roe also used Jane Carr to argue against Jane Addams's economic interpretation of vice that placed the blame for white slavery on low wages and dire working conditions. Roe disputed the link between poverty and vice throughout *The Girl Who Disappeared*. Published two years after Addams's

A New Conscience and an Ancient Evil, Roe's story cleverly used "Jane" as Roe's interlocutor. Fallet's salary of seven dollars a week demonstrated Roe's awareness of the surveys and discussions about the low wages paid to working-class women, and he was undoubtedly aware of Addams's treatise. Although Roe's white slavery narratives often involved trickery, deceit, and force, he argued that good white women do not willingly lose their morals, no matter how dismal their working conditions.

Highlighting the comparison between Jane Carr and Jane Addams, Roe described the reform work conducted by Jane Carr in Chicago's dance halls. Jane Addams coordinated investigations of the dance halls for the Juvenile Protective Association, and her fictional counterpart used similar fact-finding techniques to unearth immorality at the "Red Bird hall": "Ever since that first night at one of the big public dance halls Jane had been carrying on a quiet investigation. She was surprised to find conditions as bad as they were at the Red Bird hall, and she hoped by gathering facts concerning other similar halls that she could make recreation conditions safer and better for working girls."[115]

Despite a comparable method and object of investigation, Jane Carr differed from Jane Addams in her assessment of the causes of vice. Whereas Addams regarded vice as "the most sinister outcome of economic pressure," Jane Carr (and therefore Roe) considered economic circumstances not nearly as important.[116] When asked to rank-order the underlying causes of white slave traffic, Jane Carr placed last on her list "the economic conditions that surround the working people."[117] Roe also developed this argument through conversations between Carr and others. For example, a social reformer named John Malcom frequently visited Jane while she worked at her office in the store's social service bureau. Malcolm asked her opinion about the economic causes of vice: "'You will admit, though, won't you, that many girls do go wrong because of low wages and lack of work?' 'No, Mr. Malcolm, I cannot admit that many of them do, but I do say that some of them, perhaps fifteen per cent, go down because of these reasons.'"[118]

For Roe, working conditions did not weaken the will of working-class women, as in Addams's account. Morality was a preexisting disposition that people either possessed or lacked. Roe's story about Jane Carr and his support of women's suffrage suggested that women have a crucial role in the fight against white slavery. Although he prioritized the passage of legislation and other maneuvers in the male-dominated polity, Roe understood native-born white women as possessing political and sexual agency that conferred abilities and responsibilities critical for the nation's moral health. Roe argued, "Once a slave, then a plaything, and now a rival to man in all the walks of life, woman has proved her worth. Given education and freedom in the final analysis she will solve the white slave problem."[119]

Roe's understanding of white womanhood did not make motherhood a prerequisite for feminine morality. Unmarried working-class women like Jane could proudly serve their country through moral vigilance, and "fallen women" or white slaves could become true citizens through moral practices. This gave women agency, but it infused whiteness, as a racial category, with moral requirements. By making racial purity contingent upon sexual purity, Roe constructed whiteness as something that women could lose. Although young women could lose whiteness by flirting with vices typically practiced by foreigners, he argued that they could regain racial purity through an adherence to native-born American morality: a moral code that transcended economic circumstance.

Like his discourse about white femininity, Roe rhetorically conflated manliness and whiteness, making men's sexual practices a source of racial status. The plot thread concerning Steve, the immoral barber who becomes a detective, outlined Roe's ideas about Anglo-American manhood. After rescuing Jane, Steve continues to cavort with gamblers and pimps in saloons. He becomes a "well known hanger-on in the poolrooms, which fringe the vice districts."[120] Roe's description of Steve connected immorality with foreignness. The picture of Steve in *The Girl Who Disappeared* bolstered Roe's argument that whiteness is something achieved through moral practices. The illustration Roe included in his text shows Steve playing cards with three men. The light of the pool hall illuminates part of his visage, making half of his face white and the other half black. To his right, a man with a large nose, perhaps a Jew or an Italian, smokes a cigarette. This image suggests the racial contamination that accompanies vice. Steve is partially blackened by his associates and his eagerness to throw down his cards.

Police arrest Steve after his employer discovers that he has been stealing small amounts of money from the cash register. They place Steve in a cell at Chicago's Harrison Street Station, the only native-born white among the seven people in the cell: "It was almost night and the half dozen cellmates— two negroes, one Italian and three Chinamen—had departed, leaving Steve all alone in the cell."[121] Like Roe, Steve felt assaulted by the smells surrounding the jail: "The odors coming from the corned beef and cabbage and the fried onions, mingled with the stench and foul air of the prison, had taken away all the appetite that Steve had. So he was lying full length on the one little bench in his cell, his face a pallid white, upturned to the black ceil-

"He spent his evenings gambling with these exploiters of womanhood." From Clifford Roe, *The Girl Who Disappeared* (Naperville: World's Purity Federation, 1914).

ing, his arms folded across his breast, when he heard a gruff voice call out, 'Get up there, old man, the State's Attorney wants to see you upstairs.'"[122] This description juxtaposed Steve's white face with the foul odors that marked other races. Steve's crimes placed him, physically and morally, with African Americans, Italians, and Chinese. Like his friends at the gambling house, these associations in the jail tarnished him on some elemental level.

Roe describes how he offered Steve a chance to plead guilty to petty larceny as long as he promised to live an upright life. Despite Steve's guilt by association, Roe gives him a chance to redeem himself. He tells Steve:

> The detectives know that there is no one in the world who will prosecute an habitual criminal quicker that I will, but when a fellow has made a mistake once and will probably never make a mistake again, because he has the right

stuff in him to see the error of his ways, I believe in giving him another chance. Now, Steve, that is just what I am going to offer you. I am going to offer you another chance to make a man out of yourself, and in order to do that you must try to set things right and make amends for what you have done.[123]

Like Jane Carr's admonitions to Fallet, Roe urged Steve to draw upon his moral power—his "right stuff." Tapping this inner strength would allow him to "make a man" out of himself. Roe's extension of sympathy to Steve is out of pace with his track record of relentless white slavery prosecutions, though he perceived the foreign-born white slavers as lacking the inherent moral potential of someone like Steve. Like Jane, Steve had an internal power that made him racially distinct. Roe assigned these characters two roles in protecting their race. Through their police and investigative work, they monitored the sites where native-born whites mingled with other races. In their other role, they upheld the integrity of native-born whites by drawing on their "right stuff."

Steve accepts Roe's offer and begins to live a pure life. Eighteen months later, Roe employs him as a white slave detective. While Steve investigates white slavery cases for Roe, Jane launches her own inquiries into Chicago dance halls. John Malcolm tells Jane about the disappearance of a girl named Fannie: "'This has all the earmarks of a white slave case,' said Malcolm, after he had finished reading the letter. 'Here is a green girl, unaccustomed to large city life, who has gone to a dance hall where it is well known that procurers go to get their girls.'" Jane asks Malcolm if they have a chance to rescue the girl. He seems skeptical but tells Jane that "our white slave prosecutor" has just returned to Chicago and that he has with him "the best detective that I know of for tracing just such a case as this."[124]

Later that night, Jane goes to Red Bird hall to investigate the disappearance of Fannie. Jane spots Steve at the dance hall and notices that he is with a woman who is "one of the worst in the hall." Unaware that he is Roe's detective, Jane assumes that Steve is still living a life of shame. She quickly notifies a police officer after she sees Steve talking to a little girl in the dance hall, and the officer promptly arrests Steve. The next morning, Malcolm informs Jane of her mistake, noting that Steve is "the greatest and most successful detective we have in catching the white slavers."[125]

Finding themselves allies in the fight against white slavery, Steve and Jane renew their friendship. Soon after their incident at Red Bird hall, Steve resumes his detective work in Philadelphia, eventually locating and prosecuting the man who originally procured Jane. Roe concludes his story with a description of Jane and Steve on a train heading toward the rural home of Jane's parents in order to get married. They each pledge that they will continue their fight against white slavery. Jane says, "You and I, Steve, can devote our lives to saving other girls as you saved me."[126]

*　*　*

Jane Addams's Hull House was inspired by the promise of assimilation. She wanted to draw the color line such to include immigrant groups within the boundaries of whiteness, and economic problems that confronted new immigrant groups presented the chief obstacles to their assimilation. Solving these problems and providing a safe haven for immigrants eliminated the economic pressures that often forced women into prostitution. Addams's writings challenged the idea of freestanding agency or an idea of "free will" that women either possessed or lacked. For Addams, economic realities conditioned morality. The image of the white slave that drove Addams's crusade was neither willful nor entirely helpless. Addams thought that economic and environmental solutions to white slavery succeeded precisely because of the plasticity of women's morality upon entering the city.

Clifford Roe wanted to draw the color line between new immigrants and native-born whites. Immigrant groups invaded Chicago with their foreign foods, vile manners, and, worst of all, their new methods of procuring prostitutes. Because he saw little hope in making immigrants more like native-born Americans, Roe aggressively prosecuted foreign-born participants in the vice trade. His nativism also fit with a particular view of white femininity and masculinity; the internal virtue of white men and women kept them distinct from immigrants, and drawing on this moral compass was ultimately the solution to the white slavery problem. Native-born whites risked losing whiteness through their immorality—but possessing the "right stuff" ensured their racial strength.

Roe's investigations of white slavery drew interest from John D. Rockefeller Jr., who had spent six months as the foreman of a white slave grand jury investigation in New York City. After the conclusion of the grand jury, Rockefeller expressed the desire for Roe to investigate white slavery in New York City as he had done in Chicago. He wrote to his colleague Harold Swift, "When Mr. Roe has finished his work in Chicago, should the matter be taken up seriously here, it might be desirable to consider him as the person to lead in and direct such a campaign here." Rockefeller hired Roe as an undercover investigator in New York City on May 1, 1911, and paid him $5,000 for his year-long investigation. Rockefeller instructed Roe to keep his inquiry a secret and suggested that he tell people that he was opening up a new law practice in New York, adding, "I am sure you fully agree with our view and that you will see to it that the information does not leak out in any possible way."[127] Roe's investigation was part of a larger effort on behalf of Rockefeller to understand and combat prostitution.

5

John D. Rockefeller Jr. and the "Negro Alleged Slave Trader"

In New York City, the African American population nearly tripled between 1890 and 1910.[1] The Great Migration heightened the availability of intimate contact between whites and blacks, prompting a variety of racist responses.[2] In 1910, New York politicians attempted to establish a state law barring interracial marriage. The "Act to Amend the Domestic Relations Law, in Relation to Miscegenation," proposed to nullify all marriages "contracted between a person of white or Caucasian race and a person of the negro or black race."[3] Although this effort failed, white New Yorkers pursued segregation in other ways. This chapter shows how white slavery stories and anti-vice activism helped shape the color line in New York City between African Americans and native-born whites.

In November 1909, muckraking journalist George Kibbe Turner published a scandalous article in *McClure's* that accused New York politicians of supporting the white slave trade. Two months later, a judge from New York's Court of General Session charged a grand jury to investigate Turner's allegations and appointed John D. Rockefeller Jr. as foreman. As a result of an undercover investigation and sting operation stemming from the grand jury probe, police arrested an alleged white slave procurer, a mixed-race woman named Belle Moore. During her trial, the prosecutor tried to characterize Belle Moore as a depraved trafficker in white girls, while the defense attorney assailed the morality of the investigators. Testimony in *People v. Belle Moore* designated certain intimacies as violating the color line, thereby clarifying what it meant to be "white" or "colored" and contributing to segregation efforts in

New York City. This event demonstrates how New York reformers used the white slavery issue to police racial boundaries between native-born whites and those of African descent. Efforts to curtail white slavery in New York City coincided with the strengthening of the "one-drop rule" in the North. As a monolithic category of "colored" or "black" effaced distinctions of people who had different "proportions" of African ancestry, white slavery narratives added sexual content to the meaning of whiteness and blackness.

The Politics of Prostitution in New York City

By the end of the Civil War, there were over 600 brothels in New York City, and prostitution flourished in hotels, the "furnished room districts," and tenement housing. In the late nineteenth and early twentieth centuries, prostitution in the city generated annual profits ranging from $15 to $20 million.[4] Those outside the sex trade quickly realized its moneymaking potential. Brothel owners and pimps operated their businesses through a system of unofficial licensing and organized payments that created financial ties among the procurers, pimps, brothel madams, police, and Tammany district leaders. Brothel owners usually paid an "initiation fee" of several hundred dollars for opening a house, followed by monthly "protection fees" to the local police captain's "wardman" or collector. Some estimate that the total Tammany Hall graft from prostitution, saloons, and gambling during this period was about $7 million a year.[5] Reform organizations openly criticized the strong connections between the city government and the sex trade, and by 1909 prostitution became a heated partisan issue in New York City.

George Kibbe Turner published several accounts of white slavery that stirred public debate in New York City and Chicago. Turner's 1909 article in *McClure's*, "The Daughters of the Poor, A Plain Story of the Development of New York City as a Leading Center of the White Slave Trade of the World, under Tammany Hall," accused immigrant "slum politicians" of aiding "cadets" or "pimps" in their nefarious business. Turner's article had an immediate impact on public discussions of New York City politics.[6] Similar to his analysis of Chicago's prostitution problem discussed in chapter 4, Turner explicitly blamed eastern European Jewish immigrants for developing white slavery in New York.[7] According to Turner, although "the Jewish race has for centuries prided itself upon the purity of its women," they practiced white slavery under the aegis of Tammany Hall.[8] Turner also claimed that Italian immigrants were procuring white slaves in the city's dance halls.[9]

In "Daughters of the Poor," Turner detailed the techniques used to trap girls, citing immigrant dance halls as places where pimps ensnared fresh white slaves.[10] He argued that Jewish white slave traders made false promises of marriage to catch their prey. While Jews engaged in trickery, Italians often used physical force: "Fear is more efficacious with this class than any other, because of the notorious tendency of the low-class Italian to violence and murder."[11] Turner cited employment agencies as centers of white slave procuring, but he disputed accounts of white slavery that emphasized drugging. He declared, "The tale of drugging is almost invariably a hackneyed lie—the common currency of women of the lower world, swallowed with chronic avidity by the sympathetic charitable worker."[12]

Turner closed his article with a question and recommendation: "Shall New York City continue to be the recruiting-ground for the collection for market of young women by politically organized procurers? The only practical way to stop it will be by the defeat of Tammany Hall."[13] With its reputation under attack, Tammany Hall had to disprove its connection to the vice trade or at least gesture toward a solution. Two months after the publication of "Daughters of the Poor," Tammany supporter Judge Thomas O'Sullivan commissioned a grand jury to investigate prostitution in New York City.

The Rockefeller Grand Jury

Many regarded the commission of the Rockefeller grand jury as a "Tammany trick" designed to soothe the public without disturbing the city government's protection of vice.[14] Rockefeller's biographer and confidant Raymond Fosdick suspected that Judge O'Sullivan's Tammany sympathies directed the particularities of the jury selection, suggesting that "perhaps as a method of clothing it with respectability he designated the younger Rockefeller to serve as its foreman. Certainly the organization anticipated no very searching study of the problem." Rockefeller later remarked to Fosdick that "they couldn't have picked anybody who knew less about it."[15] He begged the judge to be excused, but despite Rockefeller's protest of ignorance about the vice trade, the judge maintained his appointment.

Judge O'Sullivan approved the grand jury to convene for only thirty days, but at the end of that period it refused to adjourn and sat for another six months. After the grand jury depleted the original fund established for the investigation, Rockefeller donated $250,000 of his own money. He read the relevant literature in the field, consulted experts on public health, and gathered the testimony of prostitutes, investigators, settlement house workers, policemen, and underworld figures. Under the direction of Rockefeller and

District Attorney James Bronson Reynolds, the grand jury interviewed several individuals who studied the prostitution, including George Kibbe Turner, former New York City chief of police Theodore Bingham, and Chicago white slave crusader Clifford Roe. Rockefeller and Reynolds also looked at "many of the confidential reports made by the special agents employed by these various commissions and investigating bodies."[16]

The jury tried to determine from the informants if white slavery dealers and procurers operated an organized business based upon forced prostitution. The judge gave the grand jury explicit instructions to uncover any structured and systematic syndicate of white slave procurers; it was not enough to prove that coercive prostitution occurred in New York City. In his grand jury deposition, George Kibbe Turner, author of the scandalous *McClure's* article, denied that such a syndicate existed. When asked, "You are satisfied that the popularly accepted use of the word syndicate cannot be used as applied to the so-called White Slave Traffic, properly, can it?," he replied, "No, I don't think so. I think there have been in existence people who own two or three houses, but so far as a general syndicate, I don't think it exists."[17]

Although Turner's retreat from his previous allegations posed an initial setback for the grand jury, Rockefeller and Reynolds solicited other testimony that described connections and collaborations among those in the prostitution trade. The grand jury report acknowledged that in the early twentieth century, prostitutes increasingly came under the control of men, and the "pimp," "pander," or "cadet" emerged to supplant female brothel owners and freelance prostitutes. Immigration Commissioner Jeremiah Jenks stated that under the pimping system, the "girls were practically sold for some hundreds of dollars and they practically come into a condition of slavery under the charge of the keepers of the houses or under the charge of some man who has control of them."[18] Former immigration commissioner Marcus Braun sent Rockefeller a set of documents he had collected while researching the vice trade in Europe. In a letter that accompanied a report of his investigations, he argued that pimping constituted a form of slavery.[19] Others testified that pimps established business networks and binding rules that approximated a "syndicate." Although they had no formal organizations, pimps acted with "mutual interest" in ways that protected them from police interference. Braun testified that they gathered in saloons and created informal rules and collaborative ties. He claimed that they pooled their resources to buy police protection and that they cooperated to maintain authority over their prostitutes.[20] The testimony of former chief of police Theodore Bingham also confirmed these observations.[21]

These testimonies suggested that New York City housed an informal network of pimps and procurers who used coercion to control prostitutes, but the grand jury did not uncover the well-organized syndicate of white slavers that the judge had commissioned the jury to find. Specifically, the final report of the grand jury stated:

> There are in the County of New York a considerable and increasing number of these creatures who live wholly or in part upon the earnings of girls or women who practice prostitution. With promises of marriage, of fine clothing, of greater personal independence, these men often induce young girls in their neighborhood to go and live with them and after a brief period, with threats of exposure or of physical violence, force them to go upon the streets as common prostitutes and to turnover the proceeds of their shame to their seducers, who live largely, if not wholly, upon the money thus earned by their victims.[22]

Although the grand jury failed to uncover a well-organized white slavery racket as depicted in many white slavery narratives, the grand jury report suggested that coercion permeated the vice trade. Next, District Attorney Charles Whitman (who had been elected on an anti-Tammany ticket) and Assistant District Attorney James Reynolds commissioned two undercover investigators to purchase prostitutes in a sting operation. They hired George Miller, an investigator from the Anti-Saloon League and the Immigration Commission, and Frances Foster, a child welfare worker from Boston.

The Sting Operation

George Miller, hired by the district attorney's office in February 1910, posed as an Alaskan brothel owner who hoped to establish a new house in Seattle. Prior to that, the Department of the Interior had employed him as an investigator for the National Immigration Commission, where his detective work led to the arrest of over seventy people involved in the prostitution trade.[23] Much of his undercover work for the district attorney's office occurred in New York City's Tenderloin district in "black and tan" saloons that catered to African Americans and whites.[24] Miller established a rapport with members of New York's interracial sex trade and eventually purchased four prostitutes after weeks of negotiations. He bought two Jewish girls for $40 from a Russian Jew named Harry Levinson and two white girls for $120 from a woman named Belle Moore. Levinson pleaded guilty and offered to help the district attorney in exchange for a lenient sentence.[25]

John D. Rockefeller Jr. after the arrest of Belle Moore and Harry Levinson. The *New York Daily Tribune* called him the "head of the grand jury through which important white slave arrests were made yesterday." April 30, 1910, 1.

Discussion of these events reverberated throughout New York City. In fact, a local newspaper reported that a businessman named Harry Levinson legally changed his name because of the flood of angry letters he had received from strangers, colleagues, and relatives due to the press reports of his namesake.[26] Yet attention to Levinson waned in early May, and the district attorney's office directed its focus on Belle Moore, the woman accused of selling white children into a life of prostitution.

The district attorney's office charged Belle Moore with the compulsory prostitution of women.[27] The jury found her guilty, and the judge sentenced her to the maximum term allowed by the statute: five years in prison. During the trial, attorneys and journalists attempted to characterize Belle Moore, the investigators, and the victims as either promoting or damaging the integrity of the white race. The attorneys used an interlocking discourse of gender, sexuality, and race: they attacked or lauded the manhood or womanhood of their witnesses by assessing their willingness to cross the color line. Likewise, they portrayed their witnesses as race traitors or race exemplars by mobilizing hegemonic notions of masculinity and femininity. Newspaper accounts of the trial amplified these representations. Journalists and attorneys reinforced a particular understanding of whiteness and blackness by articulating, with varying degrees of success, four types of sexual actors: the white slave, the white slave procurer, the New Woman, and the bohemian.

New York City Assistant District Attorney James Bronson Reynolds, who led the prosecution of Belle Moore, an alleged white slave procurer. From Ernest Bell, *Fighting the Traffic in Young Girls* (Chicago: G. S. Ball, 1910).

White Slaves and Racial Purity

The Rockefeller inquiry intended to uncover evidence of white women forced into prostitution. Investigator George Miller testified that during his first meeting with Belle Moore, he said, "I don't want colored girls. I want white girls, girls weighing less than one hundred pounds, not more than one hundred ten at most, must be naturally good looking, well built and be able to get twenty or twenty-five dollars in any whorehouse."[28] During Miller's second meeting with Belle Moore, another investigator named Frances Foster accompanied him, posing as "Frankie Fuller," the prospective manager of his brothel in Seattle. She reiterated Miller's request for racially pure girls and testified that she told Belle Moore, "I did not want a girl that showed any stain of colored blood, because I was afraid to put her in my house with white girls. I said that colored girls would not do because I was afraid to put them in there because it would make trouble for her."[29]

The construction of white womanhood in the white slavery narrative linked racial and sexual purity. Accordingly, investigators not only sought "white" as opposed to "colored" girls but also sexually innocent girls. Miller told the grand jury that Moore visited orphan asylums where she "got girls for rich men and farmed them out."[30] He testified that Moore allowed him to inspect the child prostitutes. "She called in a small colored girl and a white girl. The white girl said she was eleven years old, and the colored girl between twelve and thirteen. Both were pretty well developed. She left [sic] the big nigger in the parlor take the other girl in the room, and she told her to sit on the bed, and pushed her over and pulled up her skirt, and showed me her privates and asked me what I thought of it."[31] Frances Foster testified before the grand jury that the girls gave their ages as seventeen and eighteen but added, "They look younger." Moore reportedly assured her that the "girls are not as old as they say or as I told you." Perhaps to emphasize their innocence, Foster told the grand jury that the girls were upset because "Alice" had to leave her doll at the brothel where she formally worked and "Edith" was unable "to take away her Teddie Bear."[32]

Assistant District Attorney Reynolds accepted and reinforced the investigators' portrayal of the victims' innocence. After the arrest of Belle Moore, he consistently tried to portray the girls she reportedly procured as virtuous children. When discussing the case with the *New York Times,* he described one girl as "so little and so childish that she wept when they took her from one house to another because she had to leave her Teddy bear behind." The article continued:

> It was Belle Moore, Mr. Reynolds explained, who sold the other two girls. They gave their ages as 17 and 18, but even Belle Moore says they are younger. It is understood that they are only 15. And these are white girls. It was one of them who was so disconsolate over the loss of her Teddy bear. The other whom the purchase freed from a house where she had been kept ever since last September, brought nothing with her except a tattered doll, which she still cherished. It was dearer to her than anything else in all her unlovely world.[33]

During the trial, Reynolds continued to pepper his description of the victims with "anecdotes of the wept-for Teddy bear and the cherished 'dolly.'"[34]

The description of the white slaves' tokens of childhood worked to fix the sexual innocence of the girls, and they also couched the victims' blamelessness in racial terms. The *Times* emphasis that "these are white girls" placed them in a racial category for their readers, but the report does not locate the victims within the nineteenth-century constellation of white races, nor does it refer to them as "Anglo-Saxon girls," as it might have a decade or two earlier.

Ultimately, the facts revealed during the course of the trial did not substantiate the district attorney's claim that Moore trafficked in innocent girls. In fact, the two "girls" that Moore sold to undercover investigators were experienced prostitutes in their twenties. At the trial, the alleged victims shocked courtroom observers with their age and demeanor. Alice Milton "confessed to 23, and looked the part, despite a cluster of brown curls, which she carefully arranged on either shoulder as she entered the room." She wore a "mammoth scarlet hat, and throughout her testimony swung a patent-leather toe in the neighborhood of the stenographer's left ear."[35] The other victim, Belle Woods, was twenty-five and previously married. Although Miller told the grand jury that the women were never consulted about their transfer, Woods testified that Miller and Moore discussed the plan with both women and offered them money for their move to Seattle. Woods said, "All I remember is he asked us to go to Seattle, made arrangements for us to go to Seattle, and I said 'Yes, I would go.'"[36]

Perhaps anticipating the public's inevitable discovery that he greatly exaggerated the victims' sexual innocence, District Attorney Reynolds suggested that Belle Moore had abducted and intended to sell the investigators an eleven-year-old girl named Helen Hastings. The *New York Daily Tribune* described Hastings as "white, not more than eleven years old, about 4 feet 6 inches in height, with short, curly brown hair, dark blue eyes and good teeth."[37] The prosecutors, district attorney's office, and New York newspapers continued to insinuate that Moore intended to sell the girl despite Moore's avowal that the girl was neither a prostitute nor for sale. In fact, there is reason to believe that Helen Hastings did not exist. Police failed to find the girl after conducting a thorough search. The *Evening World* interviewed the residents in Moore's apartment complex and reported, "All are quite positive Belle Moore never had a little white girl in her flat." One resident said, "I'm sure she wouldn't bring a white girl here. She couldn't do it and escape detection."[38]

According to Miller, he first noticed Helen Hastings at Belle Moore's apartment. The eleven-year-old was lying on a bed, chewing gum, and "prattling away with no apparent consciousness of her situation." District Attorney Reynolds commanded Miller to return to Moore's apartment, giving him "orders to pay any price for the child." Miller returned the next day and asked about the girl, but Belle Moore "made it plain that the little girl was not for sale." Again, Miller asked to see her, but she told him that Helen Hastings broke her leg and was being cared for somewhere else. Detectives failed to locate Hastings after searching local hospitals.[39]

After Belle Moore's arrest, Reynolds wanted to charge her with kidnapping and murdering the girl. Although he dropped this threat at the beginning of the trial, press reports continued to characterize Helen Hastings as a victim of white slavery and possibly foul play. The *New York Times* reported that the investigators hoped to buy Hastings from Moore, but "just as the purchase was about to be completed," Moore told them that the girl had left the apartment.[40] Another article stated that the agents were in "the midst of the negotiations when she disappeared."[41] The press criticized District Attorney Reynolds for not ordering the investigators to immediately remove the child from danger. The *Evening World* reported, "That an agent of the District-Attorney, in order to make a case against an alleged procuress, abandoned an eleven-year-old white child to a negro, was admitted to-day by Assistant District Attorney James B. Reynolds, the professional investigator, who is in charge of the John D. Rockefeller Jr. Grand Jury 'white slave' investigation."[42] Reynolds simultaneously defended the investigation and highlighted the dangers posed by interracial vice districts. He said, "If he [Miller] had stopped to rescue every white girl of tender years that he found in 'black-and-tan' joints we would not have got anywhere with the efforts to get at the root of the traffic in these girls."[43] Reynolds added, "You must remember, too, that [Miller] had no reason to suppose that the girl would not be within reach after the negotiations for the other two had been completed."[44]

The district attorney's descriptions of Alice Milton, Belle Woods, and Helen Hastings rhetorically connected white racial purity with childhood innocence. Although Alice Milton and Belle Woods were not sexually naive children, the district attorney's persistence in characterizing them as white slaves suggests the cultural power of this narrative and the bond between racial and sexual purity it invokes. The victims Reynolds described did not have sexual desires that would lead them to associate with people outside of their racial category; they upheld racial purity with their sexual innocence. They also physically embodied racial purity. Frances Foster deployed the logic of the "one-drop rule" when she refused girls who showed "any stain of colored blood." This understanding of race marked a person with any African ancestry as "colored," "black," or "mulatto" and placed them firmly outside the categories of "Anglo-Saxon," "white," and "Caucasian." The one-drop rule has a long history stretching back to the eighteenth century, but white northerners invested it with new meaning in the early twentieth century.

Gender and Racial Transgression

BELLE MOORE, THE MULATTO PROCURESS

According to the prosecutors and the press, Belle Moore viciously undermined the social division between "white" and "colored" persons by corrupting "white" girls. The *Evening Post* described her as "a so-called black-and-tan pro-curer, who was holding and selling white girls for the use of both colored and white men."[45] Reporters and trial attorneys variously referred to her as a "mulatto," a "negro," a "negress," and "colored." The interchangeable terms used to describe Belle Moore suggest a growing notion of monolithic blackness. In the nineteenth century, the term "colored" referred exclusively to mulattos, but it eventually came to refer to anyone with African ancestry.[46]

Representations of Moore reflected a historical shift in racial thinking. Moore, whether a "mulatto," a "negress," or "colored," became part of an overarching group implicitly defined against "white." Despite reports of her light skin color, descriptions of Moore do not insist on her mulatto status as somehow different from "negro" or "colored." Whites in the nineteenth century debated the qualities shared by mulattos. George Fredrickson notes that some northern abolitionists portrayed mulattos as a "superior human type" whose mixed blood took "the rough edges off the overly aggressive Anglo-Saxon."[47] Others argued that this mixture made them restive and rebellious. Although debates about "amalgamation" lingered in the twentieth century, the category of "colored" absorbed mulattos as the colored/white distinction sharpened.[48] As opportunities for association between African Americans and whites flourished in northern cities, mulattos moved from symbolic figures whose moral character whites could discuss in the abstract to living threats to white identity by their ability to "pass" as white.[49]

Belle Moore demonstrated some ability to "pass," albeit symbolically, in her dealings with the investigators. While discussing the price of the prostitutes, Frances Foster had assured Moore that she would pay her well. According to Foster, Moore had said that "she wasn't worried about money, and that she knew I would treat her white."[50] Foster promised to regard Moore as "white" by dealing with her as an economic equal. The provisional equality Foster bestowed upon Moore did not represent the typical relationship between African Americans and whites in New York City. The relative gains African Americans had made by moving to New York City in the Progressive Era had been met with discrimination and forms of segregation.[51] Newspapers alluded to the diminished social distance between Moore and white New Yorkers, and insinuated that her social status allowed her to become a sexual threat.

The *New York Times* described Moore as "an extremely light mulatto" who "had a rather gayly furnished apartment at 348 West Forty-first Street."[52] Another report added that she is "probably not more than 35, with a thin, rather acrid face. She has an appearance of great intelligence, and is not unsuggestive of Cassie [*sic*] in 'Uncle Tom's Cabin.' Her hat was an amazing thing of peonies and pampas grass."[53] The comparison to the mulatto character Cassy places the crusade against white slavery in the history of northern abolitionism, transposing its victims and villains. Cassy experienced sexual exploitation in *Uncle Tom's Cabin*. The slave master Simon Legree sold her children and forced her into sexual servitude.[54] The comparison between Cassy and Belle Moore, who embodied a new form of sexual danger, hints at the consequence of black independence: freed from bondage in the South, blacks threatened to enslave whites in the North. The *Evening World* upheld this rhetorical inversion when they described Moore as "the negro alleged slave trader."[55] During the nineteenth century, white abolitionists portrayed African Americans as naturally submissive, affectionate, and loyal. According to Fredrickson, this ideology of "romantic racialism" found its clearest expression in *Uncle Tom's Cabin*.[56] By 1910, this novel provided a touchstone to discuss white slavery, and its new use reflected a change in how northern whites comprehended racial difference.

Finally, trial participants used another stereotype of African American women to characterize Belle Moore: the sexually licentious Jezebel.[57] The Jezebel image depicts black women as lusty seducers.[58] During his testimony, George Miller described a meeting with Moore where young "colored" men and women played music while everyone danced and drank together until 3:30 in the morning. Miller testified that Moore entertained the group "by dancing with her skirts up over her knees and higher."[59] Yet the willingness of the investigators to drink and dance with "colored" people gave Belle Moore's defense attorney an obvious courtroom strategy.

FRANCES FOSTER, THE NEW WOMAN

Moore's defense attorney, Alexander Karlin, tried to malign the investigators by portraying their behavior as a betrayal of the white race, and newspaper accounts reaffirmed his accusations. Karlin tried to characterize Frances Foster, the thirty-two-year-old investigator, as a New Woman. New Women were highly educated, independent, and much more sexually assertive than earlier generations of women. Many eschewed marriage and motherhood in order to pursue other forms of self-definition.[60] While New Women reflected a real shift in women's opportunities and lifestyles, they also stood as a caricature, much like the archetypal "flapper," in public discourse. Belle Moore's defense attorney had little difficulty typifying Frances Foster as a New Woman in front of the all-male jury.

Over the objections of the prosecuting attorney, Alexander Karlin succeeded in eliciting several details about Frances Foster's life. Foster reluctantly admitted during cross-examination that she was married but had had no contact with her husband for the last ten years and had no children. The prosecuting attorney objected when Karlin asked, "Are you a graduate of any college?" but the judge allowed the question to stand, and Foster replied that she had graduated from Radcliffe. Karlin questioned Foster about her prior employment and discovered that she did child protective work for a Boston charity organization.[61] Karlin's follow-up questions demonstrated that Foster continued working after marrying her husband, questions she seemed hesitant to answer.[62]

Next, Belle Moore's defense attorney tried to establish that investigator Frances Foster had developed a close and improper relationship with Belle Moore:

> Karlin: From the time that you first met this defendant, under what name had you been in the habit of addressing her?
> Foster: Addressing her as Miss Belle Moore.
> Karlin: Oh, so you got so intimate with this colored procuress that you called her Belle?[63]

Karlin suggested that Foster did not maintain the proper distance from her target. By referring to his client as a "colored procuress," Karlin briefly conceded Belle Moore's crimes in order to charge Foster with violating the color line. He suggested that the jury direct attention to Foster's impropriety as a white woman instead of Moore's procuring.

Karlin's interrogation of Foster focused on her inappropriate intimacy with racial outsiders. He tried to argue that Foster violated the color line by "slumming" in racially mixed saloons and cafés. Although many members of New York's upper and middle classes visited the vice districts, it was largely a male form of recreation.[64] Karlin repeatedly mentioned that Foster visited "colored folks" in black and tan saloons to cast doubt on her morality as a white woman. Karlin asked, "Do you think it is just the kind of work for a college graduate to be engaged in, to go around negro resorts to get evidence?"[65] He interrogated Foster about her visits to black and tans in order to give the jury a concrete image of her transgressions:

> Karlin: These cafes as I understand, they are frequented by colored folks, and they have tables where drinks are served and Orchestras play certain kinds of music.
> Foster: Colored folks only, do you mean?
> Q: No, among others, colored folks go in there?

A: Yes.

Q: And the proprietors of these institutions are colored folks?

A: Yes.

Q: And drinks are served at the tables?

A: Yes.

Q: And you, a college graduate of Radcliffe College, were hanging out with the colored folks of those places?

A: We did.[66]

He pressed her on the same issue moments later: "Did you think it quite the proper thing for a college graduate to associate with colored people, as you did?"[67] Karlin emphasized that Foster, working under the persona of "Frankie Fuller" or "Alaska Frankie," did not simply observe the drinking and revelry but actively enjoyed it. The *New York Times* echoed Karlin's charges when they described "the weeks she spent in the Tenderloin, sometimes staying for hours at a stretch in restaurants, with colored men and women drinking at her elbow."[68] The *Evening World* reported that "in pursuance of her inquiries the woman attended a party where unclad girls danced."[69] Karlin's cross-examination of Frances Foster and press reports of the trial focused on the incongruity of her prestigious education and the apparent ease with which she crossed racial boundaries.

Perhaps above all, Foster's degree from Radcliffe marked her as a New Woman. That a college-educated woman involved herself in this line of work captivated news writers, and one can infer that it fascinated their readers as well. The *New York Times* reported that "there was a great stir in the courtroom yesterday morning, when the prosecution called as its second witness 'Mme. Fuller,' in the person of Mrs. Frances Foster, a Radcliffe college graduate of some years ago."[70] The *Evening Post* often referred to her as "the college woman." The *New York Daily Tribune* titled her the "Radcliffe College girl" and described her as "a fashionably dressed young woman with eyeglasses."[71] The *Evening World* termed her "the college graduate sleuth" and published her photograph under the headline "College Woman Who Helped to Set 'White Slave' Traps."[72]

Foster could not deny her education, her class status, her prior reform work, nor her estrangement from her husband. At one point, she tried to assert her naïveté by asking for the definition of "sporting resort." Karlin quickly pointed out the absurdity of Foster's question:

Mrs. Foster, are you quite so unsophisticated that you don't know what a sporting resort is? *[objected to—sustained]* As a married woman, as a woman that has prosecuted the work for the District Attorney in connection with this White Slave Inquiry since March 2nd, as a woman who has had experience in child investigating, do you mean to tell these twelve men that you require a definition of the term "sporting resort"?[73]

Foster likely knew that "sporting resort" meant "brothel" but made the query to assert her purity as a white woman. Karlin posed the rhetorical question about her lack of sophistication to underline her qualities as a New Woman and the potential immorality that accompanied new economic and social freedoms for women.

Karlin suggested that Foster's duties as a white woman superseded her duties as an investigator. Likewise, some elite commentators during this era blamed women's colleges for leading white women graduates to shirk their racial responsibilities by having only a small number of children or none at all.[74] In 1911, approximately half of the graduates of women's colleges remained single.[75] The New Woman challenged male privilege and the Victorian sexual order, but she also posed a racial threat.[76] Women's new freedoms and the national interest in white slavery coincided with sweeping fears of "race suicide," purportedly caused by falling birth rates among native-born whites. Elaine May observes, "The declining Anglo-Saxon birthrate and the increase in childlessness reinforced fears that the American middle class was losing both its vitality and its hegemony."[77] Anxieties that immigrants would outbreed whites prompted a national discussion that celebrated white male virility and white female fertility.[78] The issue of race suicide shows how sexual and racial projects that intersect at the level of public discourse offer a cultural resource that can be used in specific contexts, like a criminal trial. Karlin could ask Foster about her visits to black and tans without explicitly stating why these visits should offend the jurors. Karlin invoked a powerful configuration of ideas that tied white women's sexual freedoms to racial vulnerability.

GEORGE MILLER, THE BOHEMIAN INVESTIGATOR

Although racial projects often focus on women's sexuality, cultural understandings of race and masculinity shape and constrain men's practices. Concerns about white race suicide enjoined white men to celebrate their sexuality within the family unit, but urbanization and changing norms of masculinity prompted them to explore other forms of sexual expression. The practice of slumming and the emerging bohemian and bachelor subcultures in large urban centers defied the Victorian notion of masculine self-restraint. Also, a gay subculture flourished in turn-of-the-century New York.[79] Gay men found acceptance in Harlem's black/white vice districts and often socialized in the black and tan saloons.[80] Like his colleague Frances Foster, George Miller's investigative work in these locales exposed him to charges of sexual and racial impropriety.

George Miller began living at the Albany Hotel under the name of "Dick Morris." He tried to create the image of a wealthy bachelor looking for a good time in New York City, and he worked to befriend Steve, an African American doorman at the hotel. Miller told Steve that he would like to see various cafés and saloons and asked Steve to show him around the city. Steve eventually took Miller to a black and tan on 35th Street and introduced him to the owner, Baron Wilkins. Timothy Gilfoyle describes Wilkins's establishment: "While attractive brown-skinned women sang popular and suggestive songs, Wilkins discreetly provided private rooms to regular customers and prostitutes."[81] Miller described Wilkins's immorality to the grand jury and noted that he once "found a white woman in bed with him."[82] Yet, Wilkins proved to be a valuable contact for Miller, eventually leading him to the alleged white slavery rings of Belle Moore and Harry Levinson.

Belle Moore's defense attorney, Alexander Karlin, charged investigator George Miller with an array of deviant acts, from sharing a bed with a black man to having sex with a white girl, and attacked Miller for his frequent association with African Americans during his investigative work. Karlin used this strategy to cast doubt on Miller's manhood and his traitorous relation to the white race. Miller had to adopt a certain persona to gain the confidence of his targets, but Karlin argued that Miller's behavior was more than a mere act. Karlin suggested to the jury that Miller took excessive pleasure in associating with underworld contacts and forced him to admit that he drank with an African American waiter at the café:

> Karlin: And you stopped at Baron Wilkins' that evening about how long?
> Miller: About an hour, half an hour, I am not sure.
> Q: Drinking with this colored man?
> A: Yes, sir.
> Q: You bought champagne, didn't you?
> A: Not that night.
> Q: Did you some other night? You bought champagne pretty liberally?
> A: Yes, sir.
> Q: Well, you drank a great deal. About how many drinks did you have with this colored man, Alex Anderson[,] on the night of the 13th?[83]

He used the same rhetorical strategy by persistently mentioning Miller's interest in "colored resorts":

> Karlin: Didn't you tell Steve sometime in the month of April that you were here from Seattle to have a good time, that you would like to see the various colored resorts in New York and asked him to show you around?
> Miller: Yes, sir.
> Q: And hadn't Steve refused several times to take this sport from the Hotel Albany around to the different colored resorts?
> A: No, sir.
> Q: How many times did you talk to Steve before he finally took you to any colored resorts?[84]

Karlin suggested that Steve persistently declined Miller's request to take him to black and tan saloons in order to emphasize that the colored doorman, not the white investigator, respected the color line.

Next, Karlin added sexual impropriety to his charge against Miller. He accused Miller of sharing a bed with African American men and women. Although he probably anticipated Miller's denial, Karlin raised the possibility of this misconduct in the minds of the jurors. Karlin promised to prove "beyond a reasonable doubt that George Miller had slept with her [Moore] and had slept with another female, and slept with a colored man by the name of Alex Anderson on April 13th."[85] He reiterated these accusations when cross-examining Miller:

> Karlin: Upon your oath, Mr. Miller, will you kindly answer this question. Didn't you on the morning of the first day that you were in the apartment of this defendant occupy the same bed, first with Alex Anderson, second with Belle Moore the defendant, and third with another colored girl? Upon your oath, tell me if that is not so, Mr. Miller?
> Miller: No, sir.[86]

Karlin charged Miller with sharing an intimate space with an African American man to suggest racial and sexual misconduct. The insinuation of homosexual activity, although incriminating, did not completely rebuke Miller's masculinity. Men in the early twentieth century could have sex with "fairies" without damaging their masculinity or heterosexual status, as long as they acted characteristically masculine and assumed the insertive role in sex acts.[87] Moreover, black men typically adopted the feminine role in interracial homosexuality. Yet homosexual activity in the black and tans violated the color line, and commentators condemned it, with the same language they used to describe interracial heterosexual relationships, as "miscegenation."[88] Karlin depicted Miller as sexually degenerate, willing to associate with nonwhites to satiate his sexual desires.

Making his most grievous accusation, Karlin tried to imply that Miller had sex with Helen Hastings, the eleven-year-old white slave, at Belle Moore's apartment.[89] Karlin argued that Miller lied about his whereabouts and distorted the chronology of his actions to cover up his sexual escapades. After his first meeting with Moore, Miller had claimed that he left her apartment, went to a bar, visited a cigar stand, and then took a long walk before returning to his hotel. Karlin asked, "Are you trying to conceal anything as to the time—for those three hours, because you don't want to admit it, because you were in bed with this defendant and those girls?"[90] Under direct examination, Miller testified that

> she [Belle Moore] served the drinks, and asked us if we had a little time and could wait a while and she would go out and call in some girls. I said "All right." She was gone about fifteen minutes, and came back with a colored girl and a white girl. Alex Anderson took the colored girl and went into the second room of the parlor. Belle Moore and I and the white girl went into the first bedroom. There she ordered the girl to disrobe and exposed her to me and asked me if I would stay the night. I excused myself and said "No."[91]

Karlin took these details and raised the possibility of a less honorable scenario involving Miller and the young girl:

Karlin: She ordered somebody to disrobe?
Miller: Yes, sir.
Q: In your presence?
A: Yes, sir.
Q: And disrobe for you?
A: Yes, sir.
Q: And she told that to whom?
A: Helen Hastings.
Q: Helen Hastings?
A: Yes, sir.
Q: Did you refuse to have any sexual intercourse with this girl?
A: Yes, sir.
Q: I took it that you were quite shocked at the indecent proposal made to you? [objected to—sustained] Well, as a matter of fact, you declined to do any such thing, is that so?

Judge Crain: He answered he did not.

Q: Well, you declined to do [so], because of your conscientious
scruples as a married man? *[objected to—sustained]*[92]

Karlin's strategy of referring to Miller's "conscientious scruples as a married man" paralleled his questioning of Foster as "unsophisticated" for her ignorance of the term "sporting resort." He juxtaposed the investigators' claims to respectability with their suspected behavior.

The culmination of Karlin's accusations effectively marked Miller as a "tramp bohemian," a marginal figure in the Progressive Era's hierarchy of masculine styles that glorified the underworld and sexual irresponsibility.[93] The apparent primitivism and sexual spontaneity of African American culture influenced this conception of white manliness and at the same time provided an example against which bearers of more legitimate forms of masculinity could define themselves. The attempts of bohemians to enjoy the perceived vitality of African American culture blurred racial boundaries. The accusations that Miller enjoyed the debauchery that he was supposedly investigating show how constructions of race (stereotypes of African Americans as primitive, oversexed, and savage) shaped dominant notions of white masculinity.

The creation of the twentieth-century color line depended upon stereotypes, or what Patricia Hill Collins terms "controlling images," of African Americans, but images of white sexuality were also used to enforce racial distinctions.[94] Just as narratives of black rapists and the threat of lynching communicated a double message to both black men and white women, the white slavery narrative worked to police the sexual practices of both racial insiders and outsiders.[95] White women who navigated New York City's underworld and white men who slept with white slaves provided negative examples that helped to define the boundaries of whiteness. Frances Foster and George Miller may have tried to protect white girls by investigating the vice trade, but Belle Moore's defense attorney easily depicted their inquiry as a grave violation of the color line.

*   *   *

Although Karlin's defense of Belle Moore failed, many saw the case as a blow to Rockefeller's entire investigation effort despite the guilty verdict handed down in the trial. The judge said to Belle Moore during her sentencing:

> White slavery, as popularly understood, is that condition to which young and innocent girls are debased when sold into captivity for immoral purposes. The evidence did not show you to be guilty of such a sale. You, as the outcome

of meetings with an investigator engaged in attempting to learn whether such white slavery existed in this City, in ignorance of his calling and object, placed, with their consent, two immoral women in his charge for immoral purposes, and received from him money in the belief that he was paying you for procuring them for his for immoral purposes.[96]

A *New York Times* editorial entitled "Ill-Chosen Agents of Reform" argued that the investigators "were, too plainly, little if any better than 'provoking agents,' laboriously creating the criminality they had been sent out to find."[97] Soon after, District Attorney Reynolds penned a letter to the *Times* that defended the investigation. Although he admitted erring in his estimates of the age of the "girls," he tried to reassert their purity: "The Teddy bear and the doll were in evidence among the few belongings they begged to be allowed to take with them. I found these articles in their possession when the young women were brought to the District Attorney's office."[98] Days later, defense attorney Karlin offered a rebuttal that reiterated the problems with the case: "Passing strange—is it not?—that though Belle Moore is alleged to be a procuress whose infamous work extends over a period of nine years, it required several weeks for her to get a '17–year-old child' who was 24 years old, and who, in turn, introduced Miller to an '18–year-old child' who was a married woman 25 years old?"[99] On June 29, 1910, about a month after the trial, the grand jury concluded its investigation, and Rockefeller filed a presentment that summarized its findings. Judge O'Sullivan refused to accept the presentment, adjourned the proceedings for two weeks, and blocked the release of the report for a month. A delayed statement to the press of a "summary of the presentment" suggested that the jury found no evidence of an organized traffic in women, and newspaper headlines across the country reiterated this idea the following day.

Although they found no evidence of a formal syndicate of white slave procurers, the grand jury's report maintained that forced prostitution occurred on an alarming scale and that an informal network of relationships connected the various players in the white slave trade.[100] However, to Judge O'Sullivan and New York City mayor William Gaynor, Turner's grand jury testimony effectively exonerated New York City from any wrongdoing. When O'Sullivan finally accepted the presentment, he reminded the jury of George Kibbe Turner's questionable testimony: "You had before you the author of the most scandalous attack upon the city. He admitted under oath that his article was overstated and deceiving. He was compelled under oath to admit that he had no evidence (not even hearsay) to support his statements. . . . Your answer to the main question submitted to you is a merited rebuke to the slanderers of the cleanest great city of the world."[101] Judge O'Sullivan pointed to other testimony to disprove the existence of a white slave syndicate. He told the jury, "The witnesses who by training and observation were competent to give you information on the subject . . . were unanimous in the belief that no organized traffic in women exists in this city."[102]

Frustrated, Rockefeller appealed directly to Mayor Gaynor to take action against the vice trade. On June 30, 1910, a day after Judge O'Sullivan officially filed the presentment, Rockefeller mailed a copy of the report to Mayor Gaynor and asked about the possibility of creating a municipal commission to study prostitution.[103] Rockefeller must have been pessimistic about his potential support, given Gaynor's opposition to Reverend Charles Parkhurst's anti-vice crusade a decade earlier. Predictably, the mayor's response was unenthusiastic.[104]

Although Rockefeller was unable to elicit support for an anti-vice organization sponsored by the mayor's office, he had enough financial resources to continue his research into prostitution. Rockefeller paid Clifford Roe to conduct a year-long investigation into New York City's white slave traffic. Rockefeller also privately funded the investigative work of two detectives. In addition, Rockefeller also appealed to the American reform and philanthropic community. In December 1910, Rockefeller mailed approximately 200 copies of Reginald Wright Kauffman's *House of Bondage* to influential citizens across the country.

Months later, Rockefeller established the Bureau of Social Hygiene (BSH) so that anti-vice agitation "would not be dependent upon a temporary wave of reform, nor upon the life of any man or group of men, but which would go on, generation after generation, continuously making warfare against the forces of evil."[105] The BSH was one of the most powerful reform organizations of its day. In addition to establishing the Bedford Hills Reformatory for Women, the BSH commissioned two influential studies of prostitution, George Kneeland's *Commercialized Prostitution in New York City* and Abraham Flexner's *Prostitution in Europe*.[106] These works represented a strong departure from the white slavery stories that circulated in New York City during the prior decade. The BSH was a harbinger of the scientific tone of the "social hygiene" campaigns that eventually superseded the agitation against white slavery in the 1910s and 1920s.

6

"Yellow Slavery" and Donaldina Cameron's San Francisco Mission

In New York and Chicago, white slavery discourse embodied arguments about where and how to draw the color line. The agitation against white slavery on the West Coast invoked some of the same concerns that drove reform efforts in other cities, yet regional differences shaped the direction and outcome of anti-vice activism. In San Francisco, narratives of sexual danger implicated a different set of victims and villains and provided a discursive resource for a different set of racial projects. The trafficking in Chinese slave girls in San Francisco's Chinatown, often referred to as "yellow slavery," drew the condemnation of reformers, politicians, and journalists.

In the late nineteenth and early twentieth centuries, accounts of devious Chinamen selling women into prostitution fueled anti-Chinese sentiments on the West Coast and helped shore up the political and social dominance of native-born whites over Chinese immigrants. Like white slavery narratives, stories about Chinese prostitutes had no single political meaning and were adaptable to different reform projects. The Chinatown vice trade formed a central justification for heightened controls on Chinese immigration, yet it also attracted the benevolence of domestic missionary workers. Missionaries lamented the plight of Chinese prostitutes and worked to secure for them safe residence and some measure of social support. According to Peggy Pascoe, "Protestant women quickly came to see Chinese immigrant prostitution as symbolic of the abuse of women that flourished in western cities."[1]

Presbyterian missionary Donaldina Cameron emerged as perhaps the most important crusader in the fight against sexual slavery in San Francisco. She launched daring rescues of Chinese prostitutes in Chinatown, gaining notoriety for her perseverance and bravery in the face of angry slave owners. Some have credited her with saving over 2,000 Chinese and Japanese slaves,[2] although this is likely an exaggeration.[3] Cameron also watched over a home that provided a refuge for rescued Chinese prostitutes and domestic slaves. She wanted to inculcate the residents of her home with Christian middle-class values and hoped that they would eventually marry suitable Chinese men. Donaldina Cameron's stories of the rescue and rehabilitation of Chinese brothel slaves summoned an image of native-born white and Chinese women united by gender-based morality and divided by essential racial differences.

Prostitution and the Nativist Reaction against Chinese Immigrants

The number of Chinese living in the United States grew from approximately 63,000 to over 105,000 between 1870 and 1880. In 1890, roughly 107,000 Chinese were living in the United States, but this number plunged to 71,000 by 1910. This demographic shift was largely a product of repressive immigration policies. In 1882, Congress passed the first of three Chinese exclusion acts that drastically limited the numbers of Chinese entering the United States. The 1882 immigration act banned immigration of Chinese laborers for ten years, facilitated the deportation of Chinese immigrants, and forced Chinese Americans who legally lived in the United States to obtain identification certificates.[4] In 1902, Congress renewed the Chinese exclusion policy, and in 1904 it was extended indefinitely. Xenophobic court decisions and federal legislation supported the overwhelming anti-Chinese sentiments of native-born Americans.[5]

Antagonism against Chinese immigrants was particularly virulent in California. By 1870, roughly three-quarters of the 63,000 Chinese in the United States lived in the state, and by 1900, almost half of the Chinese living in California resided in the San Francisco Bay area.[6] The use of Chinese immigrants as strikebreakers and as a source for cheap labor provoked a strong backlash among skilled white workers in San Francisco. Craft union leaders cultivated racial hatred as a way to unify the white labor movement and to gain political power. The Workingman's Party attracted popular support by blaming the poor economic conditions of the city on immigrant Chinese laborers, and in the 1870s members gained control of the San Francisco city government. The Workingman's Party exploited the issue of Chinese prostitution, and on one occasion members declared that Chinese prostitutes were responsible for nine-tenths of the cases of syphilis in California.[7] The new city government passed a score of anti-Chinese ordinances and, according to Pascoe, "made anti-Chinese rhetoric a staple of San Francisco community life."[8]

The anti-Chinese agitation in California played on the economic insecurity of white workers, but it also embodied an important gender and sex dimension. The sex ratio among Chinese immigrants was already sharply skewed by 1882, but the new immigration laws exacerbated the imbalance between Chinese men and women living in California. Furthermore, the passage of the 1875 Page Act empowered the California commissioner of immigration to prevent "lewd or debauched" women from entering the state. This law gave broad discretionary powers to immigration officials in San Francisco and Hong Kong and opened the door for bribery and corruption.[9] Although slave traders managed to smuggle Chinese prostitutes into California, the law effectively limited immigration possibilities for all Chinese women, creating an uneven sex ratio of Chinese men to women in California. In 1880, there were eighteen Chinese men for every Chinese woman living in the state. By 1890, this number grew to twenty-two Chinese men for every Chinese woman.[10] Anti-miscegenation laws that prevented Chinese men from marrying outside of their racial category—along with the preexisting sex imbalance within the Chinese American community—destined most Chinese men living in the United States to bachelorhood.[11]

Lack of legal employment and marriage opportunities for Chinese men and women contributed to a well-developed prostitution trade in San Francisco's Chinatown.[12] Many Chinese women entered prostitution under harsh circumstances that often involved coercion and trickery.[13] Young women were purchased or kidnapped in China, then sold to private slave owners or Chinese organized crime syndicates, or "tongs," in San Francisco. Some Chinese women fell victim to schemes portrayed in white slavery accounts, including false assurances of marriage or employment.[14] Moreover, brothel owners forced Chinese prostitutes to work in small subdivided rooms, or "cribs." Reformers regarded the "crib system" as an unusually pernicious form of brothel-keeping. Pascoe argues, "The plight of Chinese immigrant women compelled to serve as prostitutes was indeed comparable to slavery."[15]

Chinese prostitution also drew attention from reformers because the sex trade involved native-born white Americans. The Chinatown vice district constituted an interracial sex market where Chinese and white working-class men paid for Chinese prostitutes.[16] White men were regular clients of San Francisco's Chinatown brothels and opium dens. Chinatown brothels attracted white laborers because men could purchase sexual services that would cost almost twice as much in brothels outside the district.[17] Moreover, police and government officials shared in the profits of prostitution through bribes and fees.

The prostitution problem became part of the fabric of anti-Chinese agitation in San Francisco's Chinatown. Between 1866 and 1905, California residents passed eight laws designed to restrict the importation of Chinese women for prostitution.[18] Officials often applied anti-vice laws unfairly to Chinese sex workers, making prostitutes and their owners subject to tough fines and sentences.[19] Public debates about Chinatown's vice trade helped to cement a rhetorical connection between immoral sexual practices and Chinese immigration. Writing for the *North American Review* in 1897, Charles Holder proclaimed, "Slavery of the most horrible and debased nature is being carried on wherever the Chinese have a foothold."[20] Holder described San Francisco as the headquarters of the traffic in Chinese prostitutes. He explained:

> The large Chinese settlement in San Francisco has made this traffic in human beings not merely possible, but a business followed as a means of profitable investment, under the protection and patronage of two Chinese societies, and here, in the heart of an American city, we find one of the best-organized slave marts of modern times, fostered by as motley a band of criminals as could be produced in any portion of the uncivilized world; a band numbering at least three thousand, who derive their support directly or indirectly from the sale and barter of female slaves.[21]

Like white slavery narratives, dramatic accounts of Chinatown rescues sparked the interest of law enforcement officials, politicians, and wealthy philanthropists. According to Pascoe, stories of Chinese slave girls "fed the white American taste for exoticism and formed a unique genre in the popular mythology of American race relations. Missionary women called them 'rescue' stories and saw them as skirmishes in the righteous battle against sexual slavery."[22] Reform efforts targeting Chinese sexual slavery often overlapped with the agitation against white slavery, and popular books about white slavery often included separate chapters that addressed "yellow slavery."[23] Although San Francisco stood as the reputed headquarters of the Chinese slave traffic, moral entrepreneurs from Chicago and New York helped popularize the issue.

MORAL ENTREPRENEURS AND "YELLOW SLAVERY"

Jean Turner Zimmermann, superintendent of the Chicago Women's Shelter, wrote three books about white slavery: *Chicago's Black Traffic in White Girls*, *White or Yellow?: A Story of America's Great White Slave Trade with Asia*, and *Vere, of Shanghai*. In *White or Yellow?* Zimmermann recalled her missionary work in Hong Kong, Shanghai, and San Francisco's Chinatown and offered her thoughts on the traffic in Asian and American prostitutes.[24] She described an organized scheme whereby procurers captured white girls and forced them to work as prostitutes in east Asian cities. In return, slave traders kidnapped Chinese women and sold them to brothels in San Francisco. Zimmermann wrote, "John Chinaman, dove-tailing with the immense area of commercialized vice in San Francisco plays an exceedingly prominent part in the trade in women—white women shipped out—yellow slaves shipped in—centering in San Francisco."[25] Although Zimmermann stated, "I have the highest regard for and love the Chinese," she could scarcely hide her virulent racism when describing her foray into San Francisco's Chinatown: "We were surrounded on every side by hundreds, even thousands of Chinese. . . . From all sides came the smirk of hideous yellow faces."[26]

Ernest Bell, another Chicago anti-vice crusader, described the sex trade between east Asia and the United States in his popular white slavery book, *Fighting the Traffic in Young Girls*. In a chapter titled "The Yellow Slave Trade," he compares the forced prostitution of Asian women to chattel slavery: "The poor slave girls, as shown by court proceedings at Hong Kong, had the same terror of being 'sold into California' that the negro slaves in this country had of being 'sold down the river.'"[27] Bell argued that immigration restrictions, although necessary, inflated the profits for traffickers in Chinese slaves. He claimed that Chinese women were sold into slavery in Hong Kong, sometimes by their own parents, and then resold to San Francisco slave traders.

James Bronson Reynolds, who played a critical role in white slavery investigations in New York City, also had much to say about the Asian prostitution trade. At a public conference in Chicago on January 31, 1907, Reynolds delivered a speech titled "Lessons from the Orient." He used the issue of Asian prostitution to argue for tougher immigration laws. Reynolds advocated deporting immigrant prostitutes who had lived in the United States for less than three years. He declared, "It ought to be possible for the various officials to go to these dens, and see the number of inmates who had been there less than three years, and send them back to their country."[28] On February 8, 1909, Reynolds delivered a speech entitled "The Nations and the White Slave Trade" at the inaugural meeting of the Illinois Vigilance Association. He argued that the worldwide scope of the white slave traffic necessitated immigration restrictions: "American citizenship should not be a cloak for the protection and promotion of vice. . . . Provisions should be made by law so that protection of American citizenship should bring good character as its credential."[29] Reynolds, like Zimmermann and Bell, based some of his opinions on the first-hand reports of Katharine Bushnell.

THE RETURN OF KATHARINE BUSHNELL

Katharine Bushnell—Frances Willard's friend who had investigated white slavery in midwestern lumber camps—fought to eliminate the prostitution trade between California and Asia. After the WCTU sponsored her United States speaking tour, Bushnell left to work with British reformer Josephine Butler in the 1890s. Butler convinced Bushnell and her friend Elizabeth Andrew to travel to east Asia to investigate vice conditions near British military stations.[30] After their tour of India, China, and Japan, they returned to San Francisco to warn people about the sexual threat posed by Asian immigrants. Soon after the San Francisco earthquake of 1906, they published an article in the journal of the American Purity Federation titled "Recent Researches into the Japanese Slave Trade in California." They blamed the proliferation of Japanese prostitution on the moral cowardliness of Japanese men:

> There seems sometimes to be lacking in Japanese men that instinct of protection toward their womankind that finds its higher expression in chivalry toward all women, and its lower, in Oriental lands, in a jealous shutting away of the wife from other men, and the rearing of daughters in chastity to enhance their value in the matrimonial market. *Every* general and sweeping assertion does injustice to some individual cases, but we cannot for that reason refuse to note and comment on general moral peculiarities, as they vary among different peoples.[31]

In criticizing the lack of chivalry among Japanese men, Bushnell and Andrew maintained that the moral dispositions of men are racially based. They argued that native-born white men have an instinct to protect their families that Japanese men lack. Bushnell and Andrew used the stereotype of the cunning and mischievous Asian to explain why Japanese men shield their daughters from other men. The idea that Japanese men cloister their daughters "to enhance their value in the matrimonial market" suggested to the reader that the Japanese had monetary motives instead of a concern for moral purity.

Bushnell and Andrew also argued that the trade in Japanese slaves harmed American women. They claimed that racial differences separated Asians and native-born whites, but they also asserted a common identity among women that surmounted race. They maintained that there is "a solidarity in womanhood" that makes an injury against one an injury against all:

Alas! when Japanese men are willing to bring their women in large numbers to this country for sale—women bought for a few dollars there, and sold for hundreds, sometimes thousands, of dollars here—and when American capitalists are investing in this slave-traffic, while the officers of the law declare they can do nothing about releasing these Japanese slaves, because they do not protest against the inhuman treatment they receive, the outlook for American womanhood becomes very dark. Whether we count it so and wish it so, or not, there is a solidarity in womanhood which must be reckoned with, now that the Orient is brought so close to the Occident. Women rise or fall together. Either the Japanese slave trade in women must be exterminated speedily or it will go beyond control, and result in the downfall of American womanhood.[32]

Bushnell and Andrew denounced Americans for investing in prostitution and criticized police who ignored the conditions in the Chinatown vice district. According to Bushnell and Andrew, Anglo-Saxon men have a moral responsibility to protect not just "their own" women but also all women. In arguing that "women rise and fall together," they suggested that sexual violence that occurs outside the United States ultimately harms American women. Like other feminists of their era, their commitment to women's rights was wedded to an ideology of Anglo-Saxon superiority. Andrew and Bushnell's aspirations for gender equality and women's suffrage developed in their early days with the WCTU, but they fought their battles in a racial terrain distinct from the situation in Chicago and midwestern lumber towns.

With their 1907 book, *Heathen Slaves and Christian Rulers,* Bushnell and Andrew wanted to write "a sketch which would enable Americans to understand the social conditions that are being introduced into our midst from the Orient." Bushnell and Andrew warned Americans of the pernicious influence of the vice trade in Asian countries and claimed that there were over 1,000 Chinese brothel slaves toiling in California. They declared, "[T]he Christian public of America should realize that in the Oriental slavery of its Pacific coast it faces a flood." According to Bushnell and Andrew, slavery was endemic to Chinese culture because "every well-to-do heathen Chinese family keeps a slave or two." The moral weakness of Chinese men threatened to influence native-born American men, causing them to lose their reverence for all women. Bushnell and Andrews explained: "And beside the peril arising directly from the flood of Orientals who are accustomed to dealing with women as chattels, there will be the peril from a debased American manhood. Men cannot live in the midst of such slavery as this, tolerate it, defend it, make gain through it, patronize it, without losing all respect for woman and regard for her rights."[33]

Like Frances Willard and Jane Addams, Bushnell and Andrew used the issue of forced prostitution and sexual slavery to argue for white women's suffrage. They appealed to racial unity when claiming political power for white women: "The yellow flood is sure to come, and we must make ready for it. We must realize what may happen to American women if almond-eyed citizens, bent on exploiting women for gain, obtain the ballot in advance of educated American women."[34] Like Willard's argument about "the plantation negro" ignorantly exercising voting rights that properly belonged to native-born women, Bushnell and Andrew contrasted the political freedom of "almond-eyed citizens" with "educated," yet politically powerless, "American women."

Xenophobic politicians, immigration officials, and reformers harnessed the issue of Chinese prostitution for different racial projects.[35] James Bronson Reynolds and Ernest Bell used the issue to advocate immigration restrictions. Reminiscent of Jane Addams's or the WCTU's use of the white slavery issue, Bushnell and Andrew used stories of Chinese brothel slavery to argue for women's suffrage and a single standard of sexual morality. These accounts spotlighted the villains of forced prostitution, creating images of Chinese men as morally weak and sexually perverse. Other reformers, however, focused on the plight of Chinese prostitutes. The remainder of this chapter examines the work of a reformer named Donaldina Cameron who devoted her life to rescuing and reforming Chinese prostitutes. She intended to help rescue Chinese slaves by encouraging them to embrace Victorian norms of white femininity. The complexities and contradictions of Cameron's racial ideology illustrate the cultural power of narratives of yellow slavery and provide an instructive contrast to anti-vice efforts in New York and Chicago.

Donaldina Cameron's Rescue of Chinese Prostitutes

Guided by ideas of social Darwinism and Christian uplift, thousands of single women served as foreign missionaries in the second half of the nineteenth century. Presbyterians were especially involved in missionary work. The number of Presbyterian missionary organizations increased from 100 in 1870 to nearly 11,000 in 1909.[36] A few missionary organizations had "Occidental" auxiliary organizations that focused on the foreign populations of American cities. According to Carol Wilson, the Presbyterian Occidental Board was organized in 1873 "to undertake the only foreign mission enterprise ever carried on within the United States."[37] Donaldina Cameron emerged as a prominent leader in these domestic missionary efforts. One writer declared that "the tide really began to turn against the tongs and brothels in 1895, when

Donaldina Cameron entered the fight. Within a few years she would become a living legend."[38]

Cameron was born to Scottish sheepherders in 1869. Her family moved to California in the early 1870s and established a sheep ranch in the Los Angeles area. Cameron began a teacher-training course after graduating from high school but quit after her first year. Her interests turned to missionary work after Evelyn Browne, a family friend, regaled Cameron with stories of her adventures in San Francisco's Chinatown. Browne, president of the Occidental Board of Foreign Missions, and her colleague Margaret Culbertson rescued Chinese slave girls from brothels and private slave owners. Sponsored by the Occidental Board of Foreign Missions, Culbertson ran a rescue home located in the heart of San Francisco's Chinatown at 920 Sacramento Street. Often referred to as "Nine-twenty," the Presbyterian Mission Home housed Chinese girls and young women whom Culbertson had rescued from slavery. In 1895, Cameron moved to San Francisco to work with Culbertson at the mission home and earned a salary of twenty-five dollars a month. Culbertson died two years later, and Cameron took over as superintendent of the home.[39]

Cameron supervised the mission home using a highly structured schedule of tasks and activities. To rehabilitate the women, she urged them to accept and practice the tenets of Victorian femininity, including housekeeping, religious piety, and marriage. Cameron integrated Bible instruction and religious services into the daily routine of the home. She wrote, "We endeavor to urge upon our Chinese girls the importance of being good housekeepers. And then we encourage them to marry Christian Chinese."[40] Chinese residents of the mission home lived under strict rules and supervision. Old and young residents alike were kept constantly busy with daily chores like sewing, cooking, and cleaning. The mission staff limited residents' contact with people outside the home and read all incoming and outgoing mail. Residents who wanted to leave had to obtain written permission from the staff, who determined the conditions of their departure and return. Cameron read roll call every morning, and women who were absent or tardy were assigned extra tasks as punishment.[41] Under these rigorous conditions, many of the rescued prostitutes escaped from Nine-twenty. Lucie Hirata commented that, given the demands of the mission home, "it is not difficult to see why many prostitutes refused to run away to the Mission Home, or why a number of women who had been 'rescued' by the missionaries later escaped from their saviors."[42] Laurene McClain explained that mission home staff "attributed the problem of runaways to the fact that many had led 'undisciplined' lives as slaves, so were not willing to put up with the austere environment at the home."[43]

Although Cameron emphasized that the day-to-day reform work within the home was the most important aspect of the mission's activities, she built her reputation based on her dramatic rescues of Chinese slave girls. Two rescues in particular secured Cameron's status as an important anti-vice crusader: the rescue of thirty prostitutes following the Trans-Mississippi Exposition and the well-publicized rescue of a Chinese slave named Kum Qui. Her rescue stories received wide exposure and were reprinted in several anti-vice books.[44] These stories also demonstrate the complicated relationships among Chinese prostitutes, their liberators, and law enforcement officials.

"THE MONGOLIAN MAIDENS"

The Trans-Mississippi Exposition opened in Omaha, Nebraska, in 1898. Like the 1893 World's Fair in Chicago, it featured a number of exhibits representing the cultures of foreign lands. About seventy women participated in the Chinese exhibit and were allowed entry into the United States as an exception to the exclusion acts passed during the prior decades. After the close of the exposition, Chinese slave traders reportedly transported the women to San Francisco and sold them to brothels in Chinatown. A report from the Occidental Board of Foreign Missions described the situation faced by Cameron and her colleagues:

> [T]he United States by special act of Congress waived its stringent laws prohibiting the importation of Chinese women, and allowed about 70 of the Mongolian maidens to be brought over. They were to be returned to their native land within six months after the close of the exposition. Unfortunately, no bonds were given assuring a return, neither were any steps taken to insure their identification. Here was the wily Chinaman's golden opportunity. At the close of the exhibit there was a quiet slipping away of the whole 70. Not one was left for deportation. They simply vanished in the familiar Chinese method.[45]

Leaders of the mission home opposed the Chinese exclusion acts because they created a sex imbalance that prevented Chinese immigrants from establishing stable families. The homosocial environment of Chinatown created conditions that posed a great danger to Chinese women; the "wily Chinaman" threatened to exploit women in Chinatown's slave trade using the "familiar Chinese method." Although they opposed immigration restrictions, the leaders of the Occidental Board of Foreign Missions characterized Chinese men as a potential threat to the relatively small number of Chinese women living in San Francisco.

After the close of the Omaha exposition, Cameron aided police in their search for the women reportedly sold into prostitution. After an exhaustive exploration of Chinatown, they located about thirty young women and took them back to the mission home. Although Cameron characterized them as rescued victims, some of the Chinese women resisted their confinement. Cameron gave an account of the situation in her report of the mission home's activities: "What pandemonium reigned for a time when these half-frenzied creatures found themselves prisoners! They shrieked and beat themselves with their hands; they spat upon the furniture and clean floors, and cursed in English and Chinese. The scene was one of horror and yet pathos. Some were liberated that day; but a number were left in our care until further investigation could be made. They neither ate nor slept for the first day and night."[46] Cameron's description of the rescued slaves as "half-frenzied creatures" belied an attitude of Anglo-American superiority that drew on racialized notions of evolutionary progress and civilization. This understanding of civilization and savagery, central to thinking about race and gender in the Progressive Era, influenced reformers who fought white slavery in Chicago and New York. Yet unlike white slavery narratives in those cities, Cameron described the prostitutes, not the procurers, as savage. Chinatown's slavery problem stemmed, in part, from the untamed disposition of its victims. Their cursing and spitting demonstrated that they lacked and needed the civilizing influence offered within the mission home. While some women may have eagerly sought liberation from the slave traders, Cameron's account also suggested that many of the women were unhappy with being "rescued."

This incident also demonstrated the close link between Cameron's rescue efforts and the work of law enforcement and immigration officials. Some suggested that police allowed Cameron to accompany them on their raids because of her knowledge of Chinatown's underworld and her intuition in finding trap doors and hidden rooms.[47] But law enforcement officers' convenient use of the mission home resources stands as perhaps a more likely explanation for police support of Cameron. She assisted law enforcement by allowing them to use the mission home as an inspection point for Asian immigrants. Federal officials treated the home as a temporary holding cell before they deported the women or turned them over to Cameron's supervision.[48] Carol Wilson, Cameron's friend and biographer, noted that "in addition to utilizing the quarters at Nine-Twenty for temporary detention of would-be Oriental immigrants, the government agents had more than once made use of the large chapel room as a corral in which to round up the half-wild creatures herded together in the periodic raids in search of those illegally in this country."[49] The thirty women from the Omaha exposition gathered together at the mission home proved Cameron's importance to San Francisco law enforcement. One of the thirty who stayed at the home was a young woman named Kum Qui. She became the focal point of Cameron's next dramatic and well-publicized rescue.

THE RESCUE OF KUM QUI

During the final week of March 1900, the owner of a Chinese slave appeared at the door of the mission home. He was accompanied by a constable who held an arrest warrant for a young woman named Kum Qui on charges of stealing jewelry. Cameron denied that the woman was a resident of the home, but they produced a search warrant and forced their way inside the building. The men quickly spotted the woman and took her away to Palo Alto. Undeterred, Cameron followed them to the jail and remained by Qui's side in the holding cell. Near midnight, a jailer opened the cell and released Qui to three men who had arrived with bail. Cameron raced after them as they dragged Qui into a waiting buggy, but the men grabbed Cameron, threw her to the ground, and rode off with the frightened woman.[50]

A Palo Alto justice of the peace met up with the men who had escaped with Kum Qui and held an impromptu trial on a remote road. At two-thirty in the morning, Qui pled guilty to the charge of larceny, and one of her escorts paid a five-dollar fine decreed by the judge.[51] Meanwhile, Cameron went into the village to find help. Panicked that she could not locate the girl, Cameron called a San Jose sheriff. Rumors quickly spread about the incident, igniting a lynch mob that materialized in Palo Alto the following morning. According to Cameron's biographer:

> By morning the college town was thoroughly incensed by news of the outrage, which had spread among citizens and also among the Stanford University students. Local papers and San Francisco dailies carried columns of reports and cartoons, and by night a mass meeting was called to denounce the public official who had participated in the affair. Handbills were circulated throughout the town and university, the Campus one reading: "On to Palo Alto! Our reputation is at stake. Bring your own rope. No. 3 Hall. 8:00 o'clock tonight."[52]

The evening after Kum Qui's abduction, three hundred citizens of Palo Alto, many of them Stanford students, marched the city's streets with lanterns and torches. The crowd converged on the jail that had held Kum Qui and attacked it. Some cried, "Burn it up" and "Tear it down," as they destroyed the surrounding fence and ripped wood paneling from the structure. An account from the mission home described the scene: "The indignation of the students of Stanford University and the citizens of Palo Alto and San Jose was aroused by this outrage to white heat, and every assistance was freely given for the rescue of Kum Qui and the punishment of her abductors."[53] The crowd then marched to the center of town and burned an effigy of the justice of the peace who had aided in the girl's kidnapping.[54]

Palo Alto officials called a public meeting at a nearby town that drew an audience of thousands. To boost attendance, a prominent Palo Alto citizen paid $500 to charter a train from Palo Alto to transport Stanford students to the gathering. Cameron's recitation of the abduction garnered front-page newspaper coverage the next day and was arguably the highpoint of the meeting.[55] The *San Francisco Chronicle* reported that Cameron "proved by her beauty and modest manner that she was a refined and cultured woman, and it seemed amazing how men could subject such a woman to such vile indignities as she related as having been perpetuated at Palo Alto."[56] Several speakers accused B. A. Herrington, a San Jose attorney with a large Chinese practice, with engineering the plan to abduct Qui. As Herrington rose to defend himself, the crowded jeered, and some yelled, "Hang him!" After the meeting, Palo Alto police arrested a man named Wong Fong on abduction charges and later arrested Herrington after he tried to leave town. Days after the meeting, immigration officers deported Kum Qui to Shanghai.[57]

While her biographers cite the Kum Qui incident as an example of Cameron's bravery and persistence, it also revealed the depth of anti-Chinese sentiment at the time.[58] Kum Qui's abduction stirred mob violence not unlike lynch mobs in the South. The designated enemies were not only the Chinese abductors but also an American attorney who worked with the Chinese. The kidnapping and rescue of Qui occurred during a volatile time in the relationship between Christian missionaries and Chinese. During the opening months of 1900, Chinese nationalists, worried about foreign influences on the Qing dynasty, murdered Christian missionaries and converts who were living in China. The Boxer Rebellion gained force during the summer, mere months after the Kum Qui incident. Although neither Cameron nor her biographers mentioned the Boxer Rebellion, it formed an important backdrop to the missionary activities occurring in Chinatown. Missionaries viewed the Boxer Rebellion as an ominous turning point in the moral trajectory of China. For instance, Jean Turner Zimmermann declared that the Boxer Rebellion raised "its serpent head for the final destruction of everything in Asia that made for human progress, just government, and the coming freedom of the yellow world."[59] While less violent than either a southern lynch mob or the massacres promulgated by the Boxers, the reaction to Kum Qui's kidnapping exposed the volatility of anti-Chinese nativism.

Marriage and Moral Reform in Cameron's Mission Home

Cameron's rescues boosted her reputation among American missionaries and anti-vice activists, but she claimed that the true reform work occurred within the daily rhythms of the mission home. Cameron's description of the reform activities within the home reveals a racial ideology that approximated the pluralist ideas of Jane Addams. Yet whereas Addams thought that women's sexual morality was contingent upon economic circumstances, for Cameron the moral worthiness of the mission home's residents was contingent upon their training in domestic femininity. Their moral status depended upon certain sex/gender practices. Cameron's approach toward the Chinese, more so than Addams's approach to European immigrants, complicates the historical and cultural distinction between nativism and pluralism.

On one hand, Cameron professed her love for Chinese culture and opposed immigration restrictions. She saw herself as a protector of Chinese women, fighting on behalf of Chinatown's most vulnerable residents. Cameron told her biographer, "I loved the Chinese. I never remember feeling anything foreign about them."[60] She referred to the Chinese as a "loveable and gifted race" in a taped interview with another biographer.[61] In a letter written to a friend toward the end of her life, Cameron declared, "In all credit to the Chinese people, I never had occasion to fear them, because, although I often went alone into the Chinese quarters at night, no Chinese man ever threatened or frightened me (I wish I could say that of the Anglo-Saxon race)!!"[62] Her comment, penned in 1962, displays a respect for Chinese men notably lacking in the writing of anti-vice crusaders like Jean Turner Zimmermann or Katharine Bushnell. Cameron arguably had more sympathy for the Chinese than did some of her co-workers. Mary Field, who lived with Cameron at the mission home, described the Chinese residents as "vulgar, filthy, lazy, and helpless" and concluded, "We know how hard it is to deal with the ignorant and degraded of our own race, but the low-caste Mongolian woman is a harder problem. She is more conscienceless, more suspicious, more fiery and voluble, and utterly bereft of reason—half-devil and half-child."[63] In a 1984 letter to the editor of the *Pacific Historian,* a leader in the mission home recalled that "nothing angered Miss Cameron more than the racial discrimination to which Chinese were subjected in housing, employment and education." She also added that the first Chinese woman to graduate from Stanford University was a former resident of the mission home who had lived under Cameron's supervision.[64]

On the other hand, Cameron displayed a contempt for the Chinese typical of nativists and those favoring immigration restrictions. On one occasion, Cameron declared that "the Chinese themselves will never abolish the hateful practice of buying and selling their women like so much merchandise. It is born in their blood, bred in their bone and sanctioned by the government of their native land."[65] She variously referred to the mission home residents as "always ignorant and often bad; of a widely different race, manner and religion," "wild, young and untamed creatures," "alien and heathen," and "shamefully neglected, much abused and despised daughters of a heathen nation."[66] While Cameron noted the racial shortcomings of the mission home residents, she attributed her own bravery to her "Highland Scotch background."[67]

Some of Cameron's actions also called into question her professed love for the Chinese. Cameron assisted immigration officials in locating and deporting illegal immigrants. She also contracted with fruit growers in northern California to use the mission home residents for labor, sometimes sending twenty to thirty women to work for a month or two in the fields.[68] Furthermore, despite working with the residents of Chinatown all her life, she never learned to speak Chinese.[69] According to McClain, "Cameron showed a certain disdain for things Chinese. Her admiration for some facets of Chinese civilization—its art and literature—was tempered by an abhorrence for the slavery which she claimed was inherent in Chinese culture."[70]

Cameron's contradictory opinions of the Chinese mirrored her understanding of Chinese prostitutes as an amalgam of savagery and civilization. Like the "half-frenzied creatures" that were rescued after the Omaha exposition, the residents of the mission home were incomplete projects of womanhood. The descriptors "half-frenzied," "wild," and "untamed" reflect ideas about gender and evolutionary progress that comprised Cameron's racial ideology. Although they were wild, uncontrollable, and frenzied, the mission home environment offered the promise of transforming Chinese prostitutes into exemplars of womanhood. Along these lines, a mission home pamphlet about Cameron's rescues, titled *Strange True Stories of Chinese Slave Girls*, described the Chinese residents in terms of an unfinished sculpture:

> These rescued and transformed lives might well be compared to Michael Angelo's [*sic*] statue of David, carved with exquisite grace and perfection of form. This wonderful work of art, has stood for centuries, admired by thou-

sands of pilgrims from all over the world who visit Florence every year. But the very thrilling thing in the story of this noble statue is that it was the stone's second chance. A sculptor began work on a splendid piece of marble, but lacking skill he only hacked and marred the beautiful block of stone, and at last cast it aside as quite worthless. It lay thus abandoned for years. At last Michael Angelo saw it and at once perceived its possibilities. Under his skillful hand the rude block of stone was transformed into the fair and marvelous beauty which appears in the statue of David.[71]

Cameron maintained that the environment of the mission home transformed Chinese women. The Christian setting and the daily domestic routines of the home compelled the women to embrace white Victorian femininity. Cameron explained:

> It is difficult for one of Christian parentage and training to realize the struggle which goes on in the recreation of this little rescued alien. Yet slowly, there takes place a marvelous change. The cheerful wholesome life of the Mission Home transforms body and soul. Family prayers are conducted in the pleasant dining-room, where the large family gather around light, clean, white breakfast tables. . . . The music floats through open windows down the hillside, falling like a benediction on the ears of poor heathen Chinatown, just below.[72]

She declared that the mission home transformed the residents' subjectivity and allowed them to become eligible for marriage. Cameron considered the residents' marriage to respectable Chinese men as the hallmark of success for the mission home.

According to Cameron's biographer Mildred Martin, "Donaldina became an Oriental matchmaker for her daughters."[73] Between 1874 and 1928, about 266 residents of the home married Chinese suitors.[74] Cameron had a strong influence in the creation of mission home brides, selecting suitable mates for the rescued women and supervising them during their courtship. Reports from Cameron's mission home suggested that the marriages restored morality to the Chinese prostitutes. For example, one report described the courtship and marriage between resident Qui N'gun and a man named Wong John: "There was such a beautiful letter came to Qui N'gun with this ring that one cannot help quoting a few words of it: 'Dear Qui N'gun,' wrote Wong John, 'when you look at the white stone in this ring you must know that I mean that for your own pure good life, and when you look at the blue stone it means I will always be true to you.' Could any Anglo-Saxon lover have said it better?"[75] Cameron was heartened that the Chinese couple displayed a commitment to Anglo-Saxon mores during their courtship. The report also suggested the Americanizing influence that followed from Cameron's tutelage: "The young people wore American dress. Miss Cameron gave away the bride. . . . Mrs. Wong John will have a pleasant American home in the City of Brotherly Love, and we all hope will prove to have the sweetest and best of womanly gifts—that of homemaking."[76]

Although the traditional Chinese wedding gown was red, Cameron required the mission home brides to be dressed in white (a color associated in China with funerals). Laurene McClain cites Cameron's insistence on donning the mission home brides in white as another example of Cameron's ethnocentrism, yet it also represented a symbolic whitening of former prostitutes.[77] Cameron used the term "white" to refer to sexual purity, but the racial and sexual meanings of the term subtly overlapped as the mission home residents began to approximate the moral purity of middle-class native-born white women. Like Frances Willard's slogan, "a white life for two," the white wedding gown stood as a symbol of sexual purity that shaded into racial meaning. Wilson explained the alchemic effect of the white wedding on the former prostitutes: "Literal indeed has been the fulfillment of the Biblical prophecy, 'Though your sins be as scarlet, they shall be as white as snow.' Though their 'sins' have been involuntary, the result of ignorance and evil forces, nevertheless no contrast could be more dramatic than that between the sad girls rescued from dark corners, and the smiling white-clad brides who yearly go forth from the broad steps of Nine-Twenty."[78]

The "white" environment of the mission home rubbed off onto the rescued women. Like an expert sculptor working on a piece of discarded white marble, the mission home transformed the body and soul of its residents into respectable and marriageable women. With engagement rings and white wedding dresses, mission home residents rejected the practice of arranged marriage and embraced companionate marriage based on mutual love and affection. Adapting to the practices of native-born middle-class women, the Chinese women became part of a universal womanhood. The "half-wild creatures" rescued from slavery became transformed under Cameron's care and guidance.

* * *

In her incisive analysis of women's moral reform efforts in the American West, Pascoe argues that historians have too often focused on the ethnocentrism and racism in Cameron's mission home and overlooked the real benefits Cameron provided for her residents. Although the gender ideologies of Chinese and middle-class whites were dissimilar, Cameron did not impose a Victorian gender system on an entirely unwilling audience. Chinese immigrants used the mission home to escape exploitation and the patriarchal control of their families. Chinese men living in San Francisco also used the home to locate suitable mates. While some residents escaped after being "rescued," many used the mission home for their own gain. The home provided an important resource for disadvantaged residents of Chinatown.

In chapter 4, I argued that Jane Addams's adherence to racial pluralism and Clifford Roe's conception of racial nativism fit with specific ideas of sexual morality. In some ways, Cameron's mission home for Chinese prostitutes and slaves bears some resemblance to Addams's Hull House in its aims and motives. Both efforts intended to provide a safe haven for immigrants and a space for their gradual assimilation into urban America. Cameron and Addams focused on the victims of forced prostitution instead of its villains. They worked to restore respectability to exploited and despoiled women. In certain respects, however, Cameron's conception of sexual morality was closer to the ideas of Roe than of his colleague Addams. Both Roe and Cameron viewed women as sharing an essential moral disposition that could be actualized by certain cultural practices. For Cameron, Chinese women had the potential for virtue, but their natural moral disposition was corrupted by slavery and prostitution. Cameron's acceptance of the cult of true womanhood led her to believe that the mission home residents carried the special moral potential shared by all women. Whereas Addams discerned an inextricable connection between economic circumstances and morality, Cameron tied morality to essentialist ideas of womanhood. The cooking and cleaning required of the mission home had significance beyond its practical aspect because it allowed the residents to live out the tenets of Victorian femininity, while the marriage of mission home residents represented the ultimate expression of women's special moral status.

The Hull House and the San Francisco Mission Home catered to a different clientele and had different expectations for Americanizing their residents. Native-born whites deemed European immigrants much closer to themselves as a racial group when compared to those of the "Mongolian race." The racial distinctiveness of Chinese immigrants was hardly in doubt, even from those sympathetic to their troubles. I have argued that their marriage to Chinese suitors symbolically whitened the rescued slaves, but Cameron by no means viewed the married mission home residents as racially "white." Practices like housekeeping and marriage conditioned their moral status, bridging the moral distance between Chinese and native-born white Americans, but it did not erase the racial boundaries between them.

On balance, Cameron's racial ideology stood in sharp contrast to the rabid anti-Chinese prejudices that characterized San Francisco at the turn of the century. Yet reformers who held a very different opinion of Chinese immigrants often used Cameron's stories of abducted Chinese slaves. Opponents of Chinese immigration reprinted her stories and used her narratives to exemplify Chinese sexual depravity.[79] They praised her humanitarianism yet advocated immigration policies that Cameron believed contributed to the vice trade. By focusing her attention on the victims of brothel slavery, Cameron avoided some of the racist stereotypes of "yellow slavers" that fueled anti-Chinese hatred, but others used her accounts to mobilize precisely those stereotypes.

I have tried to show how narratives of Chinese women forced into prostitution provided a discursive resource for different approaches to Chinese immigration. Reformers used stories of "yellow slavery" to herald the threat of the "yellow peril." These stories acted as a vehicle for nativist arguments against Chinese immigration. The use and appropriation of these stories, however, also supported racial projects aimed to help Chinese immigrants living in San Francisco. Donaldina Cameron's narratives of forced prostitution emphasized the importance of protecting Chinese women from the often harsh environment of Chinatown. The stories of Chinese prostitutes constituted an important aspect of discussions about race and immigration in California, and they also comprised a key component of the nationwide fight against forced prostitution.

Conclusion:
The Demise of White Slavery

White slavery narratives and anti-vice activism performed the ideological work necessary for gender and racial formation. They clarified the boundaries of racial categories and allowed native-born whites to speak of a collective "us" as opposed to a "them." Crusades against white slavery helped build racial hierarchies by emphasizing moral and sexual differences between Anglo-Saxons or native-born whites on one hand and new European immigrants, Chinese, and African Americans on the other. Reformers used white slavery stories to make arguments about the moral character and proper distance between racial groups.

The crusades against white slavery demonstrate the importance of gender and sexuality in creating racial hierarchies. Constructions of the white slave, the wicked woman, and the desperate shop girl allowed for different arguments about the membership requirements for white America. These different images show that race is not a designation of biological descent but a conception of group-belonging, predicated on ideologies of sexual purity and danger. Seemingly sensationalistic white slavery narratives illuminate a real contest over who has and who does not have the full privileges of American citizenship and racial whiteness.

Each reformer articulated a distinct relationship between sexual morality and racial belonging, and I have tried to preserve both the nuances of their ideologies as well as the historical contingencies that shaped their crusades. For some reformers, white slavery narratives contributed to a nativist agenda that asserted the racial superiority of native-born whites. The depiction of immigrants and African Americans as sexual predators was a central feature of the crusades against white slavery in Chicago, New York City, and San Francisco. Clifford Roe and James Reynolds told stories about forced prostitution to underline the purportedly un-American qualities of new immigrants and African Americans. Their characterization of prostitution fit with a legalistic approach to white slavery exemplified by the trial of Belle Moore and the creation of the Mann act. Clifford Roe prosecuted southern and eastern European immigrants accused of white slavery in Chicago, while Reynolds drew upon the white slavery scenario to help prosecute Belle Moore, even though she did not match the stereotype of the notorious "white slaver." In drawing moral boundaries between white slave traders and respectable city-dwellers, these reformers also drew racial boundaries between native-born whites and racial Others. They used arguments about sexual danger to mark racial difference.

Scholars that interpret the crusades against white slavery as a moral panic often argue that white slavery narratives represented a strategy of social control used by white men to maintain their hegemony. This body of scholarship has rightly highlighted the nativism, racism, and class bias of moral reform, but solely focusing on the repressive impulses of sex reform overlooks the often polyvalent nature of these crusades. Even the social control agenda of anti-vice reformers did not work from the simple cultivation of fear; these reformers also asserted that native-born white men and women have a moral responsibility to maintain the integrity of the white race. In the trial of Belle Moore, investigators Frances Foster and George Miller were attacked on the witness stand for lacking racial integrity and sexual morality. Clifford Roe admonished white men and women to draw upon the "right stuff" within them to protect themselves from vice and to guard the boundaries of their racial group. The historical evidence presented in this book supports the interpretation of white slavery crusades as a project of social control, but it points to a broad set of actors whose associations and sexual practices required restraint.

In contrast to the anti-vice efforts of Roe and Reynolds, Donaldina Cameron and Jane Addams expressed, to some extent, a pluralist racial ideology. Cameron and Addams did not insist that immigrant residents of the Hull House and the San Francisco Mission Home reject the cultural practices of their native land. They viewed assimilation not as the erasure of racial distinctiveness but rather as a gradual process of urban adaptation. Consistent with their ideology, Cameron's and Addams's narratives of forced prostitution departed from the standard white slavery abduction scenario. They attributed blame to environmental circumstances that placed women in difficult situations. Addams, more so than Cameron, understood the underlying importance of social class in structuring the vice trade. Both considered immigrant women as the primary victims of sexual coercion in the modern city.

In many ways, Cameron and Addams represent a more humanitarian approach to the prostitution problem. Yet, their reform efforts did not mark a departure from racial thinking. Pluralists reify racial categories by emphasizing the uniqueness of immigrant groups. As Walter Benn Michaels argues, racial pluralists make lateral distinctions among groups that shore up racial differences: "The pluralist denial of hierarchy made possible the escape from the common scale and the emergence of an unmeasurable and hence incomparable racial essence."[1] Although the pragmatic outcome of their crusade is in many ways more admirable when compared to the legalist approach of nativists, they still tried to draw a color line. Addams viewed economic aid in the same way that Cameron viewed moral inoculation—as a way for immigrants to live well in American cities.

Reformers also used white slavery narratives to make a strong claim for women's suffrage and political power. Frances Willard, Katharine Bushnell, and Jane Addams argued that if women were allowed to vote, they would have the ability to pass laws that would protect vulnerable young women from exploitation. Stories of abduction and forced prostitution provided striking examples of gender inequality and the failure of the first sexual revolution to ensure female sexual autonomy. But despite their shared commitment to women's rights, they made different attributions of blame that articulated distinct racial projects. Willard and Bushnell blamed white slavery on the viciousness of immigrant men. They built their arguments for suffrage on the apparent injustice that immigrants and African Americans shared voting rights that were denied native-born white women. Willard and Bushnell opposed immigration because they thought that foreigners posed a sexual threat to native-born white women. Their feminist arguments were intimately connected to a racial ideology that positioned Anglo-Saxons, or native-born whites, as more evolutionarily advanced and civilized than African Americans and new immigrant groups.

The efforts to stop forced prostitution in the Progressive Era preclude easy generalizations about their political tendencies and complicate any neat portrait of "Progressivism." The rhetorical plasticity of white slavery stories made them ideal vehicles to express concern about the direction of social change in turn-of-the-century America. Anti-vice efforts in the Progressive Era not only provide a window into the reaction to African Americans and different immigrant groups but also show importance of gender and sexuality in creating racial inequality and hierarchy.

This book has engaged, supplemented, and challenged contemporary scholarship on social inequality. It is indebted to a score of interdisciplinary studies on race, gender, and culture as well as monographs and articles about the historical events and personalities that animate these pages. While readers will ultimately draw their own conclusions about its contribution, I hope a few core lessons emerge from this exploration of anti-vice activism that prompt a fresh, if not critical, look at the scholarship with which this study dialogues. In particular, this study makes two strong arguments related to the ontological relationship between race, gender, and sexuality and the interconnections between material inequality and culture.

While many have pointed to the need to consider intersecting forms of social inequality, relatively fewer studies have investigated the glue that holds those intersections together. The case studies explored in this book have shown how discourse related to gender and sexuality has provided the scaffolding upon which racial distinctions rest. In U.S. history, racial membership means many things to many people, but notions of family, birthright, and lineage have been elemental components of racial thinking since colonial times. Sexual practices that potentially reshuffle racial membership give racial groups ever-present crisis tendencies, challenging the very idea of "race." Sexuality as a generative principle of racial classification and, importantly, declassification means abandoning the study of race as an autonomous subject. This should be an uncontroversial claim given the popularity of intersectional approaches to studying inequality. I would argue, however, that gender and sexuality must be placed in the foreground when explaining racial inequality, racial group-making, and the concept of race itself.

Moreover, this book has shown how cultural production and reception are constitutive elements of racial group-making. Individuals, activists, and state actors used sexual stories to create and enforce racial boundaries. In turn, racial stereotypes and controlling images implicated specific visions of authentic manhood and womanhood. Much of this boundary-drawing, distinction-making, and scapegoating relied on cultural production: a woman gives a speech about white slavery that deliberately references chattel slavery; a man draws an illustration for an anti-vice book that depicts a white slave procurer with dark features and a slightly crooked nose; another details the economic pressures put upon working-class women; a journalist describes a heroic brothel raid; a district attorney uses a colorful turn of phrase. The cultural realm is no less real or important than the more obvious manifestations of racial and gender boundary-policing revealed in arrests, deportations, criminal trials, and physical violence. In fact, the cultural confers a taken-for-granted quality to social action such that the most extreme manifestations of xenophobia, nationalism, racism, and sexism seem like an appropriate, indeed necessary, response to external and internal threats to dominant social groups. The structure of narrative with its victims and villains and self-contained beginnings and conclusions offers a form of cognitive comfort for those engaged in racial and gender projects, whatever their political valence.

The attention to culture requires that we take a new approach to understanding the white slavery phenomenon.[2] Much of the past scholarship on white slavery and anti-vice activism, particularly the moral panic interpretation, posited a stimulus-response model of social action. Deeper structural changes (urbanization, immigration, and changes in the labor force), often unrecognized by those responding to them, created an almost-inevitable hysterical reaction embodied in the core components of the white slavery narrative. This account positions anti-vice activism and white slavery narratives as dependent variables that record or reflect social change outside of the conscious grasp of those responding to it. Obviously, the material context of anti-vice activism is indispensable for understanding it, and for that reason I introduced the topic by discussing large-scale social changes in urban America to which crusaders responded. Yet, existing scholarship too often clings to a form of modernization theory whereby the expressive, creative, and ideational aspects of white slave crusades merely index something deeper and realer. Just as we should view gender and racial group-making as linked processes, we should adopt a dialectical view of meaning-making and structure. As others have previously noted, the theoretical opposition between structure and culture is no longer useful or sustainable.[3] As this book has, I hope, made clear, cultural production and consumption are welded to enduring economic and political institutions. The crusades against white slavery cannot be viewed solely as an outcry against perceived urban ills, and, likewise, white slavery narratives were more than a form of lurid entertainment or creative expression.

This study has attempted to harness a wide range of theoretical insights in order to make sense of anti-prostitution crusades. I have also made comparisons and analyses of anti-vice activism in order to speak to core theoretical issues related to race, gender, and culture. I will conclude this exploration of white slavery by examining some of the events that pushed white slavery off the national stage.

The Closing of Red-Light Districts

Public concern about white slavery waned in the years leading up to World War I. The publication of white slavery narratives dropped precipitously after 1917, and many anti-vice organizations changed course or became a shadow of their former selves. As red-light districts closed in major U.S. cities, anti-vice movements became victims of their own success.[4] The new tenor and focus of anti-prostitution efforts changed the dominant image of the prostitute from a helpless victim to a diseased predator.

In New York City, prostitution drastically declined in visibility with the passage of a 1915 state law that prohibited solicitation in theaters, saloons, cabarets, and streets. Brothels no longer publicized their location, and prostitutes no longer openly advertised in nightclubs. Prostitution became almost entirely clandestine as streetwalkers disappeared from major boulevards.[5] Prohibition, immigration restrictions, changes in real estate ownership, and changing sexual norms all contributed to the decline of both prostitution and anti-prostitution efforts in New York City.[6]

Chicago's Levee district closed in 1914 after the chief of police established a "Morals Squad" to conduct brothel raids. In July 1914, a raid went awry when "Morals Men" and undercover detectives separately converged on a poolroom. The two detectives mistook the men from the Morals Squad as criminals and opened fire. A gunfight ensued, causing the death of one detective and serious injuries for the other three men. The public massacre appalled Chicagoans.[7] Embarrassed by this scandal, Mayor Carter Harrison launched an aggressive attack against the Levee district and revoked the liquor licenses of thirty-three saloons that tolerated prostitution on their property. From 1911 to 1914, police arrested ever-increasing numbers of people for violating vice laws. In 1915, Harrison's efforts received a major boost when the Illinois Senate passed the "Red Light Injunction and Abatement Law." Illinois lawmakers modeled this act after a similar piece of legislation passed in Iowa in 1909. The law allowed citizens to sue brothel owners on the grounds that brothels were a public nuisance.

California also passed a "Red Light Abatement Act" that effectively eliminated the flagrant vice trade in San Francisco's Chinatown and Barbary Coast. The California state legislature enacted the Red Light Abatement Act in 1914, granting law enforcement officials the power to close buildings used for prostitution. The law also permitted all movable property within the building to be sold. California granted voting rights to women in 1911, allowing clubwomen and the WCTU to back the bill as fully enfranchised citizens. The bill drew strong support from middle-class women because, instead of targeting prostitutes, the act made property owners liable for the activities of their renters.[8]

The legal suppression of prostitution accompanied cultural changes that helped shove the white slavery narrative of abduction and forced prostitution from public consciousness. The co-optation of anti-vice groups by social hygiene organizations moved discussions of prostitution into the domains of science and medicine. Also, theories of female delinquency helped supplant the image of feminine innocence and vulnerability central to many white slavery accounts. Politicians, news media, and the public began to view prostitution as a serious menace to public health and military preparedness.

The Rise of "Social Hygiene"

As shown in chapter 3, organizations primarily staffed by women inaugurated the crusades against white slavery in the United States. The WCTU, the American Purity Alliance, and the American Purity Federation drew attention to coercive prostitution in the late nineteenth century and approached the issue with an overriding concern for the welfare of working-class women. Beginning in the early twentieth century, men with backgrounds in science and public health displayed an increasing interest in controlling prostitution and eradicating venereal disease. "Social hygiene" organizations developed alongside the crusades against white slavery and eventually displaced women-dominated moral reform organizations. As the twentieth century moved forward, a scientific discourse of social hygiene gradually replaced white slavery storytelling.

Prince Morrow spearheaded social hygiene efforts to combat the spread of venereal disease in the United States. According to his associate Edward Keyes, Morrow had little interest in the topic before attending a conference for physicians about venereal disease in Brussels in 1902. Keyes stated, "On his return he became a burning zealot. A missionary at heart. From then on he wrote numberless articles and speeches which went throughout the country and aroused great interest."[9] Morrow founded the Society for Sanitary and Moral Prophylaxis in 1905 and the American Federation for Sex Hygiene in 1907. He brought a distinctly scientific approach to bear on the problem of sexual immorality and stressed the need for widespread sex education. Although Morrow supported the work of feminist purity crusaders, his organizations largely displaced moralistic messages about sexual sin and feminist messages about sexual exploitation with scientific explanations of disease and public health. He fought for a comprehensive program of sex education to remove the shame attached to venereal diseases and the causes of their transmission.[10]

The creation of the American Social Hygiene Association (ASHA) in 1913 effectively signaled the co-optation of anti-vice and purity organizations by social hygienists. ASHA came into existence from the merger of the American Federation for Sex Hygiene with the American Vigilance Association. The American Vigilance Association had long been the providence of anti-vice crusaders like Clifford Roe and Edward Janney. The union of the movements generated some conflicts between reformers from New York and Chicago and between reformers representing the older model of anti-vice activism and the new model of social hygiene.[11]

John D. Rockefeller Jr. played an important role in the creation of ASHA and explicitly rejected an older style of moral reform represented by Janney and others. Rockefeller told James Reynolds that his funding of the newly created ASHA depended upon the presence of leaders with "the modern point of view with reference to this subject [prostitution]."[12] He added, "The only man I know of whom I feel should definitely be replaced is Dr. Janny [sic]. I do not know Dr. Janny personally, and I have heard many pleasant things of him as a man, but I am convinced that he is of the old school and that his connection with this movement will be a hindrance rather than helpful to its progress."[13] As ASHA gained power and prominence, the important voices in the fight against prostitution were no longer authors of white slavery tracts; they were medical doctors. David Pivar contends that "social hygienists, as they displaced purity reform, narrowed public health's scope and turned to a secular leadership."[14] David Langum, commenting on the emergence of ASHA, notes, "The co-option of the women's Purity Movement, first by men, and later by doctors, was complete."[15]

The ascendance of medical experts in the prostitution debate did not go without comment from the leaders in anti-vice organizations. Despite his ties to Rockefeller and role in creating ASHA, Roe decried the increasing attention to social hygiene and the relative decline in discussions of morality. In his 1914 book, *The Girl Who Disappeared*, Roe argued that teaching morals was much more important than teaching sex education as advocated by social hygienists. Roe's character Jane Carr declared, "I think those who are insisting upon imparting technical, scientific sex knowledge to every child belong to the extremist class. It is not necessary that one should become a specialist in sex matters nor that overemphasis should be put upon the subject."[16] Later in the story, a local pastor offered his views on social hygiene in a discussion with Jane: "Our present aim should be to encourage a right mental and moral attitude. Depend upon it, the remedy for the great social cancer of vice with all its terrible attendant diseases and death, will not be found in a technical study of sex hygiene except as an aid in teaching teachers."[17]

The tension between the rising social hygiene movement and the old guard of anti-vice reform also appears in the correspondence between Mary Cobb and William Robinson. Cobb was a friend of Rose Chapman, who led the WCTU's Social Purity Department. Robinson was an editor of science journals who supported the social hygiene movement. Robinson rebuked Cobb's call to teach the principles of sexual morality in public schools and wrote, "You speak the language of the tenth century; I speak the language of the twentieth, or rather the 25th. You speak the language of gloom and reaction; I speak the language of joy and progress. You speak the language of the shackled theologian; I speak the language of the free scientist."[18] After 1910, the gender division within the early-twentieth-century anti-vice crusades manifested itself as a conflict between scientific sex education and moral education.

The rise of social hygiene transformed the racial—as well as gender—politics of anti-vice activism. Anti-prostitution discourse increasingly pointed to internal threats to white hegemony. The social hygiene movement also brought scientific legitimacy to the connection between sexual immorality and the decline of the white or Anglo-Saxon race. Charles Eliot, president of Harvard and honorary president of ASHA, declared in 1916, "If the civilization of the white race is to survive, it must be saved through the diffusion and adoption of sound policies in regard to social hygiene, carried enthusiastically and persistently into action."[19] Prince Morrow declared that venereal diseases were a "racial poison" that threatened civilization. Morrow placed a high responsibility on mothers to protect their "biological capital." He wrote: "We have thus come to recognize the dominant influence of the mother in relation to the health, as well as the life of the race." Echoing fears of "race suicide," Morrow criticized women of the "better classes" who squander their energy on "strenuous social duties and amusements of fashionable life" that should properly be directed toward "the upbuilding of the child." He concluded, "Sex is not only the cardinal fact in the individual life, but also the most vital of all facts in the racial life."[20] The expansion of the social hygiene movement drew strength from the development of eugenics, linking illicit sex to racial decline and degeneration.[21] Although Morrow personally favored education over negative eugenic measures, support grew for the latter. By 1923, forty-three states had established institutions for the feebleminded, and by 1931, thirty states had passed laws allowing for the sterilization of persons considered "unfit" for parenthood.[22]

Female Delinquency

The social hygiene movement not only replaced the organizational power of the anti-vice movement but also transformed the dominant representations of prostitution. White slavery narratives depended upon images of innocent white women who lacked sexual agency. As the twentieth century progressed, this notion of innate female innocence yielded to theories of female delinquency; images of female delinquents supplanted images of entrapped victims.[23] The depiction of autonomous females instead of white slaves or passive victims of seduction was a more realistic and enlightened image of womanhood, yet it also provided a rationale for gender discrimination. Kristin Luker argues that the social hygiene movement represented a "double-edged sword" for young women: "The new judicial and penal apparatus of the expanded, more efficient regulatory state fell most heavily on the prostitutes themselves, and the kinds of behavior that constituted prostitution had been expanded so broadly as to include vast numbers of women guilty only of having sexual relations outside of marriage."[24]

As the United States approached World War I, the military made a link between prostitution and national security. The federal government spent over $5 million in order to protect troops from the supposed threat of diseased prostitutes.[25] Over 50,000 men viewed the film *Fit to Fight,* which stressed the dangers of venereal disease and the importance of a single standard of morality. While the military inculcated soldiers with orders to remain sexually chaste, it forcefully prosecuted unescorted women near military bases. Local governments enacted laws that allowed for the detention of any woman "reasonably suspected" of carrying venereal disease, and by March 1918, thirty-two states had enacted similar measures.[26] John D'Emilio and Estelle Freedman note that the military "suspended writs of habeas corpus, arrested women en masse, and forcibly held more than fifteen thousand in detention centers for periods averaging ten weeks. No men were arrested for patronizing prostitutes."[27] Barbara Hobson argues that the effort to eradicate prostitution in the name of national security represented "one of the most blatant examples of sex discrimination in the history of American justice."[28]

Military and medical authorities viewed prostitution as a major source of disease and argued that its repression was crucial to the health and efficiency of American troops. In response to the supposed threat of infectious women, the federal government created the Committee on Training Camp Activities (CTCA) in 1917. The head of the CTCA was Raymond Fosdick, one of the founders of Rockefeller's Bureau of Social Hygiene. In 1918, the CTCA adopted an aggressive campaign of compulsory physical examination and quarantine of women suspected of having venereal disease. Over half a million dollars in federal funds were spent on the creation and maintenance of forty-three detention homes for women suspected of being lewd and immoral. According to the War Department, 18,000 women were quarantined in federally funded institutions, and thousands more were forced to submit to examinations before being detained in local jails.[29]

The creation of the CTCA and the aggressive action against female sexual delinquency threw into bold relief the ideological positions of the mostly male social hygienists and the mostly female moral reformers. Maude Miner was a female probation officer who wrote an influential anti-prostitution book, *The Slavery of Prostitution,* in 1916 and was appointed to the CTCA by Raymond Fosdick. Miner resigned soon after her appointment, however, when the coercive policies of the federal effort became increasingly apparent. Miner rejected the clear sex bias in the CTCA's approach and criticized the fact that CTCA officials made no effort to detain men suspected of harboring venereal disease during the war.[30]

Perhaps it is fitting that this account of the fight against white slavery in the United States should end with Katharine Bushnell, the woman who sparked the crusades against forced prostitution with her investigations of midwestern lumber camps. Bushnell, with Miner, was one of the few who had the courage to publicly condemn wartime measures intended to protect soldiers from venereal disease. She decried the medical inspections of women by "the vile masturbating hand of a doctor." Bushnell protested the CTCA's activities in California and argued that they allowed "a betrayal of the elementary rights of a free people."[31] She maintained that the CTCA's policy of medical inspection ruined women's claim to virtue. In a 1917 letter to the district attorney in San Francisco, Bushnell wrote, "For, should it happen that by mistake (and many such mistakes have been made in other countries) a young virgin is haled [*sic*] to the examination, or a respectable woman, no insult could be greater, no humiliation deeper, no mental wrong could be inflicted upon her of greater intensity, than to be examined. . . . Many a young woman has gone straight from the examination room to a suicide's death."[32]

White slavery no longer loomed as a threat promising to send young women to an early grave. Now, the medical and legal apparatus established to combat prostitution and immorality endangered the purity of womanhood. For Katharine Bushnell, the cycle of anti-vice reform had come full circle. By the beginning of World War I, agitation against white slavery had been transformed into a system of state surveillance.

Notes

Introduction

1. There is considerable debate among historians about the definition and character of both progressivism and the progressive movement. Classic works on the Progressive Era include Robert Weibe, *The Search for Order 1887–1920* (New York: Hill and Wang, 1966); and Richard Hofstadter, *The Age of Reform* (New York: Vintage, 1960). Rogers Smith makes a useful distinction between right, left, and centrist progressives. See Rogers Smith, *Civic Ideals: Conflicting Visions of Citizenship in U.S. History* (New Haven: Yale University Press, 1997), 412–29.

2. Shelley Stamp, "'Oil upon the Flames of Vice': The Battle over White Slave Films in New York City," *Film History* 9 (1997): 351–64.

3. See Marlene D. Beckman, "The White Slave Traffic Act: Historical Implications of a Federal Crime Policy on Women," *Women and Politics* 4 (1984): 85–101. For an insightful analysis of the Mann act and its legacy, see David Langum, *Crossing the Line: Legislating Morality and the Mann Act* (Chicago: University of Chicago Press, 1994).

4. Kevin Mumford, *Interzones: Black/White Sex Districts in Chicago and New York in the Early Twentieth Century* (New York: Columbia University Press, 1997).

5. Using a slightly wider time frame, Glenn summarizes these changes: "The period from Reconstruction through the Progressive era (1870–1930), was one of considerable ferment in meanings of citizenship and labor and in race, gender, and class relations owing to the abolition of slavery, industrialization, urbanization, massive immigration from southern and eastern Europe, and imperialist expansion into Latin America, the Caribbean, and the Philippines." Evelyn Nakano Glenn, *Unequal Freedom: How Race and Gender Shaped American Citizenship and Labor* (Cambridge: Harvard University Press, 2002), 3.

6. On the link between white slavery and liberalism, see Pamela Haag, *Consent: Sex-*

ual Rights and the Transformation of American Liberalism (Ithaca: Cornell University Press, 1999), 63–94; on the relationship between white slavery stories and American legal practice, see Frederick Grittner, *White Slavery: Myth, Ideology, and American Law* (New York: Garland, 1990); on white slavery stories as a critique of monopoly capitalism, see Mara Keire, "The Vice Trust: A Reinterpretation of the White Slavery Scare in the United States, 1907–1917," *Journal of Social History* 35 (2001): 5–41; on white slavery and the development of modern journalism, see Gretchen Soderlund, "Covering Urban Vice: The *New York Times*, 'White Slavery,' and the Construction of Journalistic Knowledge," *Critical Studies in Media Communication* 19 (December 2002): 438–60.

7. M. Joan McDermott and Sarah J. Blackstone have argued that white slavery narratives reinforced patriarchal definitions of sexuality by frightening women about the consequences of independence and nonmarital sex. M. Joan McDermott and Sarah Blackstone, "White Slavery Plays of the 1910s: Fear of Victimization and the Social Control of Sexuality," *Theatre History Studies* 16 (1996): 141–56. Margit Stange offers a Marxist/feminist reading of these texts to show how they discussed the market for women as brides and prostitutes in consumer capitalism. *Personal Property: Wives, White Slaves, and the Market in Women* (Baltimore: Johns Hopkins University Press, 1998). See also Mark Connelly, *The Response to Prostitution in the Progressive Era* (Chapel Hill: University of North Carolina Press, 1980); Jo Doezema, "Loose Women or Lost Women?: The Re-emergence of the Myth of White Slavery in Contemporary Discourses of Trafficking in Women," *Gender Issues* 18 (2000): 23–50; Grittner, *White Slavery;* and Ruth Rosen, *The Lost Sisterhood: Prostitution in America 1900–1918* (Baltimore: Johns Hopkins University Press, 1982).

8. See Brian Donovan, "The Sexual Basis of Racial Formation: Anti-Vice Activism and the Creation of the Twentieth-Century Color Line," *Ethnic and Racial Studies* 26 (2003): 708–28; Mumford, *Interzones*, 14–18, 99–116; Mary Odem, *Delinquent Daughters: Policing Adolescent Female Sexuality in the United States, 1885–1920* (Chapel Hill: University of North Carolina Press, 1995), 1–38; and David Pivar, *Purity and Hygiene: Women, Prostitution and the 'American Plan,' 1900–1930* (Westport, Conn.: Greenwood Press, 2002), 188–98.

9. Kathleen Blee, *Women of the Klan: Racism and Gender in the 1920s* (Berkeley: University of California Press, 1991), 74–86; Joanne Meyerowitz, *Women Adrift: Independent Wage Earners in Chicago, 1880–1930* (Chicago: University of Chicago Press); Odem, *Delinquent Daughters.*

10. Michèle Lamont, "Introduction: Beyond Taking Culture Seriously," in *The Cultural Territories of Race: Black and White Boundaries,* ed. Michèle Lamont (Chicago: University of Chicago Press, 1999), ix–xx.

11. See Nicola Beisel, *Imperiled Innocents: Anthony Comstock and Family Reproduction in Victorian America* (Princeton, N.J.: Princeton University Press, 1997). Gusfield shows the link between moral struggles and class politics in his analysis of class and status politics in the Woman's Christian Temperance Union. See Joseph

Gusfield, *Symbolic Crusade: Status Politics and the American Temperance Movement* (Urbana: University of Illinois Press, 1966).

12. Michael Omi and Howard Winant, *Racial Formation in the United States: From the 1960s to the 1990s* (New York: Routledge, 1986).

13. Developments in historical scholarship on gender, particularly the work of Gail Bederman, Nicola Beisel, Mary Poovey, and Judith Walkowitz, influenced my research methods. See Gail Bederman, *Manliness and Civilization: A Cultural History of Gender and Race in the United States, 1880–1917* (Chicago: University of Chicago Press, 1995); Beisel, *Imperiled Innocents;* Mary Poovey, *Uneven Developments: The Ideological Work of Gender in Mid-Victorian England* (Chicago: University of Chicago Press, 1989); and Judith Walkowitz, *City of Dreadful Delight: Narratives of Sexual Danger in Late-Victorian London* (Chicago: University of Chicago Press, 1992). New cultural history, exemplified in the work of Lynn Hunt and Judith Walkowitz, highlights narrative or storytelling as a way individuals and groups engage in power struggles. Guided by this approach, I focus on reformers' "process of articulation" (Bederman, *Manliness and Civilization,* 23) in order to map different configurations of ideology. See also Victoria Bonnell and Lynn Hunt, eds., *Beyond the Cultural Turn: New Directions in the Study of Society and Culture* (Berkeley: University of California Press, 1999); and Victoria Bonnell and Lynn Hunt, eds., *New Cultural History* (Berkeley: University of California Press, 1989).

14. See Victoria Bonnell, "The Use of Theory, Concepts and Comparison in Historical Sociology," *Comparative Studies in Society and History* 22 (1980): 156–73.

Chapter 1: White Slavery and the Intersection of Race and Gender

1. Scholars often impose the racial categories of the late twentieth or early twenty-first century onto historical actors that understood and talked about race in very different terms. Throughout this book, I try to specify the meanings of racial categories used by different historical subjects. Yet I try to offer a readable text by using terms familiar to an early-twenty-first century audience. I often use the term "native-born white" to refer to what many in the nineteenth and early twentieth centuries would regard as "Anglo-Saxon." I use the term "African American" to refer to Americans of African decent. The changing use and meanings of the terms "white," "Anglo-Saxon," "black," "mulatto," and "colored" will be addressed later in this study. For a discussion of the shifting terminology used to describe African Americans, see James F. Davis, *Who Is Black? One Nation's Definition* (University Park: Pennsylvania State University Press, 1991). For a defense of the term "African American" in contemporary writings about race, see Orlando Patterson, *Rituals of Blood: The Consequences of Slavery in Two Centuries* (Washington, D.C.: Civitas, 1998), xxi–xxii.

2. See Rogers Smith, *Civic Ideals: Conflicting Visions of Citizenship in U.S. History* (New Haven: Yale University Press, 1997), 441.

3. For a compelling exploration of this "whitening" process, see Matthew Jacob-

son, *Whiteness of a Different Color: European Immigrants and the Alchemy of Race* (Chicago: University of Chicago Press, 1998).

4. During the last fifteen years, the topic of racial whiteness in American history and contemporary culture has drawn a great deal of attention, creating a body of scholarship that Ware and Black refer to as "American whiteness studies." See Vron Ware and Les Back, eds., *Out of Whiteness: Color, Politics, and Culture* (Chicago: University of Chicago Press, 2001), 14. See also Theodore Allen, *The Invention of the White Race: Volume 1 Racial Oppression and Social Control* (New York: Verso, 1994); Ruth Frankenberg, *White Women, Race Matters: The Social Construction of Whiteness* (Minneapolis: University of Minnesota Press, 1993); Grace Elizabeth Hale, *Making Whiteness: The Culture of Segregation in the South, 1890–1940* (New York: Vintage, 1998); Jacobson, *Whiteness of a Different Color;* Ian F. Haney Lopez, *White by Law: The Legal Construction of Race* (New York: New York University Press, 1998); Steve Martinot, *The Rule of Racialization: Class, Identity, Governance* (Philadelphia: Temple University Press, 2003); David Roediger, *The Wages of Whiteness: Race and the Making of the American Working Class* (New York: Verso, 1991); and David Roediger, *Towards the Abolition of Whiteness: Essays on Race, Politics, and Working Class History* (New York: Verso, 1994), and *Colored White: Transcending America's Racial Past* (Berkeley: University of California Press, 2003).

5. Robert Connell, *Masculinities* (Berkeley: University of California Press, 1995). J. Ann Tickner argues "there can be no such thing as hegemonic femininity because masculinity defines the norm." *Gendering World Politics* (New York: Columbia University Press, 2001), 16. Others have found value in the concept as an expression of the standards of womanliness that women are pressured to adopt. See Diana Crane, "Gender and Hegemony in Fashion Magazines: Women's Interpretations of Fashion Photographs," in *Gender, Race, and Class in Media: A Text-Reader,* ed. Gail Dines and Jean M. Humez (Thousand Oaks, Calif.: Sage Publications, 2002), 314–38.

6. Gail Bederman provides a powerful account of these changes in white manliness; see *Manliness and Civilization: A Cultural History of Gender and Race in the United States, 1880–1917* (Chicago: University of Chicago Press, 1995), 1–44. For a discussion of Roosevelt's personification of Progressive Era masculinity and its link to imperialism and white racial dominance, see Bederman, *Manliness and Civilization,* 170–215; and Joane Nagel, "Masculinity and Nationalism: Gender and Sexuality in the Making of Nations," *Ethnic and Racial Studies* 21 (March 1998): 242–69.

7. Carroll Smith-Rosenberg, *Disorderly Conduct: Visions of Gender in Victorian America* (Oxford: Oxford University Press, 1985), 178.

8. See Ruth Bordin, *Alice Freeman Palmer: The Evolution of a New Woman* (Ann Arbor: University of Michigan Press), 1–13; Estelle B. Freedman, "The New Woman: Changing Views of Women in the 1920s," *Journal of American History* 61 (September 1974): 372–93; and James R. McGovern, "The American Woman's Pre–World War I Freedom in Manners and Morals," *Journal of American History* 45 (September 1968): 315–33. Viewing them as a threat to male power and privilege, many men at the turn

of the century were openly critical of New Women and accused them of sexual deviance. See Smith-Rosenberg, *Disorderly Conduct*, 245–96.

9. See Mary Odem, *Delinquent Daughters: Policing Adolescent Female Sexuality in the United States, 1885–1920* (Chapel Hill: University of North Carolina Press, 1995).

10. Elaine Tyler May, *Great Expectations: Marriage and Divorce in Post-Victorian America* (Chicago: University of Chicago Press, 1980).

11. Ibid., 94.

12. Beth Bailey, *From Front Porch to Back Seat: Courtship in Twentieth-Century America* (Baltimore: Johns Hopkins University Press, 1989).

13. Alan Hunt, "Regulating Heterosocial Space: Sexual Politics in the Early Twentieth Century," *Journal of Historical Sociology* (March 2002): 1–34.

14. Kathy Peiss, *Cheap Amusements: Working Women and Leisure in New York City, 1880–1920* (Philadelphia: Temple University Press, 1986).

15. Barbara Meil Hobson, *Uneasy Virtue: The Politics of Prostitution and the American Reform Tradition* (Chicago: University of Chicago Press, 1997), 16.

16. Martinot traces the roots of racial group-making in America to seventeenth-century proscriptions on interracial marriage and changes in the colonial class structure. Martinot, *Rule of Racialization*.

17. Ibid., 62.

18. On the concept of "racial projects," see Michael Omi and Howard Winant, *Racial Formation in the United States: From the 1960s to the 1990s* (New York: Routledge, 1986).

19. Mara Loveman, "Is 'Race' Essential?" *American Sociological Review* 64 (1999): 894.

20. See Eduardo Bonilla-Silva, "Rethinking Racism: Toward A Structural Interpretation," *American Sociological Review* 62 (June 1997): 465–79. For analyses of the intersection of racial and class domination, see Allen, *Invention of the White Race*; Martinot, *Rule of Racialization*; Roediger, *Wages of Whiteness*; and Roediger, *Towards the Abolition of Whiteness*.

21. Bonilla-Silva, "Rethinking Racism," 469.

22. Ibid., 470.

23. Bonilla-Silva writes, "On the basis of this structure, there develops a racial ideology (what analysts have coded as 'racism')." Ibid., 474.

24. For much of U.S. history, the category of "whites" was a symbolic position intimately tied to socioeconomic power, not simply a description of skin color. See Allen, *Invention of the White Race*; Noel Ignatiev, *How the Irish Became White* (New York: Routledge, 1995); Roediger, *Wages of Whiteness*; and Roediger, *Towards the Abolition of Whiteness*.

25. Allen, *Invention of the White Race*.

26. Roediger, *Wages of Whiteness*; Ignatiev, *How the Irish Became White*. Richard Jensen has suggested that historians have greatly exaggerated the extent to which native-born whites considered the Irish racially distinct. For a critique of Roediger and Ignatiev, see Richard Jensen, "'No Irish Need Apply': The Myth of Victimization," *Journal of Social History* 36 (Winter 2002): 405–32.

27. Omi and Winant, *Racial Formation,* 55. With their concept of "racial formation," Omi and Winant attempt to capture the role of ideology and the interdependent cultural and structural elements that constitute racial categories. Different
"racial projects," affecting both representations of race and the redistribution of
resources along racial lines, create racial formations. Racial formation processes
occur "through a linkage between structure and representation. Racial projects do
the ideological 'work' of making these links." Omi and Winant, *Racial Formation,*
56. While the racial formation perspective explains the transformation of racial categories based on racial projects, racial ideologies are interdependent with other systems of representation. Ann Laura Stoler contends that "racial discourse operates
in a mobile discursive field" that ties forms of racial thinking to other ideologies. See
"Racial Histories and Their Regimes of Truth," *Political Power and Social Theory* 11
(1997): 191.

28. On racial group-making, see Thomas C. Holt, "Marking, Race-Making and the
Writing of History," *American Historical Review* 100 (1995): 1–20; Loveman, "Is 'Race'
Essential?"; Kent Redding, *Making Race, Making Power: North Carolina's Road to Dis-
enfranchisement* (Urbana: University of Illinois Press, 2003); and Loic Wacquant, "For
an Analytic of Racial Domination," *Political Power and Social Theory* 11 (1997): 221–34.

29. Loveman, "Is 'Race' Essential?"

30. Mary Poovey, *Uneven Developments: The Ideological Work of Gender in Mid-
Victorian England* (Chicago: University of Chicago Press, 1989).

31. The resources that make up the structural aspects of social life depend upon
culture-bound lenses of interpretation, or what William Sewell calls "cultural
schemas." See William Sewell, "A Theory of Structure: Duality, Agency, and Transformation," *American Journal of Sociology* 98 (1992): 1–29.

32. According to Pierre Bourdieu, the power to bestow legitimate names, categories, and credentials in the social world depends upon one's "symbolic power,"
which is composed of social networks, material wealth, and cultural capital. See *Language and Symbolic Power* (Cambridge: Harvard University Press, 1993).

33. Jacobson, *Whiteness of a Different Color,* 138.

34. Barbara Fields, "Ideology and Race in American History," in *Region, Race, and
Reconstruction,* ed. J. Morgan Kousser and James M. McPherson (Oxford: Oxford
University Press, 1982), 151.

35. On moral boundary work, see Nicola Beisel, *Imperiled Innocents: Anthony Comstock and Family Reproduction in Victorian America* (Princeton, N.J.: Princeton University Press, 1997); Michèle Lamont, *The Dignity of Working Men: Morality and
Boundaries of Race, Class and Immigration* (Cambridge: Harvard University Press,
2000); and Michèle Lamont and Virág Molnár, "The Study of Boundaries in the Social Sciences," *Annual Review of Sociology* 28 (2002): 167–95.

36. For an overview of the development of intersectional research on inequality, see
Karen Brodikin Sacks, "Toward a Unified Theory of Class, Race, and Gender," *American Ethnologist* 16 (1989): 534–50. Much of the work on intersectionality has come

from a body of scholarship referred to as Critical Race Theory. See Kimberle Crenshaw, "Demarginalizing the Intersection of Race and Sex: A Black Feminist Critique of Anti-discrimination Doctrine, Feminist Theory and Anti-racist Politics," *University of Chicago Legal Forum* 139 (1989): 139–67; Richard Delgado, *Critical Race Theory: An Introduction* (New York: New York University Press, 2001); and May Jo Wiggins, "The Future of Intersectionality and Critical Race Feminism," *Journal of Contemporary Legal Issues* 677 (2001): 677–89.

37. For example, Evelyn Nakano Glenn offers a valuable framework with which to analyze the relationship between gender and race: "Race and gender are defined as mutually constituted systems of relationships—including norms, symbols, and practices—organized around perceived differences." *Unequal Freedom: How Race and Gender Shaped American Citizenship and Labor* (Cambridge: Harvard University Press, 2002), 12. See also Evelyn Brooks Higginbotham, "African-American Women's History and the Metalanguage of Race," *Signs* 17 (1992): 251–74.

38. Noting that "race and sex each reinforce and magnify the other," Joane Nagel traces the various links between sex and race historically and cross-culturally. *Race, Ethnicity, and Sexuality: Intimate Intersections, Forbidden Frontiers* (Oxford: Oxford University Press, 2003), 57. The categories of gender and sexuality are obviously interrelated. Notions of acceptable sexual expression are rooted in cultural norms of masculinity and femininity. In turn, hegemonic understandings of masculinity and femininity depend upon heteronormative ideas of female and male behavior. See Pepper Schwartz and Virginia Rutter, *The Gender of Sexuality* (New York: Rowman and Littlefield, 1998).

39. Michel Foucault, *The History of Sexuality, Volume I* (New York: Vintage, 1984); Ann Laura Stoler, *Race and the Education of Desire: Foucault's History of Sexuality and the Colonial Order of Things* (Durham, N.C.: Duke University Press, 1995).

40. Abby Ferber, *White Man Falling: Race, Gender, and White Supremacy* (Boulder: Rowman and Littlefield, 1998).

41. See Tessie Liu, "Teaching the Differences among Women from a Historical Perspective: Rethinking Race and Gender as Social Categories," *Women's Studies International Forum* 14 (1991): 571–83; Stoler, *Race and the Education of Desire;* Ann Laura Stoler, "Making Empire Respectable: The Politics of Race and Sexual Morality in 20th-Century Colonial Cultures," *American Ethnologist* 16 (1989): 634–59.

42. Liu, "Teaching the Differences," 577.

43. See Joane Nagel, "Ethnicity and Sexuality," *Annual Review of Sociology* 26 (2000): 107–33, and "Sexualizing the Sociological: Queering and Querying the Intimate Substructure of Social Life," *Sociological Quarterly* 41 (2000): 1–17.

44. James Davis concludes, "The castelike Jim Crow system was firmly entrenched by 1910." *Who Is Black?*, 53.

45. John D'Emilio and Estelle Freedman, *Intimate Matters: A History of Sexuality in America* (New York: Harper and Row, 1988), 108.

46. See J. Davis, *Who Is Black?* See also Joel Williamson, *The Crucible of Race:*

Black/White Relations in the American South since Emancipation (New York: Oxford University Press, 1984).

47. See J. Davis, *Who Is Black?* Segregation statutes and a stricter one-drop rule did not solidify physical boundaries between African Americans and whites. While southern whites could regulate and punish public transgressions of the color line, private relationships were more difficult to control. Anti-miscegenation laws in the South prohibited African Americans and whites from marrying one another, but interracial sexual relationships were often kept safely from public scrutiny. See Martha Hodes, *White Women, Black Men: Illicit Sex in the Nineteenth-Century South* (New Haven: Yale University Press, 1999).

48. Patterson, *Rituals of Blood*, 176–79.

49. See Bederman, *Manliness and Civilization*. See also Jacquelyn Dowd Hall, "'The Mind That Burns in Each Body': Women, Rape, and Racial Violence," in *Powers of Desire: The Politics of Sexuality*, ed. Ann Snitow, Christine Stansell, and S. Thompson (New York: Monthly Review Press, 1983), 328–49.

50. D'Emilio and Freedman, *Intimate Matters*, 216.

51. Spectacle lynchings counted for approximately 34 percent of all lynchings in Georgia and 40 percent of lynchings in Virginia. See Fitzhugh Brundage, *Lynching in the New South: Georgia and Virginia, 1880–1930* (Urbana: University of Illinois Press, 1993), 36.

52. See Hale, *Making Whiteness*.

53. See Patterson, *Rituals of Blood*.

54. According to Grace Hale, "Spectacle lynchings brutally conjured a collective, all-powerful whiteness even as they made the color line seem modern, civilized and sane. Spectacle lynchings were about making racial difference in the new South, about ensuring the separation of all southern life into whiteness and blackness." *Making Whiteness*, 203. She notes that "by the late 1930s representations of lynchings worked almost as well as lynching themselves." Ibid., 227.

55. For a thorough discussion of how whites portrayed blacks as sexually aggressive in the nineteenth century, see Winthrop D. Jordan, *The White Man's Burden: Historical Origins of Racism in the United States* (New York: New York University Press, 1974). On the creation of the "black beast rapist" myth, see Hall, "'The Mind That Burns,'"; and Martha Hodes, "The Sexualization of Reconstruction Politics: White Women and Black Men in the South after the Civil War," *Journal of the History of Sexuality* 3 (1992): 402–17.

56. Bederman, *Manliness and Civilization*, 46.

57. Hall, "'The Mind That Burns,'" 335.

58. Historian Vron Ware writes, "The rest of the country condoned lynching because of a readiness to believe that it was a spontaneous outburst of revenge against black rapists and child molesters." See *Beyond the Pale: White Women, Racism, and History* (New York: Verso, 1992), 181.

59. See Barbara Holden-Smith, "Lynching, Federalism, and the Intersection of

Race and Gender in the Progressive Era," *Yale Journal of Law and Feminism* 31 (1996): 31–78.

60. Cited in Williamson, *Crucible of Race,* 128.

61. On Felton's racism, see Williamson, *Crucible of Race,* 124–30. Felton's crusade against black rapists elicited surprisingly strong support from northerners as women's rights activists in the North fanned the fears about dangerous African American men. Frances Willard, president of the WCTU, refused to issue a formal denunciation against lynching for several years, citing the danger African American men posed to white women. Carrie Chapman Catt, president of the International Woman Suffrage Alliance, compared organized prostitution in India and South Africa to the threat posed by African Americans in the United States. In a letter to John D. Rockefeller Jr., she said, "White women are actually sold to the Kaffirs of that country [South Africa], with the result that the Kaffirs who have always respected the virtue of their own women are assaulting and raping white women here and there as the negroes do in our own South." See Carrie Chapman Catt to John D. Rockefeller Jr. (JDR Jr.), July 21, 1911, Record Group (RG) 2, box 10, folder 87, Rockefeller Boards, Rockefeller Family Archives, Rockefeller Archive Center (RAC), Sleepy Hollow, New York. On Willard's reluctance to condemn lynching, see Bederman, *Manliness and Civilization,* 65–67; and Glenda Elizabeth Gilmore, *Gender and Jim Crow: Women and the Politics of White Supremacy in North Carolina, 1896–1920* (Chapel Hill: University of North Carolina Press, 1996), 46–47.

62. See George M. Fredrickson, *The Black Image in the White Mind: The Debate on Afro-American Character and Destiny, 1817–1914* (New York: Harper and Row, 1971); and Jordan, *White Man's Burden.* See also Jacobson, *Whiteness of a Different Color.*

63. Jacobson, *Whiteness of a Different Color.*

64. Ignatiev, *How the Irish Became White.*

65. Jacobson, *Whiteness of a Different Color,* 176, 172.

66. Ibid., 7.

Chapter 2: The New Abolitionism

1. The most prolific white slavery authors led, or were important members of, various anti-vice and reform organizations. Clifford Roe, author of three white slavery books, was the executive secretary of the American Vigilance Association. Ernest Bell, who wrote the immensely popular *Fighting the Traffic in Young Girls,* was president of the Midnight Mission. Rev. F. M. Lehman and Rev. N. K. Clarkson, authors of *White Slave Hell,* were members of both the Midnight Mission and the White Cross Society. Edward O. Janney, author of *The White Slave Traffic in America,* acted as chairman of the National Committee for the Suppression of the White Slave Traffic and later as an executive officer of the American Vigilance Association. Norine Law wrote *Shame of a Great Nation* as a representative of the American Purity Federation. As the following chapters will show, these reformers and their organizations played a critical role in the national fight against white slavery.

2. For books that focus on a single white slave victim, see Virginia Brooks, *My Battles with Vice* (New York: Macauley, 1915), and *Little Lost Sister* (Chicago: Gazzolo and Ricksen, 1914); Guy Phelps, *Ethel Vale the White Slave* (Chicago: Christian Witness, 1910); and Clifford Roe, *The Girl Who Disappeared* (Naperville: World's Purity Federation, 1914). Books that include several white slavery stories include John Abbot, *The "White Slave" Traffic and the Social Evil* (Milwaukee: Pollworth Press, 1910); Jane Addams, *A New Conscience and an Ancient Evil* (New York: Macmillan, 1912); Ernest Bell, *Fighting the Traffic in Young Girls* (Chicago: G. S. Ball, 1910); Theodore Bingham, *The Girl That Disappears: The Real Facts about the White Slave Trade* (Boston: Gorham Press, 1911); Sidney Kendall, *The Soundings of Hell* (Los Angeles: Charlton Edholm, 1903); Herr Glessner Creel, *Prostitution for Profit: A Police Reporter's View of the White Slave Traffic* (St. Louis: National Rip-Saw Publishing, 1911); John Dillon, *From Dance Hall to White Slavery* (Chicago: C. C. Thompson, 1912); Elizabeth Goodnow, *The Market for Souls* (New York: Mitchell Kennerley, 1912); Leona Prall Groetzinger, *The City's Perils* ([Chicago?]: s.n., 1912); Robert Harland, *The Vice Bondage of a Great City or the Wickedest City in the World* (Chicago: Young People's Civic League, 1912); Edward O. Janney, *The White Slave Traffic in America* (Baltimore: The Lord Baltimore Press, 1911); F. M. Lehman and N. K. Clarkson, *The White Slave Hell, or With Christ at Midnight in the Slums of Chicago* (Chicago: The Christian Witness Company, 1910); H. M. Lytle, *Tragedies of the White Slaves* (Chicago: C. C. Thompson, 1910); Charles Locke, *White Slavery in Los Angeles* (Los Angeles: Times Mirror, 1913); Robert Moorehead, *Fighting the Devil's Triple Demons* (Philadelphia: National Publishing Company, 1911); Samuel Paynter Wilson, *Chicago and Its Cess-Pools of Infamy* (1910); C. C. Quale, *Thrilling Stories of White Slavery* (Chicago: Hamming, 1912); Clifford Roe, *Panders and Their White Slaves* (New York: Fleming H. Revell, 1910), and *Horrors of the White Slave Trade* (London: Stationers Hall, 1911); Madeline M. Southard, *The White Slave Traffic versus the American Home* (Louisville: Pentecostal Publishing, 1914); and Jean Turner Zimmermann, *Chicago's Black Traffic in White Girls* (Chicago: Chicago Rescue Mission, 1910), and *White or Yellow? A Story of America's Great White Slave Trade with Asia* (Chicago: Zimmermann, 1916).

3. For analyses of the role of captivity narratives in U.S. history, see Christopher Castiglia, *Bound and Determined* (Chicago: University of Chicago Press, 1996); and Richard Slotkin, *Regeneration through Violence: The Mythology of the American Frontier, 1600–1860* (Middletown: Wesleyan University Press, 1973). Frederick Grittner notes that the American captivity genre also employed anti-Catholic and anti-Mormon themes. For his analysis of white slavery narratives as a representation of the captivity genre, see *White Slavery: Myth, Ideology, and American Law* (New York: Garland, 1990), 15–37.

4. Castiglia, *Bound and Determined*; Slotkin, *Regeneration through Violence*.

5. See Mary Odem, *Delinquent Daughters: Policing Adolescent Female Sexuality in the United States, 1885–1920* (Chapel Hill: University of North Carolina Press, 1995), 16–20. Reformers considered seduction a central cause of prostitution. See Patricia

Cline Cohen, *The Murder of Helen Jewett* (New York: Vintage, 1998), 405–6; and Barbara Meil Hobson, *Uneasy Virtue: The Politics of Prostitution and the American Reform Tradition* (Chicago: University of Chicago Press, 1997), 56–66.

6. Jane Larson argues that "the topic of seduction allowed them to openly criticize the dominant construction of gender and sexuality in their societies." See "'Women Understand So Little, They Call My Good Nature "Deceit"': A Feminist Rethinking of Seduction," *Columbia Law Review* (March 1993): 378.

7. For an analysis of the creation and implementation of state anti-seduction laws, see Pamela Haag, *Consent: Sexual Rights and the Transformation of American Liberalism* (Ithaca: Cornell University Press, 1999); Larson, "'Women Understand So Little,'"; Lea VanderVelde, "The Legal Ways of Seduction," *Stanford Law Review* 48 (1996): 818–901; and Larry Whiteaker, *Seduction, Prostitution, and Moral Reform in New York, 1830–1860* (New York: Garland, 1997). For analysis of purity crusades as a strategy of conservative social control, see Carol DuBois and Linda Gordon, "Seeking Ecstasy on the Battlefield: Danger and Pleasure in Nineteenth-Century Feminist Sexual Thought," in *Pleasure and Danger: Exploring Female Sexuality,* ed. Carole S. Vance (London: Pandora Press, 1989), 31–49; Odem, *Delinquent Daughters;* and Suzanne Marilley, "Frances Willard and the Feminism of Fear," *Feminist Studies* 19 (1993): 123–45. For a valuable description of different strands of feminist thinking in Victorian social reform, see Elizabeth Pleck, "Feminist Responses to 'Crimes against Women,' 1868–1896," *Signs* 8 (1983): 451–70.

8. Timothy Gilfoyle, *City of Eros: New York City, Prostitution, and the Commercialization of Sex, 1790–1920* (New York: Norton, 1992), 274.

9. See David Roediger, *The Wages of Whiteness: Race and the Making of the American Working Class* (New York: Verso, 1991), 66–74.

10. Edward Bristow, *Prostitution and Prejudice: The Jewish Fight against White Slavery, 1870–1939* (New York: Schocken Books, 1982), 36.

11. F. G. Tyrrell, *The Shame of the Human Race: The White Slave Traffic* (St. Louis: National Rip-Saw Publishing, 1908).

12. Norine Law, *The Shame of a Great Nation: The Story of the "White Slave Trade"* (Harrisburg: United Evangelical Publishing House, 1909), 118.

13. Bingham, *Girl That Disappears,* 15.

14. Cited in David Pivar, *Purity and Hygiene: Women, Prostitution and the 'American Plan,' 1900–1930* (Westport, Conn.: Greenwood Press, 2002), 83.

15. Groetzinger, *City's Perils,* 1.

16. Charlton Edholm, *Traffic in Girls and Work in Rescue Missions* (1899), 13.

17. Lytle, *Tragedies of the White Slaves,* 1.

18. J. Dillon, *From Dance Hall to White Slavery,* 8.

19. Many regard the Progressive Era reaction to white slavery as a definitive moral panic. The moral panic concept accounts for exaggerated reactions to putative social problems. For an interpretation of anti-vice activism as a moral panic, see Mary deYoung, "Help, I'm Being Held Captive: The White Slave Fairy Tale of the Pro-

gressive Era," *Journal of American Culture* 6 (1983): 96–99; Jo Doezema, "Loose Women or Lost Women?: The Re-emergence of the Myth of White Slavery in Contemporary Discourses of Trafficking in Women," *Gender Issues* 18 (2000): 23–50; Grittner, *White Slavery;* David Langum, *Crossing the Line: Legislating Morality and the Mann Act* (Chicago: University of Chicago Press, 1994); and M. Joan McDermott and Sarah Blackstone, "White Slavery Plays of the 1910s: Fear of Victimization and the Social Control of Sexuality," *Theatre History Studies* 16 (1996): 141–56. Some have questioned the utility of the concept in explaining the reaction to forced prostitution. For instance, Ruth Rosen suggests that sensationalized accounts of white slavery wrongly undermined the credibility of genuine victims of the practice. Based on vice commission data, she estimates that upwards of 10 percent of brothel inmates were coerced into prostitution. She concludes, "There is strong evidence of a white slave trade and its operations." See *The Lost Sisterhood: Prostitution in America 1900–1918* (Baltimore: Johns Hopkins University Press, 1982), 125, 133. Others have criticized moral panic research for its polemic quality and conceptual fuzziness. See Benjamin Cornwell and Annulla Linders, "The Myth of 'Moral Panic': An Alternative Account of LSD Prohibition," *Deviant Behavior* 23 (2002): 307–30; Alan Hunt, "Anxiety and Social Explanation: Some Anxieties about Anxiety," *Journal of Social History* 32 (1999): 509–28; Sheldon Ungar, "Moral Panic versus the Risk Society: The Implication of the Changing Sites of Social Anxiety," *British Journal of Sociology* 52 (2001): 271–91; and P. A. Waddington, "Mugging as a Moral Panic: A Question of Proportion," *British Journal of Sociology* 37 (1986): 245–59. In countering the moral panic account of Progressive Era white slavery campaigns, Barbara Hobson contends, "To view antiprostitution as a psychological clearinghouse for a host of social disorders is to discount the economic and social problems reformers were addressing." See *Uneasy Virtue,* 140.

20. Bingham, *Girl That Disappears,* 5.

21. See Gilfoyle, *City of Eros,* 259–69; Hobson, *Uneasy Virtue,* 141–47; and Rosen, *Lost Sisterhood.*

22. Janney, *White Slave Traffic,* 13.

23. Bell, *Fighting the Traffic,* 14.

24. Law, *Shame of a Great Nation,* 184.

25. Ibid., 138.

26. Lehman and Clarkson, *White Slave Hell,* 150.

27. Bell, *Fighting the Traffic,* 215–16.

28. Ibid., 268.

29. Ibid., 285.

30. From 1860 to 1910, the number of people living in municipalities of 2,500 people or more grew from approximately 6.2 million to approximately 44 million. Charles Glabb and Theodore Brown, *A History of Urban America* (New York: Macmillan, 1976).

31. For a discussion of the connection between the white slavery genre and ur-

banization, see Mark Connelly, *The Response to Prostitution in the Progressive Era* (Chapel Hill: University of North Carolina Press, 1980).

32. On the role of confidence men in American culture, see Karen Halttunen, *Confidence Men and Painted Women: A Study of Middle-Class Culture in America, 1830–1870* (New Haven: Yale University Press, 1982).

33. Reginald Wright Kauffman, *The House of Bondage* (New York: Moffat, Yard and Company, 1910).

34. Ibid., 21.

35. Lehman and Clarkson, *White Slave Hell*, 55.

36. Ibid., 64.

37. Lytle, *Tragedies of the White Slaves*, 70.

38. Ibid., 71.

39. See Kathy Peiss, *Cheap Amusements: Working Women and Leisure in New York City, 1880–1920* (Philadelphia: Temple University Press, 1986).

40. Lehman and Clarkson, *White Slave Hell*, 369. The image of the octopus as a sprawling menace echoes Frank Norris's *Octopus: A Story of California* where he describes the exploitation of farmers at the hands of a giant railroad conglomerate. White slavery narratives embodied a critique of big business and monopoly capitalism. For an analysis of white slavery crusades as a critique of the "Money Trust," see Mara Keire, "The Vice Trust: A Reinterpretation of the White Slavery Scare in the United States, 1970–1914," *Journal of Social History* 35 (2001): 5–41.

41. Lehman and Clarkson, *White Slave Hell*, 125.

42. Law, *Shame of a Great Nation*, 192.

43. Bell, *Fighting the Traffic*, 283.

44. Cited in ibid., 112.

45. Roe, *Panders*, 92.

46. Ibid., 80.

47. Lehman and Clarkson, *White Slave Hell*, 185.

48. See Bell, *Fighting the Traffic*, 69; Law, *Shame of a Great Nation*, 159; Lehman and Clarkson, *White Slave Hell*, 184; and S. P. Wilson, *Chicago and Its Cess-Pools of Infamy*, 84–85.

49. Law, *Shame of a Great Nation*, 117.

50. Bell, *Fighting the Traffic*, 53–54; Law, *Shame of a Great Nation*, 111; S. P. Wilson, *Chicago and Its Cess-Pools of Infamy*, 64.

51. Cited in Bell, *Fighting the Traffic*, 16.

52. Law, *Shame of a Great Nation*.

53. A classic study of U.S. immigration history is John Higham, *Strangers in the Land: Patterns of American Nativism, 1860–1925* (New York: Atheneum, 1963), originally published in 1955. See also Ronald Takaki, *Iron Cages: Race and Culture in 19th-Century America* (Oxford: Oxford University Press, 1990). Commenting on the creation of the U.S. Immigration Commission in the 1900s, Stanley Lieberson notes, "Freely using the term 'race' to refer to a variety of specific groups, the commission

concluded that the various European groups could be ranked superior or inferior in terms of their inherent biological capacity." *A Piece of the Pie: Blacks and White Immigrants since 1880* (Berkeley: University of California Press, 1980), 25.

54. Lehman and Clarkson, *White Slave Hell*, 127.

55. Edward Bristow argues that the targeting of Jews as white slave traders prompted members of the Jewish community to take an active role in reform efforts aimed at eliminating forced prostitution. See *Prostitution and Prejudice.*

56. S. P. Wilson, *Chicago and Its Cess-Pools of Infamy*, 45.

57. Kevin Mumford, *Interzones: Black/White Sex Districts in Chicago and New York in the Early Twentieth Century* (New York: Columbia University Press, 1997).

58. S. P. Wilson, *Chicago and Its Cess-Pools of Infamy*, 51.

59. Bell, *Fighting the Traffic*, 25.

60. Ibid., 26.

61. Ibid., 274.

62. Madeline M. Southard, *The White Slave Traffic versus the American Home* (Louisville: Pentecostal Publishing, 1914), 10.

63. Zimmermann, *Chicago's Black Traffic.*

64. Ernest Bell Papers, box 4, folder 7, Chicago Historical Society.

65. Bell wrote, "The American people have never been so aroused and alarmed against the black traffic in white girls as they are at present." See *Union Signal*, August 4, 1910, 3.

66. Elizabeth Andrew and Katharine Bushnell, *Heathen Slaves and Christian Rulers* (Oakland: Messiah's Advocate, 1907), iv.

67. *Union Signal*, August 13, 1908, 2.

68. Law, *Shame of a Great Nation*, 164.

69. Tyrrell, *Shame of the Human Race*, 20.

70. Cited in Law, *Shame of a Great Nation*, 107; Groetzinger, *City's Perils*, 52; S. P. Wilson, *Chicago and Its Cess-Pools of Infamy*, 59; and *The Dangers of a Large City* (n.p., 1912), 15.

71. Locke, *White Slavery in Los Angeles*, 9.

72. Cited in Law, *Shame of a Great Nation*, 143.

73. *Chicago Tribune*, October 17, 1909, 4; *Dangers of a Large City*, 19.

74. S. P. Wilson, *Chicago and Its Cess-Pools of Infamy*, 47.

75. *The Light*, November 1910, 48.

76. Lehman and Clarkson, *White Slave Hell*, 128.

77. Ibid., 71.

78. *Union Signal*, April 22, 1909, 9.

79. Ibid., February 21, 1889, 8.

80. Ibid., April 22, 1909, 9.

81. Addams, *A New Conscience*, 4.

82. Olive Bell Daniels, *From the Epic of Chicago: A Biography, Ernest A. Bell, 1865–1928* (Menasha, Wisc.: George Banta Publishing Company, 1932), 56.

83. The American Purity Federation of Chicago merged with the American Purity Alliance from New York to form the National Vigilance Committee. See Pivar, *Purity and Hygiene*, 76–77.

84. *Union Signal*, October 18, 1906, 2.

85. Ibid., February 18, 1909, 3.

86. Ibid., 13.

87. See Judith Walkowitz, *City of Dreadful Delight: Narratives of Sexual Danger in Late-Victorian London* (Chicago: University of Chicago Press, 1992), 96.

88. Addams, *A New Conscience*, xi.

89. Frances Willard, *Glimpses of Fifty Years* (Chicago: Woman's Temperance Publication Association, 1889), 425.

90. Odem, *Delinquent Daughters*.

91. Cleveland Dodge to JDR Jr., January 19, 1911, RG 2, box 10, folder 86, Rockefeller Boards, Rockefeller Family Archives, RAC.

92. J. P. Morgan to JDR Jr., December 17, 1910, RG 2, box 10, folder 85, Rockefeller Boards, Rockefeller Family Archives, RAC. Historians of prostitution tend to agree that *The House of Bondage* was one of the most influential books of the white slavery genre. *The House of Bondage* went through sixteen editions in the two years after its publication. Rosen argues that the book "gained significant public attention." *Lost Sisterhood*, 114. Grittner notes, "*The House of Bondage*, Kauffman's white slave novel, had the greatest impact during the years of the panic." *White Slavery*, 109. Langum writes, "An entire genre developed around white slavery. . . . The best known was Reginald W. Kauffman's *The House of Bondage*." *Crossing the Line*, 33.

93. Stanley Fish, *Is There a Text in This Class? The Authority of Interpretive Communities* (Cambridge: Harvard University Press, 1980); Janice Radway, "Interpretive Communities and Variable Literacies: The Functions of Romance Reading," in *Rethinking Popular Culture: Contemporary Perspectives in Cultural Studies*, ed. Chandra Mukerji and Michael Schudson (Berkeley: University of California Press, 1991), 465–86, and *Reading the Romance: Women, Patriarchy, and Popular Literature* (Chapel Hill: University of North Carolina Press, 1984); JoEllen Shively, "Perceptions of Western Films among American Indians and Anglos," *American Sociological Review* 57 (1992): 709–24.

94. According to Wendy Griswold, the capacity for multivocality gives certain literary works "cultural power." "Fabrication of Meaning: Literary Interpretation in the United States, Great Britain, and West Indies," *American Journal of Sociology* 92 (1987): 1077–117. Cultural power pivots on the question of function as well as meaning. Just as some cultural objects have a greater carrying capacity for meaning, some allow for a wider range of personal and social uses. For example, Janice Radway has shown in *Reading the Romance* how middle-class women use romance novels to carve out a private space and to escape domestic stress. Similarly, social movement scholars have demonstrated that some stories are more effective than others in recruiting and rousing activists. James Jasper argues that effective narratives produced by social move-

ment leaders are often crafted to produce a "moral shock." *The Art of Moral Protest* (Chicago: University of Chicago Press, 1997), 159–62.

Chapter 3: Suffrage and Slavery

1. Paula Baker, "The Domestication of Politics: Women and American Political Society, 1780–1920," *American Historical Review* 89 (June 1984): 620–47. Louise Newman argues, "Anglo-American female activists proudly took credit for the importance of the domestic sphere (even as they critiqued it as too restrictive), using it as a locus from which to demand an expansion in political rights for themselves." *White Women's Rights: The Racial Origins of Feminism in the United States* (Oxford: Oxford University Press, 1999), 14. According to Nancy Cott, "The positive contribution of passionlessness was to replace that sexual/carnal characterization of women with a spiritual/moral one, allowing women to develop their human faculties and their self-esteem. The belief that women lacked carnal motivation was the cornerstone of the argument for women's moral superiority, used to enhance women's status and widen their opportunities in the nineteenth century." "Passionlessness: An Interpretation of Victorian Sexual Ideology, 1790–1850," *Signs* 21 (1978): 233. Theda Skocpol argues that "arguments based on notions of women's special morality, accepted by most Americans of both genders, did much to shape public opinion and legislative agendas in the early twentieth century." *Protecting Soldiers and Mothers: The Political Origins of Social Policy in the United States* (Cambridge: Harvard University Press, 1992), 21.

2. Barbara Welter, "The Cult of True Womanhood: 1820–1860," *American Quarterly* 18 (Summer 1966): 151–74. Some feminist historians have suggested that Welter's idea of "the cult of true womanhood" is too often used to describe lived reality of Victorian women. Instead, the cult of true womanhood stands as a set of normative prescriptions that were often contested. Nancy Hewitt, "Taking the True Woman Hostage," *Journal of Women's History* 14 (Spring 2002): 156–62; Mary Louise Roberts, "True Womanhood Revisited," *Journal of Women's History* 14 (Spring 2002): 150–53; Christina Simmons, "Modern Sexuality and the Myth of Victorian Repression," in *Gender and American History since 1890*, ed. Barbara Melosh (New York: Routledge, 1993), 17–42.

3. Baker, "Domestication of Politics."

4. Suzanne Marilley, "Frances Willard and the Feminism of Fear," *Feminist Studies* 19 (1993): 123–45.

5. Philip N. Cohen, "Nationalism and Suffrage: Gender Struggle in Nation-Building America," *Signs* 21 (1996): 707–27; Angela Y. Davis, *Women, Race, and Class* (New York: Vintage Books, 1981); Paula Giddings, *When and Where I Enter: The Impact of Black Women on Race and Sex in America* (New York: Bantam, 1984); Newman, *White Women's Rights*.

6. William T. Stead, *The Maiden Tribute of Modern Babylon (The Report of the "Pall Mall Gazette's" Secret Commission)* (London: Pall Mall Gazette, 1885).

7. Edward Bristow, *Vice and Vigilance: Purity Movements in Britain since 1700* (Dublin: Gill and Macmillan, 1977), 111.

8. Judith Walkowitz, *City of Dreadful Delight: Narratives of Sexual Danger in Late-Victorian London* (Chicago: University of Chicago Press, 1992), 104. See also Bristow, *Vice and Vigilance.*

9. Bristow observes that "the Criminal Law Amendment Act was a symbolic and substantial triumph for feminists and puritans. They looked to the events of the year as a turning point in the history of morals and as an example of how women might cleanse society." *Vice and Vigilance,* 114.

10. Frances Willard, "President's Annual Address," in *Minutes of the Seventeenth Annual Meeting of the National Woman's Christian Temperance Union* (Chicago: Woman's Temperance Publication Association, 1889), 19.

11. Willard wrote: "In 1885, in common with all thoughtful women who read newspapers, I was profoundly stirred by the revelations in England, the sequel of which was such legislation for the protection of woman as the world has never known. William T. Stead became, as he must ever continue, a hero in my eyes, and in my annual address in the autumn of that year in Philadelphia, as President of the National W.C.T.U., I earnestly urged upon the women the necessity of a new departure which should incorporate work for the promotion of social purity as an organized feature in the broad plans of our society." Frances Willard, *A White Life for Two* (Chicago: Woman's Temperance Publication Association, 1890), 6. For an insightful account of the WCTU's broad efforts to promote moral purity and, as a consequence, censorship, see Kathleen M. Parker, *Purifying America: Women, Cultural Reform, and Pro-censorship Activism, 1873–1933* (Urbana: University of Illinois Press, 1997).

For the sake of consistency, I will refer to the department as the Department of Social Purity, but the name changed over the years. In 1885, the WCTU changed the "Department for the Suppression of the Social Evil" to the "Department of Social Purity." In 1888, the name changed to the "Department of the White Cross and White Shield," mirroring the name of the then-prominent British purity organization. Beginning in 1892, Dr. Rose Woodallen Chapman became superintendent of the department and changed its name to the "Department of Purity." See "Course of Study for Local Unions: Evolution of Departments, 1882–83," *Union Signal,* May 24, 1906, 14.

12. Willard viewed the creation of anti-vice laws as the responsibility of like-minded men. She advocated the creation of a male Vigilance Association modeled after the National Vigilance Committee in England. Willard stated that "there is a need in this country of the organization of a Vigilance Committee, composed of men, similar to the one in operation in England. The duty of this organization would be the proper enforcement of laws against criminal vice and public immorality of all kinds. This Committee would be to the cause of Social Purity what a Citizens' League is to temperance work." Frances Willard, "President's Annual Address," in *Minutes of the Fourteenth Annual Meeting of the National Woman's Christian Temperance Union* (Chicago: Woman's Temperance Publication Association, 1886), xxxvii.

Willard's idea came to fruition with the creation of the American Vigilance Association in 1910.

13. Mary Odem, *Delinquent Daughters: Policing Adolescent Female Sexuality in the United States, 1885–1920* (Chapel Hill: University of North Carolina Press, 1995), 14–15. See also Jane Larson, "'Even a Worm Will Turn at Last': Rape Reform in Late Nineteenth-Century America," *Yale Journal of Law and the Humanities* 9 (1997): 1–71. Larson convincingly shows how the WCTU's efforts to raise the age of consent functioned as a "back door" strategy that effectively attacked a range of sex crimes, including rape and incest (46). She contends that "the scope of rape reform aspired to by these early reformers was almost as sweeping as that eventually accomplished by the modern rape reform movement almost a century later" (19).

14. William Beatty, "Katharine C. Bushnell, M.D.—Evangelist and Investigator," *Union Signal,* July–September 1997, 13–19; Dana Hardwick, "Man's Prattle, Woman's Word," in *Spirituality and Social Responsibility: Vocational Vision of Women in the United Methodist Tradition,* ed. R. S. Keller, (Nashville: Abingdon Press, 1993), 165–84.

15. Jeremy Kilar, *Michigan's Lumbertowns: Lumbermen and Laborers in Saginaw, Bay City, and Muskegon, 1870–1905* (Detroit: Wayne State University Press, 1990).

16. Ibid.

17. *Union Signal,* February 17, 1887, 9.

18. Kilar, *Michigan's Lumbertowns.*

19. Ibid.

20. Ibid.

21. Katharine Bushnell, *Dr. Katharine C. Bushnell: A Brief Sketch of Her Life Work* (Hertford, England: Rose and Sons, 1932), 5.

22. *Union Signal,* November 8, 1888, 4.

23. Hardwick, "Man's Prattle, Woman's Word."

24. *Union Signal,* February 17, 1887, 8.

25. Ibid, 9.

26. Ibid.

27. Ibid.

28. Ibid.

29. Odem, *Delinquent Daughters,* 11; Parker, *Purifying America,* 10, 103. For a discussion of the concerns of the White Cross Society, see David Pivar, *Purity Crusade: Sexual Morality and Social Control, 1868–1900* (Westport, Conn.: Greenwood Press, 1973).

30. *Union Signal,* December 3, 1903, 4.

31. Ibid., May 6, 1905, 10.

32. Ibid., November 29, 1906, 13.

33. *Minutes of the Seventeenth Annual Meeting of the National Woman's Christian Temperance Union* (Chicago: Woman's Temperance Publication Association, 1889), cclvii.

34. *Union Signal,* February 21, 1889, 8.

35. Ibid., January 10, 1889, 1.

36. Bushnell, *Dr. Katharine C. Bushnell*, 6.

37. On the National WCTU's influence abroad, see Barbara Epstein, *Woman's World/Woman's Empire: The Woman's Christian Temperance Union in International Perspective, 1880–1930* (Chapel Hill: University of North Carolina Press, 1991).

38. Bushnell, *Dr. Katharine C. Bushnell*, 2.

39. Ruth Bordin, *Woman and Temperance: The Quest for Power and Liberty, 1873–1900* (New Brunswick: Rutgers University Press, 1981); Barbara Epstein, *The Politics of Domesticity: Women, Evangelism and Temperance in Nineteenth Century America* (Middletown, Conn.: Wesleyan University Press, 1986); Joseph Gusfield, *Symbolic Crusade: Status Politics and the American Temperance Movement* (Urbana: University of Illinois Press, 1966), 76–93; Carolyn De Swarte Gifford, *Writing Out My Heart: Selections from the Journal of Frances E. Willard, 1855–96* (Urbana: University of Illinois Press, 1995), 7–14.

40. According to Marilley, "Winning the vote and sustaining organized political action became more immediate goals for self-protection than even prohibitionary laws." "Frances Willard and the Feminism of Fear," 134.

41. Gusfield, *Symbolic Crusade*.

42. Glenda Elizabeth Gilmore, *Gender and Jim Crow: Women and the Politics of White Supremacy in North Carolina, 1896–1920* (Chapel Hill: University of North Carolina Press, 1996).

43. Cited in Anna Gordon, *Frances E. Willard: A Memorial Volume* (Chicago: Woman's Temperance Publishing Association, 1898), 73.

44. Cited in Gifford, *Writing Out My Heart*, 307.

45. Ibid., 308.

46. Ibid., 306–7.

47. Ibid., 271–77.

48. Gordon, *Frances E. Willard*, 44–91.

49. Willard, "President's Annual Address," in *Minutes of the Seventeenth Annual Meeting*, 94.

50. Willard successfully used "home protection" discourse to mobilize middle-class white women. Willard argued that women's capacity for motherhood gave them moral authority that justified their political participation. She typically began her essays and speeches by focusing on the evils of drinking, but after capturing the attention of her audience, she shifted away from temperance to discuss voting and lobbying. See Marilley, "Frances Willard and the Feminism of Fear."

51. Willard, *White Life for Two*, 13.

52. Willard, "President's Annual Address," in *Minutes of the Fourteenth Annual Meeting*, 78.

53. Willard, "President's Annual Address," in *Minutes of the Seventeenth Annual Meeting*, 426.

54. Gail Bederman, *Manliness and Civilization: A Cultural History of Gender and Race in the United States, 1880–1917* (Chicago: University of Chicago Press, 1995).

55. Its size and diversity limit generalizations about a single racial ideology of the WCTU. Although the evidence presented here reveals the Anglo-Saxon nativism of its national leadership, the dominant racial ideology of the WCTU competed with other ideas within the organization. African American workers in the WCTU criticized both "white men" and "Anglo-Saxon men" for their sex crimes. For instance, National Superintendent Frances Harper openly charged white men with raping African American women. She also challenged white women's refusal to confront the sex crimes wrought by their husbands and sons. See Leslie K. Dunlap, "The Reform of Rape Law and the Problem of White Men: Age of Consent Campaigns in the South, 1885–1910," in *Sex, Love, Race: Crossing Boundaries in North American History,* ed. Martha Hodes (New York: New York University Press, 1999).

56. Willard, *White Life for Two,* 10.

57. *Union Signal,* August 1, 1901, 8.

58. George Wharton James, *Chicago's Dark Places: Investigations by a Corps of Specially Appointed Commissioners* (Chicago: The Craig Press and the Woman's Temperance Publishing Association, 1891), 132.

59. Frances Willard, *Glimpses of Fifty Years* (Chicago: Woman's Temperance Publication Association, 1889), 422. The WCTU firmly opposed the regulation of prostitution because it entailed regular medical inspections of impoverished women. Not only did this represent the tacit acceptance of prostitution, but it also gave state approval for the sexual double standard. Moreover, proposals to regulate prostitution made working-class women subject to humiliating inspections. In the late nineteenth century, reformers defeated vice regulation in New York, Chicago, San Francisco, and Philadelphia. For an analysis of the debate between those favoring regulation of prostitution and those favoring its abolition, see David Pivar, *Purity and Hygiene: Women, Prostitution and the 'American Plan,' 1900–1930* (Westport, Conn.: Greenwood Press, 2002).

60. Cynthia Blair, "Vicious Commerce: African American Women's Sex Work and the Transformation of Urban Space in Chicago, 1850–1915" (doctoral dissertation, Harvard University, 1999); Kevin Mumford, *Interzones: Black/White Sex Districts in Chicago and New York in the Early Twentieth Century* (New York: Columbia University Press, 1997); Thomas Lee Philpott, *The Slum and the Ghetto: Immigrants, Blacks, and Reformers in Chicago, 1880–1930* (Belmont: Wadsworth, 1991).

61. James, *Chicago's Dark Places,* 92.

62. Ibid., 98.

63. Ibid., 102.

64. Ibid., 102.

65. Ibid.

66. Ibid., 140.

67. Ibid.

68. Cited in Ida B. Wells, *A Red Record: Tabulated Statistics and Alleged Causes of Lynching in the United States, 1892–1894* (Chicago: Donohue and Henneberry, 1894), 59.

69. Ibid., 59. Gilmore has persuasively shown that Wells publicly criticized Willard, not because she was the most blatant fount of white racism but because she had a history of interracial cooperation. See *Gender and Jim Crow,* 56–57.

70. Bederman, *Manliness and Civilization,* 256.

71. Frances Willard, "President's Annual Address," in *Minutes of the Twelfth Annual Meeting of the National Woman's Christian Temperance Union* (Chicago: Woman's Temperance Publication Association, 1894), 130.

72. Cited in Wells, *Red Record,* 87.

73. Gilmore, *Gender and Jim Crow,* 58–59.

74. From the *Union Signal,* December 6, 1894, cited in Wells, *Red Record,* 87.

75. Gilmore, *Gender and Jim Crow.*

76. Odem, *Delinquent Daughters.*

77. See Gilmore, *Gender and Jim Crow,* 59. Gilmore concludes, "For the next few years, temperance, which had once held such promise for interracial understanding, would serve white supremacy."

78. Aaron Powell, ed., *The National Purity Congress: Its Papers, Addresses, and Portraits* (New York: The American Purity Alliance, 1896).

79. *Union Signal,* July 14, 1910, 10.

80. Ibid., November 11, 1909, 10.

81. Lillian Stevens, "President's Annual Address," in *Minutes of the Twenty-ninth Annual Meeting of the National Woman's Christian Temperance Union* (Chicago: Woman's Temperance Publication Association, 1910), 100.

82. *Union Signal,* January 17, 1907, 10.

83. *Minutes of the Twenty-eighth Annual Meeting of the National Woman's Christian Temperance Union* (Chicago: Woman's Temperance Publication Association, 1909), 329.

84. William Ferguson, "A Study of Social Vice," *Union Signal,* November 2, 1899, 3.

85. Thacher wrote:

> The immigrants during the years from June 30, 1900, to June 30, 1907, inclusive, numbered 6,667,732. Two immigrants every minute for the last seven years! It is well known that the families of foreigners increase very rapidly, so it is safe to say that this enormous number has at least doubled itself already. Thirteen and a half million out of a possible population of ninety million! In this proportion there are only seven native born Americans, with all their intelligence, high ideals, pure morals and consecrated Christianity to work with each foreigner to lift him out of his ignorance, his poverty, his lack of ambition, his low moral condition!

See *Minutes of the Twenty-sixth Annual Meeting of the National Woman's Christian Temperance Union* (Chicago: Woman's Temperance Publication Association, 1907), 215.

86. *Union Signal,* November 4, 1909, 4.

87. Ibid., May 19, 1910, 3.

88. Paul Boyer makes a useful distinction between environmental and coercive reform. *Urban Masses and Moral Order in America, 1820–1920* (Cambridge: Harvard University Press, 1992), 175–91. I will suggest in the next chapter that environmental and coercive anti-vice strategies align with pluralist and nativist racial ideologies respectively. For a critique of Boyer and a discussion of how environmental and coercive strategies overlap, see Odem, *Delinquent Daughters*, 108–10, 211 n. 39.

89. Marilley, "Frances Willard and the Feminism of Fear," 140.

Chapter 4: "The Black Traffic in White Girls"

1. Racial and ethnic pluralism denotes an acceptance of a multicultural society in civic, religious, and educational institutions. For a thorough discussion of the limits of Jane Addams's pluralist vision, see Rivka Shpak Lissak, *Pluralism and Progressivism: Hull House and the New Immigrants, 1890–1919* (Chicago: University of Chicago Press, 1989); and Elisabeth Lasch-Quinn, *Black Neighbors: Race and the Limits of Reform in the American Settlement House Movement, 1980–1945* (Chapel Hill: University of North Carolina Press, 1993).

2. In Chicago, the female labor force increased from 35,600 to 407,600 from 1880 to 1930, mirroring national trends in the expanding female labor force. Many of these women lived apart from their families and relatives. See Joanne Meyerowitz, *Women Adrift: Independent Wage Earners in Chicago, 1880–1930* (Chicago: University of Chicago Press), xvii; and Mary Odem, *Delinquent Daughters: Policing Adolescent Female Sexuality in the United States, 1885–1920* (Chapel Hill: University of North Carolina Press, 1995), 21.

3. Meyerowitz, *Women Adrift*.

4. Ibid., 108.

5. Ibid., 110.

6. Thomas Lee Philpott, *The Slum and the Ghetto: Immigrants, Blacks, and Reformers in Chicago, 1880–1930* (Belmont: Wadsworth, 1991), 7–8.

7. Stanley Lieberson writes:

> A general distinction began to develop between old and new immigrants; a distinction that sought to put a variety of characteristics together. The old immigrants were from Northwestern Europe, had come to the United States in significant numbers before 1880, were more industrious, more likely to assimilate, were closer to the native white Americans in general outlook and cultural characteristics, and were of inherently more desirable stock. The new immigrant groups, those from the remaining parts of Europe, were placed on the opposite end of the continuum with respect to all of these characteristics.

A Piece of the Pie: Blacks and White Immigrants since 1880 (Berkeley: University of California Press, 1980), 26.

8. Mary Linehan, "Vicious Circle: Prostitution, Reform and Public Policy in Chicago, 1830–1930" (doctoral dissertation, Notre Dame University, 1991), 152.

9. Lieberson, *Piece of the Pie.*

10. John Higham, *Strangers in the Land: Patterns of American Nativism, 1860–1925* (New York: Atheneum, 1963 [1955]); Lieberson, *Piece of the Pie.*

11. Philpott, *Slum and the Ghetto.*

12. Ibid., 23.

13. By 1890, two-thirds of the African American population lived from Harrison Street to 33rd Street. By 1900, the black belt extended south of the downtown area to 39th Street. Ten years later, over 30 percent of African Americans lived in predominantly African American sections of the city, and most lived in the second and third wards of Chicago's thirty-five wards. See Cynthia Blair, "Vicious Commerce: African American Women's Sex Work and the Transformation of Urban Space in Chicago, 1850–1915" (doctoral dissertation, Harvard University, 1999).

14. Lieberson, *Piece of the Pie;* Douglas S. Massey and Nancy A. Denton, *American Apartheid* (Cambridge: Harvard University Press, 1993).

15. Kevin Mumford, *Interzones: Black/White Sex Districts in Chicago and New York in the Early Twentieth Century* (New York: Columbia University Press, 1997); Philpott, *Slum and the Ghetto.*

16. Mumford, *Interzones,* 39–42.

17. Philpott, *Slum and the Ghetto,* 22.

18. Jane Addams, *A New Conscience and an Ancient Evil* (New York: Macmillan, 1912), 118.

19. See James, *Chicago's Dark Places;* Samuel Paynter Wilson, *Chicago and Its Cess-Pools of Infamy* (1910); F. M. Lehman and N. K. Clarkson, *The White Slave Hell, or With Christ at Midnight in the Slums of Chicago* (Chicago: The Christian Witness Company, 1910); H. M. Lytle, *Tragedies of the White Slaves* (Chicago: C. C. Thompson, 1910); John Dillon, *From Dance Hall to White Slavery* (Chicago: C. C. Thompson, 1912); Leona Prall Groetzinger, *The City's Perils* ([Chicago?], 1912); and Guy Phelps, *Ethel Vale the White Slave* (Chicago: Christian Witness, 1910).

20. Richard Lindberg, *Chicago by Gaslight: A History of Chicago's Netherworld, 1880–1920* (Chicago: Academy Chicago Publishers, 1996), 114.

21. Ibid.

22. W. T. Stead, *If Christ Came to Chicago! A Plea for the Union of All Who Love in the Service of All Who Suffer* (Chicago: Laird and Lee, 1894), 126.

23. Ibid., 130.

24. Joseph Baylen, "A Victorian's 'Crusade' in Chicago, 1893–1894," *Journal of American History* 51 (1964): 428.

25. Cited in Gary Smith, "When Stead Came to Chicago: The 'Social Gospel Novel' and the Chicago Civic Federation," *American Presbyterians* 68 (Fall 1990): 193.

26. Cited in Baylen, "A Victorian's 'Crusade,'" 128.

27. The Committee of Fifteen was comprised of prominent Chicagoans, including Julius Rosenwald, Clifford Barnes, and Harold Swift. They privately funded Roe's investigations. See Clifford Barnes, "The Story of the Committee of Fifteen," *Social*

Hygiene 4 (1918): 145. The Chicago Committee of Fifteen is not to be confused with New York's Committee of Fifteen. See Jeremy P. Felt, "Vice Reform as a Political Technique: The Committee of Fifteen in New York, 1900–1901," *New York History* 54 (1973): 24–51.

28. George Kibbe Turner, "The City of Chicago: A Study of the Great Immoralities," *McClure's,* April 1907, 576.

29. Ibid., 576.

30. Ibid., 582.

31. "A Prophet with Honor," *Northwestern Christian Advocate,* January 1913, 51.

32. Olive Bell Daniels, *From the Epic of Chicago: A Biography, Ernest A. Bell, 1865–1928* (Menasha, Wisc.: George Banta Publishing Company, 1932).

33. Cited in ibid., 39.

34. Ibid., 41.

35. Ibid., 52.

36. Ibid., 34.

37. Those in the Midnight Mission conceived of themselves as foreign missionaries, fighting to spread American and Christian values to non-natives: "We constantly minister at midnight in the streets of Chicago to Chinese, Japanese, an occasional Persian, Hindu or Arab, French, Polish, Russians, Germans, Italians, Jews, and almost every nationality under heaven. The Midnight Mission has some features of a foreign missionary society." Ernest Bell, *Fighting the Traffic in Young Girls* (Chicago: G. S. Ball, 1910), 414. Bell's rhetoric changed little over the years. His 1911 report to the directors' meeting of the Midnight Mission stated that "this year our eyes are fixed upon the multitudes of men, speaking forty different tongues, who throng the streets of shame—a human stockyards such as this does not disgrace London, Berlin, New York—or even Paris if we are rightly informed." See Ernest Bell Papers, box 1, folder 12, Chicago Historical Society.

38. *Union Signal,* August 4, 1910, 3; Daniels, *From the Epic of Chicago,* 63.

39. Bell, *Fighting the Traffic,* 260.

40. Ibid., 262.

41. See Kathryn Kish Sklar, "The Historical Foundations of Women's Power in the Creation of the American Welfare State, 1830–1930," in *Mothers of a New World: Maternalist Politics and the Origins of Welfare States,* ed. Seth Koven and Soyna Michel (New York: Routledge, 1993), 43–93.

42. In addition to direct help for Chicago's destitute, the Hull House garnered municipal support for playgrounds and lobbied to pass law regulating child labor in 1893. It actively distinguished itself from narrowly defined charity work. The Hull House had flexible funding, strong ties to other women's organizations, and a religious, moralistic justification for social reform. The Hull House worked with various women's organizations, recruiting volunteers through Chicago's female organizations and philanthropic societies. It solicited help from a national network of

reformers, such as the General Federation of Women's Clubs, the Chicago Women's Club, and the Mothers' Congress.

43. Jane Addams, *Twenty Years at Hull-House* (1938; repr., New York: Penguin, 1981), 98.

44. Lissak, *Pluralism and Progressivism.*

45. Ibid., 32.

46. Ibid., 29.

47. Ibid., 31.

48. Addams did not extend the same promise of assimilation to African Americans. Addams made a fundamental distinction between African Americans and new immigrants, suggesting that the weaknesses of African American families prevented them from instilling American morals in their children. While the Hull House considered new immigrants as victims of poverty and environment, it placed the blame for the poor circumstances surrounding African Americans on individual shortcomings inherited by a legacy of slavery. Until the 1940s, the Hull House prohibited African American women from staying at its boarding house and summer camps. In other endeavors, the Hull House kept the participation of African Americans to a minimum. The racial exclusivity practiced by the Hull House became increasingly apparent as the black belt extended eastward during the early twentieth century, encompassing the neighborhood location of the Hull House. See Lasch-Quinn, *Black Neighbors.*

49. Allen Davis, *American Heroine: The Life and Legend of Jane Addams* (New York: Oxford University Press, 1973), 183; Walter Lippmann, *A Preface to Politics* (New York: M. Kennerley, 1914), 78.

50. Janet Beer and Katherine Joslin, "Diseases of the Body Politic: White Slavery in Jane Addams' *A New Conscience and an Ancient Evil* and Selected Short Stories by Charlotte Perkins Gilman," *Journal of American Studies* 33 (1999): 3.

51. James Weber Linn, *Jane Addams: A Biography* (New York: D. Appleton-Century, 1935).

52. Ibid., 197.

53. Addams argued against the segregation, and toleration, of specific municipal vice districts. She disputed "segregationists" who thought that partitioning allowed for greater police control over the prostitution trade. Addams contended that segregation did not ensure the protection of white slaves because they were still subject to legal punishment. She argued, "Certainly enfranchised women would offer some protection to the white slaves themselves who are tolerated and segregated, but who, because their existence is illegal, may be arrested whenever any police captain chooses, may be brought before a magistrate, fined and imprisoned." Jane Addams, *A New Conscience,* 193–94.

54. Ibid., 49.

55. Ibid., 72.

56. Ibid., 73.

57. Cited in *White Ribbon Ensign,* July 1912, 1.

58. Addams, *A New Conscience,* 64.

59. Ibid., 69.

60. Meyerowitz, *Women Adrift.*

61. Ibid., 34.

62. Addams, *A New Conscience,* 77.

63. Ibid., 59.

64. In her otherwise trenchant critique of contemporary anti-trafficking movements, Jo Doezema uses this quote to claim that Addams engaged in pious victim-
blaming. However, taking her work as a whole and comparing it to many of her contemporaries, it is clear that Addams held a genuinely left-progressive approach to the
prostitution question. Jo Doezema, "Who Gets to Choose? Coercion, Consent, and
the UN Protocol," in *Gender, Trafficking, and Slavery* (Oxford: Oxfam, 2002), 23.

65. Addams, *A New Conscience,* 21.

66. The data in table 4.1 are derived from a content analysis of forced prostitution stories in Addams's *A New Conscience* and Clifford Roe's *Panders and Their
White Slaves* (New York: Fleming H. Revell, 1910).

67. Addams, *A New Conscience,* 69–71.

68. Ibid., 70–71.

69. Ibid., 160.

70. Ibid., 92.

71. Ibid., 24.

72. Cited in Clifford Roe, *Horrors of the White Slave Trade* (London: Stationers
Hall, 1911), 19.

73. Linehan, "Vicious Circle," 182; Frederick Grittner, *White Slavery: Myth, Ideology, and American Law* (New York: Garland, 1990).

74. *Chicago Tribune,* September 26, 1909, 1.

75. Roe, *Panders,* 14.

76. Ibid., 21.

77. Clifford Roe, *The Girl Who Disappeared* (Naperville: World's Purity Federation,
1914), 85–86. In his study of prostitution in Chicago, Walter Reckless suggests that Roe
routinely characterized straightforward incidences of prostitution in terms of abduction and sexual slavery. *Vice in Chicago* (Montclair, N.J.: Patterson Smith, 1933).

78. On dancing and dance halls as targets of moral condemnation, see Ann Wag-
ner, *Adversaries of Dance: From the Puritans to Present* (Urbana: University of Illinois
Press, 1997).

79. Louise Hadduck de Koven Bowen, *The Road to Destruction Made Easy in Chicago* (Chicago: Hale-Crossley Printing Co., 1916).

80. *Chicago Tribune,* May 21, 1908, 3.

81. The data from table 4.2 are derived from a content analysis of forced prostitution stories in Addams's *A New Conscience* and Roe's *Panders.*

82. *Chicago Tribune,* May 6, 1908, 5.

83. Ibid., May 21, 1908, 3.

84. He wrote: "There have been hundreds of foreign girls shipped into this country for immoral purposes, and yet the number of such girls is much lower than that of the girls of our own country who have been procured by the panders. In the United States, at least three-fourths of the girl slave victims have been inveigled from our own farms, homes, towns and cities; but it was the foreigner who taught the American this dastardly business." Roe, *Panders,* 211.

85. See table 4.1.

86. Roe, *Panders,* 215.

87. *Chicago Tribune,* February 20, 1908, 7.

88. Roe, *Girl Who Disappeared,* 267.

89. Roe cited in Norine Law, *The Shame of a Great Nation: The Story of the "White Slave Trade"* (Harrisburg: United Evangelical Publishing House, 1909), 120.

90. Roe, *Horrors of the White Slave Trade,* 171.

91. Roe, *Girl Who Disappeared,* 81.

92. Clifford Roe, *What Women Might Do with the Ballot: The Abolition of the White Slave Traffic* (New York: National American Woman Suffrage Association, 1912), 9; Roe, *Panders,* 184.

93. Roe, *Horrors of the White Slave Trade,* 121, 141.

94. Ibid., 133, 132, 135.

95. Ibid., 141, 148.

96. Some evidence suggests that Roe had an uneasy relationship with local religious leaders. After his 1907 crusade, Roe received invitations to speak at ministers' meetings, but he criticized their indifference: "I told the ministers of the white slave traffic and of my prosecutions. Some of them passed resolutions, but did nothing more." *Chicago Tribune,* September 26, 1909, 1.

97. Ibid.

98. Roe, *What Women Might Do,* 8.

99. Barnes wrote: "But the politicians, who know no party when their selfish interests are affected, quickly brought such pressure to bear that the attorney who was proving himself so troublesome to the vice interests was forced out of office and eventually compelled to carry on his work in an independent capacity, supported only by this small group of citizens." Barnes, "The Story of the Committee of Fifteen," 146.

100. *Chicago Tribune,* September 26, 1909, 1.

101. Roe, *Horrors of the White Slave Trade,* 196–201.

102. See Mark Connelly, *The Response to Prostitution in the Progressive Era* (Greensboro: University of North Carolina Press, 1980), 118.

103. See table 4.1.

104. Roe, *Horrors of the White Slave Trade,* 100, 101.

105. Roe explained, "The French girl slave soon became common, not only in New York, but also in Chicago, San Francisco, and other American cities. Until the last few

years the French girl brought a high price to the trader who sold her, and in conse-quence some of these procurers grew very rich. In many of the larger cities of the United States today the proprietors of the larger immoral houses are French people." Ibid., 99.

106. Ibid., 100.

107. Ibid., 41–42.

108. Roe, *Girl Who Disappeared*, 9.

109. Ibid., 12.

110. Ibid., 19–20.

111. Ibid.

112. Roe, *Panders*, 13, 14.

113. Roe, *Girl Who Disappeared*, 113, 114.

114. Ibid., 115.

115. Ibid., 261.

116. Addams, *A New Conscience*, 63.

117. Ibid., 266.

118. Ibid., 268.

119. Roe, *Panders*, 53.

120. Roe, *Girl Who Disappeared*, 55.

121. Ibid., 60.

122. Ibid., 60–61.

123. Ibid., 64.

124. Ibid., 234, 244.

125. Ibid., 251, 255.

126. Ibid., 332.

127. JDR Jr. to Harold Swift, January 12, 1911; JDR Jr. to Roe, January 26, February 2, 1911; RG 2, box 7, folder 43, Rockefeller Boards, Rockefeller Family Archives, RAC.

Chapter 5: John D. Rockefeller Jr. and the "Negro Alleged Slave Trader"

1. By 1910, 91,709 African Americans lived in the city, and most of them were southern-born, unskilled, unmarried men. Gilbert Osofsky, *Harlem: The Making of a Ghetto* (New York: Harper and Row, 1963), 17–20.

2. Mumford writes that "the Great Migration represented a significant, and en-during, challenge to the interracial taboo and ideology of sexual segregation." Kevin Mumford, *Interzones: Black/White Sex Districts in Chicago and New York in the Early Twentieth Century* (New York: Columbia University Press, 1997), 100.

3. Osofsky, *Harlem*, 42.

4. Timothy Gilfoyle, *City of Eros: New York City, Prostitution, and the Commer-cialization of Sex, 1790–1920* (New York: Norton, 1992).

5. Jeremy P. Felt, "Vice Reform as a Political Technique: The Committee of Fifteen in New York, 1900–1901," *New York History* 54 (1973): 24–51.

6. An article in *Current Literature* (December 1909, 594) declared that the white slavery issue was "so far transcending mere politics and so arresting in its national and international importance that it quickly overshadowed all the anticipated issues of the campaign, such as taxation, subways, and extravagance in expenditure."

7. Turner wrote, "About twenty-five years ago the third great flush of immigration, consisting of Austrian, Russian, and Hungarian Jews, began to come into New York. Among these immigrants were a large number of criminals, who soon found that they could develop an extremely profitable business in the sale of women in New York." George Kibbe Turner, "The Daughters of the Poor, A Plain Story of the Development of New York City as a Leading Center of the White Slave Trade of the World, under Tammany Hall," *McClure's,* November 1909, 47.

8. Ibid.

9. Turner stated, "The cadet in the past was almost always Jewish; now the young Italians have taken up the business in great numbers." Ibid., 57.

10. The man who guided Turner on a tour of the city's dance halls claimed that Turner fabricated most of the article's details about dance hall depravity. He stated that "Mr. Turner at first seemed to mistake their poor clothes and lack of knowledge of social forms as an indication that they were immoral." *New York Times,* October 28, 1909, 3.

11. Turner, "Daughters of the Poor," 58.

12. Ibid., 57.

13. Ibid., 61.

14. John Ensor Harr and Peter J. Johnson, *The Rockefeller Century* (New York: Charles Scribner's Sons, 1988). The Rockefeller investigation was only one aspect of the city's fight against prostitution. From 1902 to 1932, the Committee of Fourteen investigated and campaigned against prostitution and other perceived vices. See George Chauncey, *Gay New York: Gender, Urban Culture, and the Making of the Gay Male World, 1890–1940* (New York: Basic Books, 1994), 36. Mara Keire, "The Committee of Fourteen and Saloon Reform in New York City, 1905–1920," *Business and Economic History* 26 (1997): 573–83. On the Victorian anti-obscenity crusades of Anthony Comstock and the New York Society for the Suppression of Vice, see Nicola Beisel, *Imperiled Innocents: Anthony Comstock and Family Reproduction in Victorian America* (Princeton, N.J.: Princeton University Press, 1997).

15. Raymond Fosdick, *John D. Rockefeller, Jr.: A Portrait* (New York: Harper and Brothers, 1956), 137.

16. Rockefeller Grand Jury Presentment, RG 2, box 9, folder 7, page 6, Rockefeller Boards, Rockefeller Family Archives, RAC (hereafter "Grand Jury Presentment"). They interviewed representatives from the Committee of Fourteen, the New York Society for the Suppression of Vice, the Society for Social and Moral Prophylaxis, the Florence Crittenden Mission, the Society for Improving the Conditions of the Poor, and the Committee on Amusements and Vacation Resources for Working Girls.

17. Ibid., with supporting notes.

18. Ibid.

19. Braun to Rockefeller, April 2, 1910, RG 2, box 6, folder 38, Rockefeller Boards, Rockefeller Family Archives, RAC. Braun wrote: "I mentioned to you at the recent interview I had in your office with you, that in my seven years experience as an investigating official of this government, I failed to find any organized traffic in women, and I do not believe now, that such an organized traffic exists, nor do I believe, that with the exception of sporadic cases, innocent girls are sold or driven into this life, but nevertheless I regard every prostitute in this country more or less a white slave, just because of the existing conditions enumerated above."

20. Grand Jury Presentment, 621.

21. Ibid., 520. Bingham wrote: "It was distinctly understood that they (the pimps) always chip in to help each other out, and certain facts would show to what extent they would go, because it is a rule in that world that a woman belongs to a man, and nobody must interfere if he kills her; they must not interfere, that is the unwritten law, and while they are not bound together by any written agreement or perhaps any understood agreement, they're all in the same business and so they will chip in and help each other, but nothing more definite than a verbal understanding."

22. Ibid., 9.

23. Testimony of George Miller, Grand Jury Trial Transcript, Transcripts of the County of New York, Court of General Sessions 1883–1927, Special Collections, Lloyd Sealy Library, John Jay College of Criminal Justice, New York, case 3317, roll 420, page 527 (hereafter "Grand Jury Trial Transcript").

24. Many middle- and upper-class whites considered black and tan cafés as notorious hotbeds of immorality. Mumford writes, "The Black and Tan speakeasy attempted to offer a place in which there were no prohibitions or inhibitions." See Kevin Mumford, "Homosex Changes: Race, Cultural Geography, and the Emergence of the Gay," *American Quarterly* 48 (1996): 406. In his 1920 book about life in New York tenements, Jacob Riis observed that "the borderland where the white and black races meet in common debauch, the aptly-named black and tan saloons, has never been debatable ground from a moral standpoint. It has always been the worst of the deplorably bad." Jacob Riis, *How the Other Half Lives: Studies among the Tenements of New York* (New York: Scribner's, 1920), 156.

25. In a two-hour interview with investigators, Levinson revealed the locations of three "clearinghouses" or "stockades" where "they always have on hand an average of from five to eight women waiting to be transported to different points outside of New York City." *New York Daily Tribune,* May 5, 1910, 1. After his confession, detectives raided the buildings and found them deserted. *New York Times,* May 6, 1910, 18.

26. *Evening Mail,* May 12, 1910, 2.

27. The district attorney's office charged her with violating section 2460 of the penal code: "knowingly receiving money for and on account of procuring and placing women in the custody of another person for immoral purposes."

28. *People v. Belle Moore,* Transcripts of the County of New York, Court of General Sessions 1883–1927, Special Collections, Lloyd Sealy Library, John Jay College of Criminal Justice, New York, case 1169, roll 153, page 9 (hereafter *People v. Belle Moore*).

29. Ibid., 143.

30. Miller, Grand Jury Trial Transcript, 540–41.

31. Ibid., 561.

32. Frances Foster, Grand Jury Trial Transcript, 408.

33. *New York Times,* April 30, 1910, 1.

34. Ibid., April 20, 1910, 18.

35. Ibid., May 5, 1910, 6.

36. *People v. Belle Moore,* 239. During the grand jury proceedings, Foster and Miller offered different accounts of the prostitutes' willingness to move to a brothel in Seattle. Miller testified that their willingness was never discussed and that Moore had "absolute control" over their movements. Miller, Grand Jury Trial Transcript, 559. Foster, on the other hand, thought that the girls "very willingly entered into this arrangement." Foster, Grand Jury Trial Transcript, 399. Rockefeller asked Foster, "In other words, it was not against the girls' consent, but money was paid for securing the girls?" Before she had a chance to respond, Reynolds interjected, "Under the law, the question of consent is not involved; either with or without consent." Foster, Grand Jury Trial Transcript, 400.

37. *New York Daily Tribune,* May 4, 1910, 1.

38. *Evening World,* May 4, 1910, 4.

39. *New York Times,* May 5, 1910, 6.

40. Ibid., May 1, 1910, 20.

41. Ibid., May 3, 1910, 20.

42. *Evening World,* May 3, 1910, 1.

43. *New York Daily Tribune,* May 4, 1910, 1.

44. *New York Times,* May 5, 1910, 6.

45. *Evening Post,* April 30, 1910, 4.

46. James F. Davis, *Who Is Black? One Nation's Definition* (University Park: Pennsylvania State University Press, 1991), 6.

47. George M. Fredrickson, *The Black Image in the White Mind: The Debate on Afro-American Character and Destiny, 1817–1914* (New York: Harper and Row, 1971), 121.

48. In 1920, the category of mulatto was dropped from the U.S. census, and the Census Bureau defined "black" as anyone with any African ancestry. See J. Davis, *Who Is Black?,* 12.

49. On "passing," see Kathleen Pfeiffer, *Passing and American Individualism* (Cambridge: Harvard University Press, 2003).

50. *People v. Belle Moore,* 145.

51. Osofsky succinctly observes, "With the increased migration of Negroes from the South, the brighter side of race relations in the city—the softening of institutional prejudices—came to an end." *Harlem,* 40.

52. *New York Times,* May 5, 1910, 20.

53. Ibid., May 19, 1910, 5.

54. For an extended discussion of the role of the mulatto in nineteenth-century American literature in general and *Uncle Tom's Cabin* in particular, see Nancy Bentley, "White Slaves: The Mulatto Hero in Antebellum Fiction," *American Literature* 65 (September 1993): 501–22; and James Kinney, *Amalgamation: Race, Sex, and Rhetoric in the Nineteenth-Century Novel* (Westport, Conn.: Greenwood Press, 1985), 66–71.

55. *Evening World,* May 6, 1910, 4.

56. Fredrickson, *Black Image.*

57. K. Sue Jewell writes: "Jezebel, more commonly known as the bad-black-girl, is a cultural image that is portrayed as a mulatto or fair-complexioned African American female, who possesses features that are considered European. Thin lips, long straight hair, slender nose, thin figure and fair complexion are the physical characteristics that make up this image." *From Mammy to Miss America and Beyond: Cultural Images and the Shaping of U.S. Social Policy* (New York: Routledge, 1993), 46.

58. Patricia Hill Collins, *Black Feminist Thought: Knowledge, Consciousness, and the Politics of Empowerment* (New York: Routledge, 1990); Jewell, *From Mammy to Miss America.*

59. *People v. Belle Moore,* 14. Both Miller and Foster told the grand jury that Moore and her friends had a "circus" for their guests, which involved near-naked dancing. Miller, Grand Jury Trial Transcript, 405; Foster, Grand Jury Trial Transcript, 357.

60. Carroll Smith-Rosenberg, *Disorderly Conduct: Visions of Gender in Victorian America* (Oxford: Oxford University Press, 1985), 176–78.

61. The professionalization of child protection work offered a popular career path for female college graduates in the Progressive Era. Boston, in particular, was a home to several child protective societies. See Linda Gordon, *Heroes of Their Own Lives: The Politics and History of Family Violence* (New York: Penguin Books, 1988).

62. *People v. Belle Moore,* 156–60.

63. Ibid., 178.

64. George Chauncey writes, "Going slumming in the resorts of the Bowery and the Tenderloin was a popular activity among middle-class men and even among some women, in part as a way to witness working-class 'depravity' and to confirm their sense of superiority." *Gay New York,* 36.

65. *People v. Belle Moore,* 160.

66. Ibid., 163–64.

67. Ibid., 176.

68. *New York Times,* April 20, 1910, 18.

69. *Evening World,* May 19, 1910, 2.

70. *New York Times,* May 20, 1910, 18.

71. *New York Daily Tribune,* May 19, 1910, 1.

72. *Evening World,* May 19, 1910, 1–2.

73. *People v. Belle Moore,* 161–62.

74. Gail Bederman, *Manliness and Civilization: A Cultural History of Gender and Race in the United States, 1880–1917* (Chicago: University of Chicago Press, 1995); Elaine Tyler May, *Barren in the Promised Land: Childless Americans and the Pursuit of Happiness* (Cambridge: Harvard University Press, 1995), 61–93.

75. May, *Barren in the Promised Land,* 64. May notes that during the Progressive Era, "for the first time ever in the United States, experts from a wide range of fields began to accuse affluent and educated women of deliberately avoiding motherhood and causing a 'national decline.'" 72.

76. Smith-Rosenberg, *Disorderly Conduct;* Linda Stone and Nancy P. McKee, *Gender and Culture in America* (New Jersey: Prentice Hall, 1999).

77. May, *Barren in the Promised Land,* 63.

78. Bederman, *Manliness and Civilization;* Michael Kimmel, *Manhood in America: A Cultural History* (New York: Free Press, 1996), 157–88.

79. Chauncey, *Gay New York.*

80. Mumford, *Interzones.*

81. Gilfoyle, *City of Eros,* 210. According to a vice investigation cited in *City of Eros,* Baron Wilkins's café was "the swellest club in town" with a "high class of sporting people."

82. Miller, Grand Jury Trial Transcript, 556.

83. *People v. Belle Moore,* 39.

84. Ibid., 37.

85. Ibid., 233.

86. Ibid., 49.

87. Chauncey, *Gay New York.*

88. Mumford, *Interzones,* 400, 399.

89. Prompted by these serious accusations levied against the investigators, the prosecution challenged Karlin's depiction of Miller. The cross-examination lasted two days, during which time the prosecuting attorney made 163 objections. Judge Crain sustained 143 of these objections and chastised Karlin in open court for his aggressive tactics. At one point during Karlin's cross-examination of Miller, the judge threatened to hold Karlin in contempt of court. After sentencing Belle Moore, Judge Crain cautioned Karlin again on his courtroom strategy. *People v. Belle Moore,* 192.

90. Ibid., 52.

91. Ibid., 10.

92. Ibid., 56.

93. Kevin White, *The First Sexual Revolution: The Emergence of Male Heterosexuality in Modern America* (New York: New York University Press, 1993), 39–50.

94. Collins, *Black Feminist Thought,* 66–90.

95. Jacquelyn Dowd Hall, "'The Mind That Burns in Each Body': Women, Rape, and Racial Violence," in *Powers of Desire: The Politics of Sexuality,* ed. Ann Snitow, Christine Stansell, and S. Thompson (New York: Monthly Review Press, 1983), 328–49.

96. *People v. Belle Moore*, 290–91.

97. "Ill-Chosen Agents of Reform," *New York Times*, May 21, 1910, 8.

98. James B. Reynolds, "Belle Moore's Case," *New York Times*, May 27, 1910, 8.

99. Alexander Karlin, "White Slave Case," *New York Times*, May 31, 1910, 8.

100. They concluded from the testimony of witnesses: "We have found no evidence of the existence in the City and County of New York of any organization or organizations, incorporated or otherwise, engaged as such in the traffic in women for immoral purposes, nor have we found evidence of an organized traffic in women for immoral purposes. It appears, on the other hand, from indictments found by us and from the testimony of witnesses that a trafficking in the bodies of women does exist and is carried on by individuals acting for their own individual benefit, and that these persons are known to each other and are more or less informally associated." Grand Jury Presentment, 4.

101. Judge's address to jury, RG 2, box 8, folder 57, Rockefeller Boards, Rockefeller Family Archives, RAC.

102. Ibid.

103. Rockefeller to Gaynor, June 30, 1910, ibid. He told Gaynor, "As a private citizen may I express the hope that the recommendation made in this report regarding the appointment by your Honor of a commission to study the question of prostitution and the laws in existence with reference to it and the methods employed in its restraint in various cities of this country and Europe, may commend itself to you."

104. For a description of Parkhurst's anti-vice efforts, see David Pivar, *Purity Crusade: Sexual Morality and Social Control, 1868–1900* (Westport, Conn.: Greenwood Press, 1973), 162–66. Gaynor to Rockefeller, July 2, 1910, RG 2, box 8, folder 57, Rockefeller Boards, Rockefeller Family Archives, RAC. "I thank you for your letter, and for sending me a copy of the grand jury's report. At the same time there is no law permitting grand juries to make presentments as they please. I may not appoint the commission, but will think it over. I do not mind telling you that I have been a student of this matter for over twenty years here and abroad, and I believe I am already quite fully informed as to the way the social evil is dealt with in Europe. I doubt if the City can go to any great expense in the matter."

105. JDR Jr., Statement for Publication, January 27, 1913, RG 2, box 9, folder 67, ibid.

106. Gilfoyle writes that "both works quickly redefined the public debate on the subject in Progressive Era New York." Gilfoyle, *City of Eros*, 277.

Chapter 6: "Yellow Slavery" and Donaldina Cameron's San Francisco Mission

1. Peggy Pascoe, *Relations of Rescue: The Search for Female Moral Authority in the American West, 1974–1939* (Oxford: Oxford University Press, 1990), 13–14.

2. Mildred Crowl Martin, *Chinatown's Angry Angel: The Story of Donaldina Cameron* (Palo Alto: Pacific Books, 1977); Carol Green Wilson, *Chinatown Quest: The Life Adventures of Donaldina Cameron* (Palo Alto: Stanford University Press, 1931).

3. Pascoe, *Relations of Rescue.*

4. Rogers Smith, *Civic Ideals: Conflicting Visions of Citizenship in U.S. History* (New Haven: Yale University Press, 1997), 441–42.

5. Tomás Almaguer, *Racial Fault Lines: The Historical Origins of White Supremacy in California* (Berkeley: University of California Press, 1994).

6. Ibid.

7. Ibid.

8. Pascoe, *Relations of Rescue*, 15.

9. Lucie Hirata, "Free, Indentured, Enslaved: Chinese Prostitutes in Nineteenth-Century America," *Signs* 5 (1979): 3–29. See also David Pivar, *Purity and Hygiene: Women, Prostitution and the 'American Plan,' 1900–1930* (Westport, Conn.: Greenwood Press, 2002), 100–106.

10. Hirata, "Free, Indentured, Enslaved," 5.

11. Californians passed an anti-miscegenation law in 1880 that prevented marriage between whites and a "Negro, mulatto, or Mongolian." See Peggy Pascoe, "Miscegenation Law, Court Cases, and Ideologies of 'Race' in Twentieth-Century America," in *Sex, Love, Race: Crossing Boundaries in North American History,* ed. Martha Hodes (New York: New York University Press, 1999), 464–90.

12. Hirata, "Free, Indentured, Enslaved."

13. Ibid.; Pascoe, *Relations of Rescue.*

14. Benson Tong, *Unsubmissive Women: Chinese Prostitutes in Nineteenth-Century San Francisco* (Norman: University of Oklahoma Press, 1994); Judy Yung, *Unbound Voices: A Documentary History of Chinese Women in San Francisco* (Berkeley: University of California Press, 1999).

15. Pascoe, *Relations of Rescue*, 14.

16. Yong Chen writes, "Complicating the situation is the fact that white men frequented Chinese brothels and Chinese men called on white prostitutes. All these issues rendered houses of prostitution a revealing intersection of gender, class, and race." *Chinese San Francisco, 1850–1943: A Trans-Pacific Community* (Palo Alto: Stanford University Press, 2000), 76.

17. Neil Larry Shumsky, "Vice Responds to Reform: San Francisco, 1910–1914," *Journal of Urban History* 7 (1980): 31–47.

18. Almaguer, *Racial Fault Lines.*

19. Hirata, "Free, Indentured, Enslaved."

20. Charles Frederick Holder, "Chinese Slavery in America," *North American Review* 165 (September 1897): 290.

21. Ibid., 289.

22. Pascoe, *Relations of Rescue*, 123.

23. Ernest Bell, *Fighting the Traffic in Young Girls* (Chicago: G. S. Ball, 1910), 213–22; Edward O. Janney, *The White Slave Traffic in America* (Baltimore: Lord Baltimore Press, 1911), 41–52; Clifford Roe, *Horrors of the White Slave Trade* (London: Stationers Hall, 1911), 253–60.

24. Jean Turner Zimmermann, *Chicago's Black Traffic in White Girls* (Chicago: Chicago Rescue Mission, 1910), *White or Yellow? A Story of America's Great White Slave Trade with Asia* (Chicago: Zimmermann, 1916), *Vere, of Shanghai* (Chicago: Zimmermann, 1925).

25. Zimmermann, *White or Yellow?*, 19.

26. Ibid., 57, 16.

27. Bell, *Fighting the Traffic*, 215.

28. "Public Conference," *Philanthropist*, April 1908, 36–37.

29. "The Illinois Vigilance Association Annual Meeting," *Philanthropist*, April 1909, 18.

30. On Bushnell's work abroad, see Philippa Levine, *Prostitution, Race, and Politics: Policing Venereal Disease in the British Empire* (New York: Routledge, 2003), 104–11; Pivar, *Purity and Hygiene*, xv–xvi.

31. Elizabeth Andrew and Katharine Bushnell, *Heathen Slaves and Christian Rulers* (Oakland: Messiah's Advocate, 1907), 1.

32. Ibid., 11.

33. Ibid., iv, 148, 163, 164.

34. Ibid., 163.

35. Almaguer, *Racial Fault Lines;* Chen, *Chinese San Francisco.*

36. Louise Newman, *White Women's Rights: The Racial Origins of Feminism in the United States* (Oxford: Oxford University Press, 1999), 34.

37. C. G. Wilson, *Chinatown Quest,* 13.

38. Richard Dillon, *The Hatchet Men: The Story of the Tong Wars in San Francisco's Chinatown* (New York: Coward-McCann, 1962), 235.

39. Martin, *Chinatown's Angry Angel;* C. G. Wilson, *Chinatown Quest.*

40. Donaldina Cameron, "Report of Mission Home Superintendent," 1904, Mission Home Reports, box 3, folder 4, page 77, Mildred Martin Papers (hereafter "MM"), M0780, Department of Special Collections, Stanford University Libraries, Stanford, Calif.

41. Laurene Wu McClain, "Donaldina Cameron: A Reappraisal," *Pacific Historian* 27 (Fall 1983): 25–35; Pascoe, *Relations of Rescue.*

42. Hirata, "Free, Indentured, Enslaved," 28.

43. McClain, "Donaldina Cameron," 34.

44. Andrew and Bushnell, *Heathen Slaves;* Bell, *Fighting the Traffic*, 218–21; Janney, *White Slave Traffic,* 45–51; Zimmermann, *White or Yellow?*

45. *The Occident,* 1899, box 3, folder 2, page 17, MM.

46. Cameron, "Report of Mission Home Superintendent," 80–81.

47. Martin, *Chinatown's Angry Angel;* C. G. Wilson, *Chinatown Quest.*

48. Rescue efforts and the development of rescue homes coincided with rising anti-Chinese hostility. See Chen, *Chinese San Francisco,* 81.

49. C. G. Wilson, *Chinatown Quest,* 47.

50. Martin, *Chinatown's Angry Angel,* 55; C. G. Wilson, *Chinatown Quest.*

51. According to historian Benson Tong, Chinese brothel owners commonly used this method of abduction: "Some kidnapping cases involved complicated legal entanglements. Often, with the aid of corrupt sheriffs and constables, tongs brought charges of robbery or petty larceny against their victims. The tong would then tender bail to gain possession of the women." *Unsubmissive Women,* 151.

52. C. G. Wilson, *Chinatown Quest,* 28.

53. Donaldina MacKenzie Cameron, *Strange True Stories of Chinese Slave Girls* (San Francisco, n.d.), 3.

54. C. G. Wilson, *Chinatown Quest.*

55. See *Palo Alto Times,* April 3, 1900, 1; *San Francisco Chronicle,* April 3, 1900, 1.

56. *San Francisco Chronicle,* April 3, 1900, 1.

57. C. G. Wilson, *Chinatown Quest,* 25–35.

58. Martin, *Chinatown's Angry Angel;* C. G. Wilson, *Chinatown Quest.*

59. Zimmermann, *Vere,* 89.

60. C. G. Wilson, *Chinatown Quest,* 10. Yong Chen argues that "we must recognize that in doing what they saw as aiding helpless prostitutes the sympathetic missionary rescuers set themselves apart from anti-Chinese crusaders." *Chinese San Francisco,* 81.

61. Interview, Mildred Crowl Martin and Donaldina Cameron, July 25, 1967, box 8, MM.

62. Donaldina Cameron to Crawford, June 9, 1962, box 9, private correspondence, MM. It also demonstrates the persistence in the term "Anglo-Saxon" in twentieth-century racial thinking.

63. Mary H. Field, 1899, "Rescued Lives," Mission Home Reports, box 3, folder 4, pages 63–64, MM.

64. Lorena Logan to John Bloom, March 3, 1984, box 9, MM. Logan wrote the editor of the *Pacific Historian* to protest the publication of Laurene McClain's article "Donaldina Cameron: A Reappraisal."

65. Cited in Martin, *Chinatown's Angry Angel,* 85.

66. Cameron, "Report of Mission Home Superintendent," 1902, pages 63, 72, MM.

67. Pamphlet, "Eastfield Ming Quong, A Bay Area Landmark: Rescuing Children for 125 Years," in *Eastfield Ming Quong 125th Anniversary Celebration,* published by the *Business Journal,* November 1992, publications folder, box 6, pages 8–9, MM. Cameron wrote: "I think real courage means doing difficult things where one had a sense of danger or fear. Very truly, I did not have to combat that feeling. Perhaps my Highland Scotch background has had something to do with it, but I never anticipated danger when I went accompanied or unaccompanied on some of the raids in which I participated in Chinatown."

68. C. G. Wilson, *Chinatown Quest,* 85, 125.

69. Some evidence suggests that Cameron harbored deep regrets about not learning Chinese. In 1937, she wrote a letter to her successor at the Mission Home: "It is almost a tragedy that neither my Boards, nor I, fully comprehended the vital im-

portance of acquiring the language, and a better knowledge of the people, through residence in their own country. . . . My three months in Canton were worth all the preceding ten years that I had spent in this local Chinatown!" Cameron to Lorena Logan, February 24, 1937, box 9, personal letters, MM.

70. McClain, "Donaldina Cameron," 22.

71. Cameron, *Strange True Stories,* 9.

72. Cited in Martin, *Chinatown's Angry Angel,* 123–24.

73. Ibid., 67.

74. Pascoe, *Relations of Rescue.*

75. Mary H. Field, "A Bit of Romance at '920,'" *The Occident,* February 1900, 18, box 3, folder 2, MM.

76. Ibid., 19.

77. McClain, "Donaldina Cameron," 31.

78. C. G. Wilson, *Chinatown Quest,* 140.

79. For example, Andrew and Bushnell reprinted seven case reports of women rescued by Cameron. See Andrew and Bushnell, *Heathen Slaves,* 157–61.

Conclusion

1. Walter Benn Michaels, *Our America: Nativism, Modernism, and Pluralism* (Durham, N.C.: Duke University Press, 1995), 66.

2. Scholars have focused renewed attention on the cultural dimensions of social movements in recent years. For instance, see James Jasper, *The Art of Moral Protest* (Chicago: University of Chicago Press, 1997); Hank Johnson and Bert Klandermans, eds., *Social Movements and Culture* (Minneapolis: University of Minnesota Press, 1995); and David Myer, Nancy Whittier, and Belinda Robnett, eds., *Social Movements: Identity, Culture, and the State* (Oxford: Oxford University Press, 2002).

3. See, for example, William Sewell, "A Theory of Structure: Duality, Agency, and Transformation," *American Journal of Sociology* 98 (1992): 1–29; and Michèle Lamont, "Introduction: Beyond Taking Culture Seriously," in *The Cultural Territories of Race: Black and White Boundaries,* ed. Michèle Lamont (Chicago: University of Chicago Press, 1999), ix–xx. Jeffrey C. Alexander advocates a "strong program" for cultural sociology that gives full weight to the autonomy and independent force of culture; see *The Meanings of Social Life: A Cultural Sociology* (Oxford: Oxford University Press, 2003).

4. See Thomas C. Mackey, *Red Lights Out: A Legal History of Prostitution, Disorderly Houses, and Vice Districts, 1870–1917* (New York: Garland, 1987); Joseph Mayer, "The Passing of Red Light Districts," *Social Hygiene* 4 (1918): 197.

5. Timothy Gilfoyle, *City of Eros: New York City, Prostitution, and the Commercialization of Sex, 1790–1920* (New York: Norton, 1992), 306–15.

6. Ibid., 308–13.

7. Richard Lindberg, *Chicago by Gaslight: A History of Chicago's Netherworld, 1880–1920* (Chicago: Academy Chicago Publishers, 1996), 146.

8. Neil Larry Shumsky, "Vice Responds to Reform: San Francisco, 1910–1914," *Journal of Urban History* 7 (1980): 31–47.

9. Notes of an interview with Edward Keyes about Prince Morrow, November 12, 1946, box 1, folder 1, American Social Hygiene Association Collection (ASHA), Social Welfare History Archives (SWHA), University of Minnesota.

10. David Pivar, *Purity and Hygiene: Women, Prostitution and the 'American Plan,' 1900–1930* (Westport, Conn.: Greenwood Press, 2002), 35–37.

11. For a thorough and insightful description of the creation of ASHA and the crucial role Rockefeller played in the social hygiene movement, see Pivar, *Purity and Hygiene,* 119–38.

12. Rockefeller to Reynolds, July 11, 1913, RG 2, box 6, folder 30, Rockefeller Boards, Rockefeller Family Archive, RAC.

13. Ibid.

14. Pivar, *Purity and Hygiene,* 142.

15. David Langum, *Crossing the Line: Legislating Morality and the Mann Act* (Chicago: University of Chicago Press, 1994), 23.

16. Clifford Roe, *The Girl Who Disappeared* (Naperville: World's Purity Federation, 1914), 133.

17. Ibid., 161–62.

18. William Robinson to Mary Cobb, December 7, 1910, box 1, folder 4, ASHA, SWHA.

19. Charles W. Eliot and William F. Snow, M.D., *1900–1915 Progress,* 1916, publication 44, Collection SW45, box 1, folder 1, ASHA, SWHA, reprinted from *Social Hygiene* 2 (January 1916): 2.

20. Prince Morrow, *Eugenics and Racial Poisons* (New York: The Society of Sanitary and Moral Prophylaxis, 1912), 3, 7, 9–10, 20.

21. Pivar, *Purity and Hygiene,* 142–58.

22. Barbara Meil Hobson, *Uneasy Virtue: The Politics of Prostitution and the American Reform Tradition* (Chicago: University of Chicago Press, 1997).

23. See Mary Odem, *Delinquent Daughters: Policing Adolescent Female Sexuality in the United States, 1885–1920* (Chapel Hill: University of North Carolina Press, 1995). Hobson writes, "When World War I was declared, the prostitute was cast as the enemy on the home front. The white slave victim, a pervasive image in journals and popular novels of the prewar years, disappeared. War propaganda presented the prostitute as someone predatory and diseased." *Uneasy Virtue,* 165.

24. Kristen Luker, "Sex, Social Hygiene, and the State: The Double-Edged Sword of Social Reform," *Theory and Society* 27 (1998): 621. See also Ruth Alexander, *The "Girl Problem": Female Sexual Delinquency in New York, 1900–1930* (Ithaca: Cornell University Press, 1998); and Regina Kunzel, *Fallen Women, Problem Girls: Unmarried Mothers and the Professionalization of Social Work 1890–1945* (New Haven: Yale University Press, 1996).

25. Luker, "Sex, Social Hygiene, and the State."

26. Odem, *Delinquent Daughters.*

27. John D'Emilio and Estelle Freedman, *Intimate Matters: A History of Sexuality in America* (New York: Harper and Row, 1988), 212.

28. Hobson, *Uneasy Virtue,* 167.

29. Ibid.; Luker, "Sex, Social Hygiene, and the State."

30. Odem, *Delinquent Daughters,* 121–24.

31. Cited in Hobson, *Uneasy Virtue,* 170.

32. Bushnell to John Preston, August 27, 1917, David Starr Jordan Papers, box 95, folder 848, Stanford University Libraries.

Index

BRIAN DONOVAN is an assistant professor of sociology at the University of Kansas and a 2005–6 National Endowment for the Humanities Research Fellow. His work has appeared in *Ethnic and Racial Studies, Law and Social Inquiry,* and *Theory and Society.*